Learning and Motivation in the Postsecondary Classroom

Learning and Motivation in the Postsecondary Classroom

Marilla D. Svinicki
University of Texas-Austin

ANKER PUBLISHING COMPANY, INC.
Bolton, Massachusetts

Learning and Motivation in the Postsecondary Classroom

ISBN 1-882982-59-2

Composition by Beverly Jorgensen/Studio J Graphic Design
Cover design by Frederick Schneider/Grafis

Anker Publishing Company, Inc.
176 Ballville Road
P.O. Box 249
Bolton, MA 01740-0249 USA

www.ankerpub.com

DEDICATION

This book is dedicated to my husband, Jay, who convinced me that I had something to say and should get on with it.

About the Author

Marilla D. Svinicki has a Ph.D. in psychology from the University of Colorado at Boulder and is director of the Center for Teaching Effectiveness and associate professor of educational psychology at the University of Texas at Austin. She is also the editor in chief of the series *New Directions for Teaching and Learning*. She has published two edited books and many chapters on the topic of learning in postsecondary classrooms. Her teaching and research interests are in the areas of learning and motivation as translated into teaching practice.

TABLE OF CONTENTS

PREFACE

Purpose of This Book

Research and theory about learning and motivation have come a long way since I first started my career in the early 1970s. We now have a lot to offer those who teach at the postsecondary level, but until now, little has been done to bring this wealth of information to the faculty in the trenches. Those who do the research seldom publish in venues that are read by faculty outside their discipline, and faculty are reluctant to venture into the professional journals in which this information is published. Even if they did, much of the writing is at a level that requires a lot of prior knowledge to be understood. The purpose of this book is to bring the findings and theories of educational psychology to the rest of the higher education community, those who teach at all the postsecondary educational institutions and have not had a resource to help them do much to adopt a scholarly approach to understanding their students' learning problems.

It has been my honor and my pleasure to stand at the intersection of these two groups: researchers in learning and faculty in the classroom. My favorite activity is to translate the more esoteric findings of my research colleagues into everyday language and examples for the teachers in the field. I believe that once they see how much is known and can be done with that knowledge, faculty will eagerly take it in and apply it to their own classes.

Organization of This Book

The book chapters revolve around the kinds of learning questions and tasks that confront most faculty and their students. For example, students in all classes have to master some basic information, and the findings from the cognitive theory of learning are very helpful in recommending ways in which instruction can be developed to help them with that task. This is the content of Chapter 2. In Chapter 3, I take that learning one step further to apply it to the problem of understanding. To be able to really use information they are learning, students have to understand it at more than a surface level. How does an instructor help students go beyond mere memorization to a level of true understanding?

At a different level, almost all courses involve students in developing new skills, such as applying their new knowledge to problems or more general thinking skills like critical analysis. In Chapter 4, I use a different base theory, social learning theory, to introduce ways of helping students master new skills. I am particularly taken with the idea of the cognitive apprenticeship as a way of teaching the more difficult thinking skills that are so highly prized in higher education.

Chapter 5 takes learning beyond the classroom as it tackles the problem of transfer. Perhaps the most prevalent criticism of education is that students cannot use what they have learned in real situations. In Chapter 5, I examine what is known about transfer and how to promote it.

Chapter 6 tackles a more recent goal of instruction: to help students learn to learn, what is called in the literature self-regulated learning. The rate of information growth today requires that students be independent learners, eventually able to plan and monitor their own learning. Educational psychology has been paying a lot of attention to this task and has developed some good strategies for students to master in order to become independent learners.

Chapter 7 addresses the very important and very popular issue of motivation. Faculty are often at a loss as to how to motivate their students to study and participate more fully in the class. In this chapter I introduce some of the wide variety of theories that have been proposed as explanations of learner motivation, and then I attempt to synthesize those theories into a set of practical strategies for instructors to follow.

The final chapter about theories is Chapter 8, which deals with individual differences in learning. This was a difficult chapter to write because there are so many strong opinions about how and why students differ in their learning. Much of what has been put forth is not as well grounded in the literature as I would like, and also not as useful when in comes down to making decisions about what to do. I offer instead some practical differences in learners that can inform instructional design more meaningfully.

All books must have a last chapter (of course), and the last chapter in this book is an attempt to illustrate how the foregoing theories can be combined into an instructional design process that is truly based on solid research. Throughout the book I have tried to strike a balance between practical examples and an informal tone and the scholarly work that backs up my conclusions. In each case I have also included some ideas about what might come next as a way of stimulating the reader's curiosity. I hope that the application of the ideas presented in this book is obvious to anyone, even someone who isn't interested in psychology. And I hope that the reader will continue to think about these issues even after finishing the book, and maybe be intrigued enough to want to go further. If that happens, there is no stopping the innovation and effectiveness in teaching that can be reached.

Marilla D. Svinicki

MY ATTEMPT TO MOTIVATE YOU
TO LEARN ABOUT LEARNING

"I can barely keep up with the latest developments in my own field. Why should I try to develop expertise in a whole new area?" That's a good question, certainly deserving of an answer. So I will attempt in this first chapter to make the case for understanding the theories and research on learning and motivation that should undergird all our decision-making in teaching. To do so, I am going to appeal to your intellectual side and your altruistic side, but then, being realistic, I'm also going to appeal to your pragmatic side because I believe that understanding the structure of learning results in better outcomes with less effort for both students and teachers.

UNDERSTANDING THEORY CAN MAKE YOU MORE EFFECTIVE AS A TEACHER

The primary responsibility of a teacher is to facilitate student learning. There are better and worse ways of doing that, but it would be hard to argue that we shouldn't be trying to be more effective at it. In order to be more effective at anything, it helps to understand the underlying mechanism. Consider the analogy of your car. You can get around in your car without knowing how it operates, right? But if you wanted to maximize fuel efficiency, it would help to understand how the car uses fuel and what you could do to get the most out of it. For example, you would know that there is an optimal mixture of fuel and air that promotes good gas mileage. And you would know that the carburetor creates this mix. To be an effective car user, then, you would recognize the importance of getting the carburetor adjusted as a way of increasing gas mileage.

Likewise, you can probably get by with teaching your classes without knowing much about how the students are learning. But if you understand how students learn, you can maximize the mileage you get out of any encounter with the students because you'll know how important it is to provide an organizational structure to new content. Your teaching will be more effective because you can be sure that the instruction taps into student strategies for learning. In this case you would be sure to provide an outline of the day's lesson for the students to make sure they get the main points of the class. You would visually highlight key ideas so that students would be more likely to include those ideas in their notes and subsequent learning. You would be sure to define and spell key terms that might be unfamiliar to the students so that they get them down correctly.

You're saying to yourself, "I already do those things; they're just common sense." Good for you. You've discovered some of the basic building blocks of learning on your own. Wouldn't you be suspicious of a theory of learning that didn't make common sense or didn't correspond to what you had observed? Just think how much more effective you would be if you knew even some basic concepts about learning that have been tested through research rather than having to discover them on your own. As we'll discuss later, understanding the structure of an area of knowledge makes you much more effective at using it for a wide range of purposes.

UNDERSTANDING THEORY MAKES YOU AND YOUR STUDENTS MORE EFFICIENT

A corollary to the effectiveness argument is a set of appeals for efficiency. The first appeals to your own need to save time in planning your teaching, and the second appeals to the need of your students to be more efficient at learning. As you probably realized above, you have discovered many of the basic ideas of learning through the process of trial and error. And your students have probably discovered some of their own strategies for learning by the same method. Indeed, the students who come to college usually have a very specific and successful set of learning strategies or they wouldn't have gotten this far. While this system works, it takes an awfully long time and a lot of frustration to find something if you don't know where to look or what to look for. Knowing how learning occurs allows you to bypass a lot of that digging around on your own and get to the business of using the information to design instruction. It won't take several semesters of tinkering to get a class right; it could happen on the first try if the design process is systematic and based on demonstrated principles of learning.

A second efficiency argument deals with the efficiency of student learning. One of the markers of effective teaching is that it leads to efficient learning. Students shouldn't have to go through contortions to learn; the instruction should point them in the right direction from the very beginning. That makes for efficient learning. Now, I should point out that the research literature on learning suggests that instruction shouldn't be too efficient; there is actually a need for students to put forth an effort to learn in order for learning to be long term (Druckman & Bjork, 1991). However, from an efficiency point of view it would be better for students to put their effort toward worthwhile concepts and be more efficient in learning the mundane or lower level concepts.

As an instructor who understands how learning happens, you can help students learn about learning efficiently. For example, many students are not aware of the need to read different types of texts using different strategies, particularly if they are new to a field. You can help them be more efficient in their study if you provide some suggestions about how to process your particular discipline's written material. The time savings in reading can then be applied to the harder work of learning.

UNDERSTANDING THEORY WILL HELP YOU SOLVE PROBLEMS

An advantage of knowing how something works is that you can continue to function even when it doesn't work. For example, if your car won't start in the morning, it helps to understand what is involved in getting it to start so that you can concentrate your efforts in those areas. We know that the tires have nothing to do with starting the car, so kicking them is a futile gesture, good only for releasing pent up frustration. However, if we know that the car needs gas because it is an internal combustion engine and a fully charged battery because there needs to be an electric spark to ignite the gas, we can start our problem solving there by checking whether the tank is filled and the battery is charged and connected to the engine. Now you're saying to yourself, "I don't need to know all that to drive a car. I just need to know that the car needs gas and the battery has to crank for the thing to start." True, but suppose you've kept the tank full and you turn the key and hear the cranking, and it still doesn't start. Now what? The more you know about how the car works, the further you can go toward figuring out what is wrong.

The same is true for teaching. If you have extremely bright and capable students, it doesn't much matter how you teach since they will be able to adapt to and cope with almost anything you throw at them. But what if your students are not in the top 1% of the population, a much more likely scenario? What if you have students who are really new to the field and don't yet have the kind of coping strategies they need? What if you do a brilliant job of presenting an enlightening and provocative lecture on the latest development in the field, and two thirds of the students don't understand a word you've said? The more you understand about how students learn, the more easily you'll be able to figure out what went wrong and what to do about it.

UNDERSTANDING THEORY WILL HELP YOU BE A MORE CREATIVE TEACHER

Most teachers are assigned a particular set of courses that they repeat once a semester or once a year. One way we keep the courses fresh is to update the material on a regular basis. This works wonderfully well except in those foundational classes that require a particular set of concepts to be taught before students move on to later courses. Then it often happens that to stay fresh the instructor adds new material but cannot drop anything from the existing material. As a result, the course grows in density until it becomes unwieldy for both students and teacher.

An alternative way to keep a course fresh is to constantly search for new ways to teach the material rather than for new material to teach. Most instructors do this by observing others and attempting to incorporate those ideas into their own classes. This works fine unless there is not a good fit between the new method and the old material. When this attempt to "adopt" fails, you need to be able to "adapt"—to find a better way of using the same idea, a task much facilitated if you understand how the given method is supposed to work. Alternatively, you can customize your own methods based on what you know about learning. The theories themselves suggest many strategies for helping students learn, both directly and indirectly. For example, if you know that learning should require some effort of a particular type on the part of the students, you can analyze your course to identify those concepts that are most important and deserving of student effort and come up with assignments that involve the students in processing the content deeply by requiring effort. An example assignment might be one in which students are required to contrast opposing interpretations of a phenomenon; the literature on learning asserts that the act of contrasting causes key features to be noticed more readily than simply listing the features, which in turn causes learning to last longer.

UNDERSTANDING THEORY IS A REFLECTION OF PROFESSIONAL SELF-DEVELOPMENT

I've now appealed to your altruistic and pragmatic sides; let me appeal to you as a professional. Theorists in the area of professional behavior (Schon, 1983) have pointed out that what distinguishes a professional in a field is his or her ability to engage in reflective practice. Reflective practice involves examining the assumptions that underlie your actions and making them consistent (Brookfield, 1995). Reflective practice also involves modifying and adjusting your practice or assumptions in the face of data. Consider yourself as a professional in your disciplinary field: What are the things that make you an expert in that area? You have 1) a vast storehouse of knowledge that is 2) well organized for quick searches and 3) a lot of case examples that help you reason through new examples. You also have 4) an inquiring attitude about the theories and assumptions of your field and 5) an interest in increasing your own understanding and advancing the field's understanding of basic and advanced phenomena (Bransford, Brown, & Cocking, 1999). The first three of these take a long time to accumulate; the last two probably existed from the very beginning of your interest in the field. These latter two also can be considered hallmarks of a professional attitude toward anything. As a professional you reflect on your theories and assumptions and try to advance their understanding both for yourself and for the field as a whole.

Now consider what would happen if you applied those same attitudes and values to your profession as a teacher. You already may have the case examples you need. You're just missing the storehouse and the organization for quick searches. The latter can be based on theories of learning or more concrete categories such as typical problems in teaching. The storehouse, I'm afraid, comes only with effort and time. But the theories that already exist can be very helpful in organizing what you have already experienced and alerting you to what to look for in new experiences. Soon you will have a storehouse of well-organized and categorized ideas that can form the basis of further growth.

UNDERSTANDING THEORY CAN LEAD TO CLASSROOM RESEARCH

One possible outcome of beginning to think about teaching in the inquiring way you already think about your discipline is that you may be inspired to start doing formal or informal research on teaching and learning in your own classes. Lee Shulman has said that one of the reasons that education seems to make so little progress is that we don't systematically study and publish our findings about different teaching events. He encourages faculty to apply their vast intellectual skills of analysis and evaluation to the act of teaching and to build a body of knowledge about teaching that is public and known to other practitioners.

It may be too grand an idea to encourage you to do extensive research for publication purposes, and, indeed, your institution may not value that kind of research. But you can still research questions that are of interest to you if you learn about theories of learning and want to see how they are operating in your class. Many of the ideas that have already been mentioned can be taken one step further and systematically studied for the effects they have on student learning. If the results are interesting to you, they might be interesting to a colleague as well. Initiating the same kind of collaborative dialogue that marks so many successful research efforts and that also raises questions about teaching will challenge your intellectual growth and contribute to the growth of the field as well.

PEDAGOGICAL CONTENT KNOWLEDGE

One caveat to the above interest in general theory and research is the question of the disciplinary specificity of learning and teaching strategies. Shulman has proposed the concept of "pedagogical content knowledge" as a way of distinguishing an understanding of how a field is learned as opposed to either knowledge of the field itself or of generic teaching concepts (Hillocks & Shulman, 1999). He suggests that there is an area of knowledge between these latter two, between knowledge of the field and knowledge of teaching. He calls it pedagogical content knowledge because it is knowledge about how to teach or learn a specific field. For example, learning astronomical concepts requires an ability to visualize that is not found in many other disciplines. One type of pedagogical content knowledge in astronomy, therefore, is helping students learn to visualize. Often, for experts in a field, these skills come so automatically that it is easy to overlook them as possible stumbling blocks when students are struggling. Developing pedagogical content knowledge means recognizing what the students might be experiencing and designing instruction to help them get around the blocks.

This does not mean, however, that the more general theories of learning and motivation are not useful. In fact, they form the foundation of pedagogical content knowledge upon which the specifics of the discipline are then built. But it is their manifestation in the discipline context that each instructor or discipline must discover. For example, all learning involves making connections between concepts and examples; it is the specific concept-example pairing that is the local instantiation of the more general principle.

ARE YOU CONVINCED?

I hope that I have given you sufficient motivation to plunge ahead and learn about theories and research in learning and motivation. Not only will it be a new challenge, but in the long run understanding how someone learns will help you help them be more effective and efficient at it.

2

HELPING STUDENTS
LEARN THE CONTENT

The most basic task of an instructor in any course is to help students learn the content. Notice that I didn't say "cover the content," because covering it is easy: Just keep talking. I said "help students learn the content," because that is, after all, one of the foundational purposes of education: to learn content. The students' job is to learn it, and the instructor's job is to make sure they do.

The "content" consists of vocabulary, definitions, facts, principles, information, and many other concrete as well as abstract concepts and the relationships among them. The content is what is written in the textbook, delivered in the lectures, and tested by most basic test formats. I distinguish between content and the other two most important categories of things that a learner must master: skills and understanding. Understanding (which is not the same as content knowledge) is the subject of the next chapter, and skill learning is the topic of Chapter 4. The present chapter focuses on learning the foundational knowledge from which the most complex forms of understanding are derived.

Unfortunately, many students equate this type of foundation knowledge learning with mastering the discipline. For too many, learning the content is synonymous with mastery. It is far from being enough learning to qualify as such in the minds of most faculty, but students have had many years of fact learning, and it is hard for them to accept that this is not all there is to achieving proficiency. Even more unfortunately, this misconception is only reinforced by the kinds of tests they experience in college: tests in which their performance is judged primarily on their ability to recall facts with only an occasional opportunity to apply those facts to a problem solution. As a result of their perception of what constitutes knowledge, many students depend on the memorization of facts to get them through their courses. Facts and details can be memorized if students are willing to put in enough effort and time, and so their memorization strategies are often rewarded with a good grade.

Most faculty would agree, however, that their own concept of understanding goes into much greater depth and doesn't rely on the surface features that form the basis for memorization. Instead they would opt for meaningful learning; learning that is connected to prior knowledge and useful for future performance. To develop this meaningful learning, a student needs to process new content at a much greater depth such that what is learned is the underlying structure of the content, not the surface features. Once the structure is understood, details can be filled in or recalled on the basis of that structural knowledge. This type of learning will last much longer and be much more useful than the surface processing represented by memorization.

THE BEST THEORIES FOR CONTENT LEARNING

According to the psychological literature, the best theories for understanding how students master meaningful content are cognitive theory, concept learning theory, and constructivist theory. All three deal with how new information is taken in and revised to make it meaningful and memorable. All three revolve around the idea that the best way to understand how students learn content is to understand how individuals think and store information in memory. All three are described in much more detail in the appendix. What is offered below is a thumbnail sketch of each sufficient to draw some conclusions about designing instruction.

Cognitive Theory

Cognitive theory is the parent theory of the three (Figure 2.1). It asserts that when new information is taken in through the senses, the learner must focus attention on key aspects of it, which then get placed in working memory, a sort of writeable/erasable type of memory that consists of what we are aware of at the moment. While in working memory, the new information is being compared with old, related information retrieved from long-term memory, our permanent storage system. If the two types of information are similar enough, the new information is added to the long-term memory structure related to the existing memories. If the two types are very different, the learner will sometimes have to create a new information structure to hold it, or the learner might modify the existing structure to accommodate this new information. In fact, this process was described by Jean Piaget, a world famous developmental psychologist who proposed it as the way we all learn. New information that fits with old information is said to be assimilated; new information that causes the learner to revise the existing structure is said to be accommodated. All the while the learner is trying to maintain a balance between old and new structures and information. The process of revising incoming information to fit into the long-term memory structure is called encoding. The purpose of most encoding is to make the new information more meaningful and memorable so it can be retrieved later to help in similar situations.

Figure 2.1
Cognitive Theory's Description of Learning

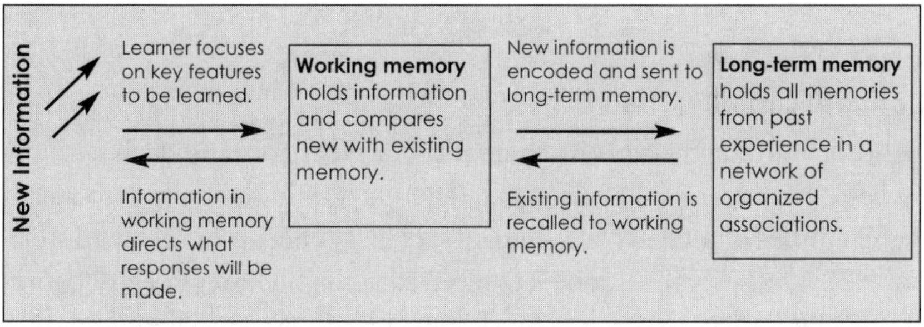

For example, in cognitive theory terms, when a student reads about the Battle of Gettysburg, whatever he pays attention to is what will get learned. He might focus on the military strategy, he might focus on the issues behind the Civil War as they are played out in that battle, or he might focus on who fought in the battle. Whatever attracts this focused attention goes into working memory to be processed for storage. The student then tries to find a similar event or fact already stored in memory to use as an anchor for this new information. Part of that stored information is the category of event of this battle (e.g., a Civil War battle) and its remembered associations (such as American wars, North versus South, blue/gray, Lincoln's speech, etc.). If after searching memory, he finds a relevant match to this current passage (perhaps his memory of other battles), the new information is marked as a Civil War battle, and he responds accordingly. This new information will become associated with all the other Civil War information he has in long-term memory. If there has never been a Civil War category before because he has never learned about it before, the learner will pick the closest category that he does have and use it to make a connection. For example, maybe he has read a lot about wars in general, so he tries to use that knowledge to connect with this new information about the Battle of Gettysburg. If, on the other hand, he has no prior exposure to anything like the Battle of Gettysburg, he may have to create a new category based on this new experience.

According to cognitive theory, learning is a constant processing of new and old information seeking connections or creating them anew. We could say that a learner has learned when his long-term memory structure becomes more organized and efficient for information storage and retrieval.

Concept Learning Theory

Concept learning theory is a subset of cognitive theory and deals with the processes that learners go through to encode new information into meaningful chunks of related characteristics, called concepts or schemata (Figure 2.2). Long-term memory is comprised of highly integrated networks of schemata all interconnected in an organized manner. These schemata control our behavior because they represent our most consistent pattern of behavior in the presence of a given set of conditions. It is especially true that when students are learning definitions and simple concepts, their behavior is best described by concept learning theory.

For example, in the case of our young friend's encounter with the Battle of Gettysburg, what he's looking for in long-term memory is actually a concept or a schema of Civil War information. Failing to find one, he creates a new schema containing all the characteristics of this particu-

Figure 2.2
Concept Learning Theory's Description of Learning

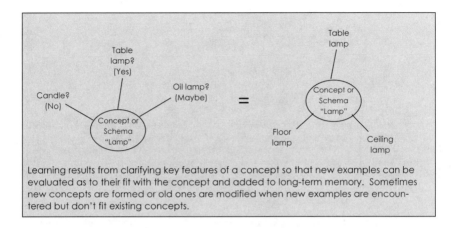

Learning results from clarifying key features of a concept so that new examples can be evaluated as to their fit with the concept and added to long-term memory. Sometimes new concepts are formed or old ones are modified when new examples are encountered but don't fit existing concepts.

lar battle. As he encounters more information about the Civil War, his war schema is enhanced or tuned by comparing Gettysburg to other battles. Battle characteristics, which show up whenever he reads about wars, become more strongly related to one another, while other characteristics like place or who's fighting get dropped from the schema because they vary so much from one battle to another. After encountering a sufficient amount of information about battles and non-battle encounters, the student has developed a pretty good concept of what battle or war is (and is not) to guide future use of the information about Gettysburg. This comparison process is the essence of concept learning. By comparing Gettysburg with other battles, other events, and other wars, the learner has grasped the concept of Gettysburg as a Civil War battle.

Constructivist Theories

Constructivist theories take learning one step deeper into the mind of the learner (Figure 2.3). Constructivists assert that learners are constantly updating their long-term memory schemata, based on their ongoing experiences. What results is a very complex and unique world view peculiar to each individual, having been constructed out of all the learner's prior experiences. Constructivists say that learners are constantly constructing their understanding of the world based on those

13

Figure 2.3
Constructivist Theory's Description of Learning

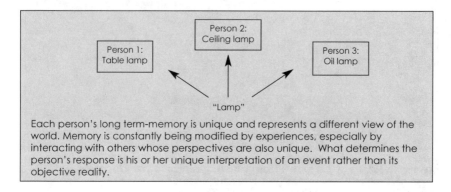

Each person's long term-memory is unique and represents a different view of the world. Memory is constantly being modified by experiences, especially by interacting with others whose perspectives are also unique. What determines the person's response is his or her unique interpretation of an event rather than its objective reality.

experiences. Therefore, everyone's construction of the world is unique even though we share a great many concepts. There are many versions of constructivist theory—some more radical than others—but the basic theory revolves around the learners' constant reconstruction of meaning out of experience.

According to constructivist theory, the student's understanding of the Civil War will change with each new encounter and will be uniquely his because no one else will have had the same experiences as he has had. Some overlap will occur where experiences are held in common, but each pattern is unique because each learner comes to the situation with a unique set of background experiences.

USING THESE THEORIES TO ENHANCE LEARNING

All three of the foregoing theories say that, during the learning of content, learners are picking out key features that define the concepts and making connections between that new information and their existing world views. Therefore, instruction should focus on helping the learners identify those features and make those connections. Eventually, the ability to recall those connections should be fluent enough to allow for permanent and efficient use of the information.

To use these theories in designing instruction, remember these important points:

1) Learning involves changing the long-term memory of the learner through new connections.

2) Students must focus on the key aspects of new information in order to learn it.

3) Students must encode information into long-term memory in order to learn it.

4) Students must have multiple exposures to using new information in order for learning to last.

What follows is a series of instructional suggestions based on these three theories.

Identify the Key Features to Be Learned

Prior to instruction you need to carefully analyze any concept that is to be learned so that the defining features (the key things that go into the definition of the concept) are identified and emphasized during instruction. An example of such an analysis is shown in Figure 2.4.

One of the most helpful teaching strategies for concept learning is giving a clear definition. The definition in essence lists the critical features of the concept. The need for a clear definition may seem obvious, but in reality, it is a very difficult thing for most experts to do because their own understanding of the concept is so rich that they have trouble breaking it down into its essence. It is also often the case that the kinds of concepts we are teaching at this basic level are not easily broken down further into clearly identified components. Nevertheless, if your students are going to have to learn basic definitions and concepts, you must first be able to highlight the defining features of that content and incorporate them into the definition. For example, the author of the history textbook our student is reading will have chosen to include key ideas about the Civil War battles that are necessary to learning what was unique about them as opposed to other wars or other events during the Civil War.

A second part of this feature analysis must involve considering what will be present in the situations in which the learners are going to use this new information, because you must think not only of what to pay attention to but also what to ignore. Actual usage situations will be full of rich details, some of which are important and some of which are not, and

Figure 2.4
Two Examples of Conceptual Learning

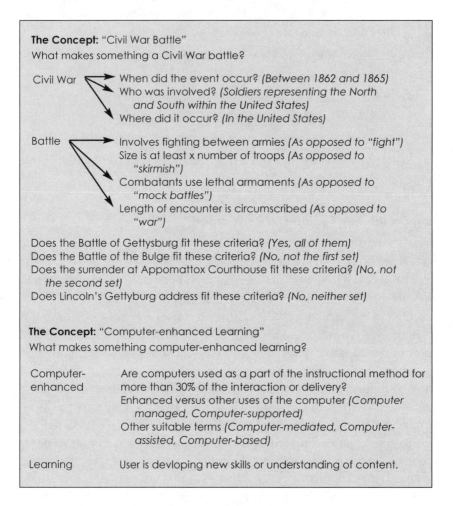

The Concept: "Civil War Battle"
What makes something a Civil War battle?

Civil War — When did the event occur? *(Between 1862 and 1865)*
Who was involved? *(Soldiers representing the North and South within the United States)*
Where did it occur? *(In the United States)*

Battle — Involves fighting between armies *(As opposed to "fight")*
Size is at least x number of troops *(As opposed to "skirmish")*
Combatants use lethal armaments *(As opposed to "mock battles")*
Length of encounter is circumscribed *(As opposed to "war")*

Does the Battle of Gettysburg fit these criteria? *(Yes, all of them)*
Does the Battle of the Bulge fit these criteria? *(No, not the first set)*
Does the surrender at Appomattox Courthouse fit these criteria? *(No, not the second set)*
Does Lincoln's Gettyburg address fit these criteria? *(No, neither set)*

The Concept: "Computer-enhanced Learning"
What makes something computer-enhanced learning?

Computer-enhanced — Are computers used as a part of the instructional method for more than 30% of the interaction or delivery?
Enhanced versus other uses of the computer *(Computer managed, Computer-supported)*
Other suitable terms *(Computer-mediated, Computer-assisted, Computer-based)*

Learning — User is devloping new skills or understanding of content.

learners will have to be able to tell which are which. The more the learning situation can be made to resemble the real world situation, the harder it will be to learn, but the better the learning will be in the long run because the learners will know what to ignore. Research strongly supports designing instruction to look like the real thing so that students will eventually be able to recognize key features regardless of the surrounding noise. In the case of history teaching, for example, instructors might have students learn about the Civil War by reading authentic, first-person accounts and picking out key ideas found in them. Here they'd have to be able to differentiate a key idea from a detail.

Focus Student Attention by Highlighting the Key Features During Learning

During instruction, the defining features identified in the foregoing analysis need to be highlighted so that student attention will be focused on them. Some ways that key features are highlighted in different media include simple things like bold print and underlining in text, verbal cueing ("The first main point is . . .") and the use of outlines projected on an overhead in lectures, and contrasting colored text and progressive disclosure on computer screens. If it is difficult for students to figure out the main features of a concept, they will not be able to give those ideas the kind of attention needed for learning. The highlighting draws attention to the ideas and gets them into working memory where they can be processed.

Both theory and research offer some cautions and some strategies about manipulating student attention. The first is that attention is limited, and you should exercise caution so as not to overload it. For example, having too many main ideas presented simultaneously or through too many channels will dilute attention. How many is too many? That's a difficult question to answer since it depends on how much the learner already knows and how well structured the information is, but research suggests that working memory can only hold seven pieces of information (plus or minus two) at one time. It's best to err on the side of less information than more. So, for example, in our history class, a 50-minute class period probably can explore three main concepts, each having only one or two subconcepts. Examples and elaborations don't count as new information because they are really just expansions of the main idea. My own rule of thumb is that at the end of the class period, a student should be able to tell me what the main ideas of the class period were without reading them from the notes. Given that restriction, you can see that if I had more than five main points, most students (or even most adults) wouldn't be able to hold that much information.

One of the values of a progressive disclosure procedure (each main point displayed in succession with the rest covered or dimmed) is that only the highlighted idea draws immediate attention. In essence, the learners know where to look. There is no overloading of working memory because the learner is focusing on one point at a time. The advantage of leaving the already covered ideas up but dimmed is that it allows the learners to see an overall structure to the information, which, as we'll see later, is an important support for deep learning.

Another strategy that attacks the same overload problem is providing the students with outline notes to which they can add their own summaries. The outline provides the main points so students don't have to expend processing attention resources on figuring out what to write in their notes. Rather, they can devote that energy to making connections between the main ideas and their own experiences or instructor examples—that is, encoding the information.

The second caution about attention deals with using multiple channels of input. While some research supports the idea of having redundant information provided both orally and visually, other studies show that adding too many additional inputs (like flashing words or cute sounds) or requiring simultaneous activity by the learner (for example, note taking) can divide the learner's attention too much. Students have learned to cope with this overload problem by becoming verbatim recorders of what the instructor says, leaving any thinking they might do until later. This is unfortunate because they cannot possibly transcribe all that the instructor says; they invariably will miss some of the elaboration that the instructor provides in the form of examples and richer details, which are important for encoding into long-term memory. DeWinstanley and Bjork (2002) report that the biggest detrimental impact of too much simultaneous information is on encoding, the most important process in learning. To get around this problem, instructors should insert strategic pauses that allow students to digest what they have heard and summarize it in their notes. (In fact, that would be a good way to teach students to use summarizing in their notes, which is a much more effective learning strategy than verbatim note taking.) Instructors should also resist the temptation to get too flashy with a presentation for fear of overwhelming student attentional capacity.

Sequence the Instruction to Support Learning

There is a science as well as an art to deciding the order in which instruction should proceed. The research literature has identified three issues that can be considered in making sequence choices. They involve: 1) whether to start with an overview or build to a climax; 2) use of a strategic sequence of examples to illustrate a concept; and 3) whether to give a lot of practice all at once or space learning out over a longer period of time.

Overview or climax? Instruction can 1) flow from the big picture to the details or 2) build from the details to a big picture climax or 3) cycle through several iterations of details and summaries before drawing a grand conclusion. In our history example, should the instructor give an overview of all the Civil War battles and then analyze each one against that overview? Or should she describe the battles and then pull together all their common characteristics into a grand, unifying summary? The choice is not driven as much by which is the best strategy for learning as it is by 1) learner preferences, 2) learner prior knowledge, and 3) goal of the instruction.

In terms of learner preferences, the research literature has supported the idea that individuals will show a preference for holistic processing (seeing the big picture first) versus sequential processing (going step-by-step to develop an idea). In reality, there is much to be said for providing an overview first before giving details, and it certainly won't harm the learners who prefer details first. From a learning standpoint, having a big picture structure available into which to plug details should facilitate most learning. In the literature, this is called giving an "advance organizer" because it provides some preliminary organization of the material to facilitate student understanding. Many textbooks provide introductory overviews or chapter objectives to accomplish this. There is an old rhetorical strategy that gives the same advice. It says, "Tell them what you're going to tell them, tell them, then tell them what you told them."

The sequencing choice will also depend on how much *prior knowledge* the students bring to the situation. Learners with a lot of prior knowledge about a subject already have an existing knowledge structure into which to plug new information and therefore don't really need a very elaborate initial overview. They can plunge directly into details and they may possibly even prefer that level of presentation because it should give them an opportunity to compare what they are receiving with what they already know and refine one or the other on the spot. There is research to support the idea that, while highly structured material is good for novices, students with prior knowledge about an area learn more with less structured presentations. The reasoning is that the lack of structure forces them to provide the structure based on their prior knowledge, and thus to process the material much more deeply (deWinstanley & Bjork, 2002). This strategy would also be supported by the constructivist theory, which says it is best for the learners to provide their own structure.

From the perspective of *learning goals*, providing an overview first favors objectives focused on building a structured knowledge base because the focus is on where the details fit into the big picture. Giving details first and building to a conclusion is better for goals that stress higher order thinking skills because the learners have to organize information on their own while the details are being presented. Humans are pattern-seeking organisms and so we do try to find patterns in any information that we encounter. An instructional sequence that moves from details to conclusion is sort of like a detective story that invites the reader to speculate who done it along the way until the climax is reached and all the threads drawn together. If the purpose of the learning is to practice this type of conclusion drawing, the sequential model works well. If the purpose is learning a fixed set of content, the learners will eventually have to go back and organize the information in light of the conclusions drawn. While this is actually a good strategy for learning, our students are unfortunately not necessarily inherently curious about our topics, and they frequently choose to simply wait until the climax (the main point) is reached, at which point they write it all down. Sometimes we can thwart this tendency by actively involving them in the inductive process along the way. For example, the history instructor could pose questions that invite the students to speculate on what the next development might be in the sequence of the Civil War. The compromise is to move iteratively through the material in a sequence of smaller loops that emphasize both big picture and the inductive process.

There is another point to consider in this overview/climax debate, and that is the content of the discipline itself. Research on differences among disciplines has outlined what we knew intuitively: There are differences between disciplines in a lot of ways that influence learning. Most relevant to this discussion are the discipline structure and its epistemology. Some disciplines are highly structured, even hierarchically structured, such that knowledge building must proceed in an orderly sequence (for example, math). Other disciplines are more loosely structured and allow knowledge building to take many routes (for example, psychology). Highly structured disciplines lend themselves to the climax model because they build up gradually. Loosely structured disciplines could probably go either way, although if the instructor doesn't like surprises, she might be better off with the overview structure. That way she can exercise more control over the direction instruction takes because she has set some boundaries up front.

In terms of epistemology, some disciplines are argued in one direction in terms of how ideas are generated. For example, biology tends to depend on the slow accumulation of lots of evidence all pointing toward the same conclusion. Physics tends to grow by debate and argument as new theories are proposed that overturn existing theories. (Although this is an oversimplification, it makes the point of how disciplines can differ.) Each of these two approaches would suggest a way to sequence instruction: either the slow, steady accumulation of data or the seesaw of contrasting theories.

Sequencing examples. Now let's consider how examples play a role in sequencing instruction. The first examples that students associate with a concept are very important because they become the benchmarks against which future judgments are made. It is particularly effective to contrast key, paradigmatic examples with increasingly complex nonexamples presented simultaneously (Decyk, 1994). Paradigmatic examples are those that are most closely associated with a concept (for example, using the example of dog as opposed to iguana to illustrate the concept of "pet"), so it is easier for learners to understand and remember them. The simultaneous presentation of the examples allows the learners to make more detailed comparisons because they don't have to hold as much information in working memory. Instead, the information resides in the simultaneously presented display, and all the learners have to do is compare the examples. (This is an example of the use of "scaffolding" in instruction. The instruction is specifically designed to provide a scaffold or support for initial learning by removing an obstacle—in this instance, one due to memory limitations.) The sequence of comparisons used can then build gradually toward a more refined and complex understanding of the concept. The sequence used should highlight the various features of the concept. For example, in teaching the concept of "love," you might start with romantic love, which for most college students would be the paradigmatic example of love, and ask if platonic love also fits their definition of love. Then move on to fraternal love or parental love and so on. Each comparison highlights a different aspect of the concept. Although this example uses a fairly abstract concept as an illustration, the same strategies are used in many disciplines to explore the qualities of their most basic concepts. For a more complete analysis of this type of example sequencing, consult Decyk (1994) or any writings on the Socratic method (Dillon, 1988) or other questioning sequences.

One particularly effective way of simultaneously contrasting concepts is the use of a comparative organizer, as shown in Figure 2.5. In this organizer the initial example of the concept being illustrated has all the qualities indicated in the columns, while the other examples lack one or more of them. The instructor can use this grid as the basis for a lecture and gradually fill it in, or, better yet, have the students work together to fill it in. (See Angelo & Cross, 1993, for examples of other student activities along this line.)

Figure 2.5
A Comparative Organizer for the Concept "Pet"

PETS	Are alive	Are confinable	Can be handled	Have available food sources	Respond to commands
Dogs	X	X	X	X	X
Cats	X	X	X	X	
Pet Rocks		X	X		
Ants	X	X		X	
Other Example					

One particularly important set of recommendations about example use comes from the concept learning literature. It is both common sense and research supported to say that it is easier to learn concrete concepts than abstractions. Unfortunately, much of what we teach in higher education resides in abstractions or generalized principles. If the learners have no personal experiences to use as connections for understanding the abstractions (which is generally the case), they will be forced to rely on memorization and very shallow processing strategies to learn the concepts. It is important that instructors provide concrete examples of new concepts as much as possible early in learning. These concrete examples will anchor students' understanding until they have sufficient experience to generalize the abstraction. Of course, it is always preferable that the learners generate their own examples, but without prior knowledge this will be difficult for them.

Spaced versus massed practice. One final aspect of sequencing is the issue of spacing of learning. Should we cluster information together all at once or space it out over several classes? On the one hand, the cognitive model would say that things have to be simultaneously present in working memory in order for connections to be made between them. Thus, we should be very attentive to making sure that everything that needs to go together gets presented in close proximity. On the other hand, as common experience and research supports, it is better to return repeatedly to information over the course of several sessions rather than experience it only once but in a really detailed and intense way. While there is some benefit for initial learning of massed practice (a lot of exposure in one shot), in general long-term retention is best produced by having students return to the information over and over again, especially in varied forms and situations. This is probably because having to retrieve information from memory anew each time makes the retrieval process more automatic, and experiencing the information in different contexts has the effect of varying the irrelevant cues and teaching the learners to ignore them, as discussed earlier.

So, for example, if our history instructor has provided a set of rules for classifying Civil War events or causes, she would reiterate them each time a new event was studied. Eventually this set of rules would become second nature for the students and shape the way they look at future events. These rules become heuristics for analyzing new information.

In addition, as I said earlier, the cognitive model asserts that working memory has a limited capacity to hold information for any length of time. There is a wonderful visual analog for this concept in the old "I Love Lucy" television series. In one episode, Lucy and Ethel are working in a candy factory assembly line, wrapping pieces as they move along the conveyer belt. They're doing fine until something interrupts their smooth flow. The candies start coming faster than they can handle so they start stuffing candies into their mouths and aprons to avoid letting an unwrapped one through. Of course, they can't keep up and eventually the whole system breaks down. Think of that image as analogous to information flowing into working memory. Too much, too fast, and the system breaks down.

If more information comes in before we've transferred other new information to long-term memory, we lose whatever came first; first in, first out. So it is a bad idea to try to present too much information all at once. Learners need spaces between information bits in order to process them and move them along. Instructors can provide these spaces by inserting strategic pauses after important points to allow students to get those points out of working memory and free up space for the next new information.

Support the Learners' Encoding of Content

We have now reached the most critical part of the learning process: encoding or the transformation of information for storage in long-term memory. Failures here are essentially failures to learn. Unless new information can be incorporated into the learner's long-term memory, it will not be available for future use. So it is critical to design instruction that supports encoding. Virtually all forms of encoding are based on making connections between old and new information or among new pieces of information. Psychologists talk about this as making the information more meaningful by making more connections and ways to access it. Let's consider the most common forms of encoding and what they imply for instruction.

Organization. The first way to improve storage is to have a good organization system. Organization enables us to do more with whatever resources we have. The same is true for memory. The more organized it is, the more we can do with it. So one of the best ways to encode information is to organize it. This actually is the most basic form of encoding, too. We are organizing organisms; we're always trying to put things into categories because it speeds up processing time. Once something has been categorized, we don't have to examine it all that closely because whatever the characteristics of the category are, that's what we'll attach to the new example. As students take in new information, their first reaction (after getting it down verbatim) is to find a way to categorize it, to organize it. For example, if I were to read off a list of 12 words, four of which were fruits, four vegetables, and four dairy products, that's how you would remember them. You'd put all the fruits together, all the vegetables, and all the dairy products. You can't help it; it's ingrained in your system. The same is true for students. They will try to organize information by whatever means they can. To make sure that students use the best, most accurate, and most efficient system, an instructor can organize the information for them. Sometimes students are accustomed to using a categorization system that we experts have long abandoned. Our history example provides a good example of this. Students automatically associate history with chronology, and so they tend to group events in the order in which they occurred. For an expert historian, this is a very naïve and ineffective strategy. The historian would much prefer organization by causal forces. In order to make sure that her students are following her lead, this history instructor will have to emphasize the organization of the content in terms of cause and effect. She may even have to refuse to give dates to break the students of their habits. To help students encode more effectively, we can organize the content by the way we present it. Something so simple as providing an outline of the day's lecture is a way to provide organization for encoding.

Elaboration. The next strategy for encoding is to elaborate on the material. When we do this, we add connections and fill in details that differentiate among concepts. The additional connections and details provide more ways for new information to connect with existing information, which makes access easier. Our history instructor elaborates on the Battle of Gettysburg by talking about the physical structure of the site and what it was before the battle. She might use memorable stories about individuals from each side who participated in the battle, how they got there, and what happened to them later. She might have the students read short stories about the battle or see a film about it. She might bring in pictures of the soldiers, the battlefield, Matthew Brady style, or clips from the PBS series. She might ask students to see if any of their relatives fought in the war. These details will enrich the students' understanding and can themselves be cues for retrieving content from long-term memory.

Imagery. This encoding strategy involves the use of images, as you might expect. In memory, a picture really is worth 1,000 words. Using vivid images or unusual images makes content easier to remember. Memory gurus advise using such images to improve memory for names. I'm suggesting it as a way to store information more efficiently. I do want to make a distinction between images as described here as an encoding strategy and images as used in an elaboration encoding strategy. Just providing a picture of something will not enhance memory. The picture has to in some way represent what is to be remembered. That is why this particular strategy requires you to use the image to make a connection between ideas (e.g., a face and a name). Pictures alone will elaborate an idea, but it takes connected images to stand alone as stored memories.

To illustrate with history again, political cartoons are the kind of images that can be encoded. Political cartoons take a complex set of ideas and distill them into a visual analogy. So if our history instructor wanted to make the point that the North's army was well equipped while the South's was not, the cartoon might depict the North's soldiers in sleek cars and the South's soldiers in donkey carts. That image conveys a strong message.

Beyond these basic strategies for encoding, there are some important caveats that influence how students store new information.

Deep versus shallow processing. Sometimes new information comes with its own built-in meaning, and sometimes the learner has to create meaning where none exists. One manifestation of this activity is shallow versus deep processing. *Shallow processing* means that the meaning of information is going to be based on surface features. An example of shallow processing is memorizing. The shallowest of shallow processing is repeating information over and over again until you can say it from memory. In this case, the surface features that have been stored in memory are things like the sound of the words, the color of the cover of the book, the visual image of words on the page, or a particularly prominent feature of someone's face; the information has no real meaning. A lot of memory tricks that you find in books depend on shallow processing. For example, we are often advised to learn names quickly by picking out some prominent feature of a person and making an association with a bizarre visual image using that feature and the person's name, like Bob = Bulb for the person with the large red nose (bulb is sort of like bob and sort of like large red nose). This would be in contrast to actually getting to know the person and learning more about him, which might allow deeper processing. Another example is memorizing the colors in a rainbow by using the memory aid "ROY G BIV." Deeper processing of that information would require learning why the colors fall in that order (i.e., because of their wavelengths).

Deep processing refers to storing information in long-term memory on the basis of its real meaning or structure. For example, learning a person's name by getting to know what they do and where they belong in your network of associations is processing your knowledge of them at a much deeper level. This level of processing allows you to access the person's name not just by his or her appearance but through multiple connections, like where you met, whom you know in common, what interests you share, and so on. Deep processing of content involves making connections between what learners are trying to encode and whatever they already know about the topic. To encourage deep processing, an instructor should use examples and situations that learners can connect with, things that are familiar and perhaps experienced personally. This, of course, means getting to know the learners and their interests and situations, not just for motivational purposes (which also are served by this strategy), but because it facilitates making deeply processed connections. In our history course, the instructor may find out which students have actually visited Civil War battlefields and connect with those experiences. Or she might have the class read a group of Civil War novels or see films based on the war. She might relate events that led to the war to current events that resulted from the war or events in other nations that had civil wars. Making students compare any of these would produce deeper processing than simply listening to a straight narrative.

Prior knowledge. This brings up the interesting effect of learner prior knowledge and experience. If there is one thing that all psychologists can agree on, it is that prior knowledge and experience affect current behavior and learning. When learners are trying to deep process information, they are almost always trying to tap into their prior knowledge, the schemata through which they interpret the world. The more prior knowledge they have about a topic, the easier it is for them to find a relevant connection or schema and to learn the material. This is one reason why it is so much easier to teach upper division courses or adults: The learners bring a lot of prior knowledge with which to connect, so the instructor doesn't have to make the connections for them.

A disadvantage of prior knowledge is that sometimes a given learner's prior knowledge is incorrect, and that can result in confusion or misunderstanding. For example, suppose one of the students in history class came from a Southern family background in which the Civil War was thought of as oppression of states' rights rather than an assertion of national unity. Now a new interpretation is being proposed in the history class, one that conflicts with what that student has been raised with. What would be the effect on learning?

This has been a particular focus of research on science education, where misconceptions abound and get in the way of learning correct information. For example, many physical principles are counterintuitive (e.g., heavy objects fall at the same speed as light objects). Unless the existence of incorrect prior knowledge is anticipated and confronted directly, it often interferes with learning the correct interpretation of events. Sometimes even new information based on real observations will be distorted to fit with the existing misconception (Guzzetti & Hynd, 1998). Constructivists are particularly sensitive to the need for designing instruction to support or contradict learners' prior knowledge. Without this experience, the learners could easily construct an internally consistent, but externally incorrect world view.

What do you do about misconceptions? A strong body of research proposes ideas for producing conceptual change, when a learner's prior conceptual understanding is incorrect, incomplete, and intractable. We'll consider this topic in more depth in Chapter 3, but here are a few conceptual change ideas.

A particularly interesting perspective on this process has been provided by Posner, Strike, Hewson, and Gertzog (1982). Their model says that four conditions must be present for learners to abandon a previously held erroneous belief. The first condition is *dissatisfaction*; the learners have to be confronted with information that makes them dissatisfied with their previous belief. The second condition is that any new explanation being offered to replace the old belief must be *intelligible*; that is, the learners have to be able to understand the new proposal fairly easily. Third, the proposed alternative must be *plausible*; the possibility that it could be used to explain any situation that the old theory did as well as that which it couldn't has to be believable. And, finally, the new proposed theory must be *fruitful*; it must be able to predict new ideas as well as explain old ones. In terms of teaching, instruction must be designed to meet these four conditions if students are to be convinced to abandon their old misconceptions and adopt our new ones.

How often do we actually pay attention to these needs rather than just assuming that students will adopt the new theories we offer simply because we said them? Not very often, I would expect, which could explain why old beliefs and incorrect prior knowledge are seldom dislodged simply by exposure to new ideas.

On the other hand, prior knowledge can be used to the instructor's advantage. It saves processing time because learners can and will make connections with it on their own. Prior knowledge that is similar in structure to new learning can be used as an analogy to help the learners make inferences about the direction that new information is likely to take (e.g., if all previous examples of concept X have these characteristics and the current instance is like X, then it must have the same characteristics and act the same way). The instructor might be able to use students' knowledge of board games to help them understand politics, for example. Or if they've mastered the reasoning behind one Civil War battle, perhaps they can use that knowledge to analyze the next one without instructor intervention.

Meaningfulness. I said earlier that learners are generally trying to find meaning in the experiences they have and the things they encounter. Instruction that helps them make new information more meaningful will result in easier and more long-lasting learning. (Note: The term "meaningful" here doesn't have the same meaning as "relevance," that is, topical, current, or even important. "Meaningful" here is a narrower, more technical use of the word as "something that has a lot of connections to a learner's prior knowledge or with other things also being learned.") One of the best ways to help learners find meaning is through the use of concrete examples with which they are familiar. It is not an overstatement to say that the basis for meaningfulness is the learner's ability to identify the points of connection between his or her own experiences and the information being learned. Instructors can provide examples from the real world, but it is usually far preferable for the learners to make their own examples. The learners' own examples will be more meaningful to them because they will have more interconnections with the learner's total experiences and world views.

There are some artificial ways of making information meaningful when there is no inherent meaning in them. These are the various mnemonic strategies that show up in "improve your memory" techniques. For example, the use of acronyms that are real words and have some relationship to the phrases for which they stand are attempts to make long phrases more meaningful (e.g., "homes" [for remembering the name of the five great lakes]—Huron, Ontario, Michigan, Erie, and Superior) or the use of phrases as substitutes for long lists that are hard to remember (e.g., "every good boy does fine" for the strings on a guitar). Today a lot of phone numbers are turned into words (e.g., 555–SAFE for a safe house for abused children). The system works because the word or the phrase is more meaningful than a long title, a set of musical notes, or string of numbers, respectively.

Another strategy for adding meaning to inherently meaningless sets of information is the use of imagery. Research has shown that placing lists of words in the context of a narrative that connects them, however bizarrely, makes the lists easier to learn and remember.

If the content you are trying to teach does involve the tedious learning of a lot of lists, and if those lists have no internal logic readily available to a novice, you could help your students a great deal if you encourage them to create meaning through the use of such strategies. Eventually if students stay in the field long enough, those memory tricks will become unnecessary because they will have had sufficient practice using the lists that the lists become automatic. Or perhaps the students will expand their understanding of the list enough to become aware of the reasons behind the existence of the list in the first place, which brings us to the last strategy for supporting encoding, and that is the one based on the underlying structure of the material.

Structural understanding. This strategy is my personal favorite when it comes to enhancing encoding because it encompasses most of the other strategies. I also think that it is structural understanding that grounds what most of us mean by "understanding." As a result, I'll delay a full discussion of this idea for the next chapter. Here I'll give a brief overview of the idea so you can see how it fits into the idea of encoding.

Encoding by structural understanding means basing the encoding on the organization of the material, how the various parts fit together as a whole. A familiar example of this type of encoding involves creating an outline of the content to be learned. The outline lays out the structure of the content—what the main ideas are and how they are hierarchically related, what the supporting data are for each main idea, and an ordering and grouping of all the information in one compact image. Many times you can simply close your eyes and picture the structure of the outline in your mind. If that doesn't help, you can use the structure as a stimulus for remembering the parts. You know that the content outline had three main headings, and you can only think of two. But because you know there's a third, that encourages you to keep thinking about what the third one is. And if you know the relationship among the three main headings, you might be able to infer what the third heading is based on the two you can remember. There are lots of ways in which we signal structure to learners. We do it verbally by using words that imply relationships (such as "for example") and visually through the use of outlines and concept maps. We'll investigate these signals further in the next chapter.

What is the bottom line with regard to structural knowledge as the basis for encoding? It is worth your while as an instructor to spend time thinking organizationally about your course's content and to design instruction around that organization. It is also worth your students' while to encourage them to think structurally by modeling such thinking yourself, by using case-based reasoning as a stimulus to their use of comparative cases as memory tools, by having them complete content organizers, and using any other strategies that encourage structural thinking.

Give Students an Opportunity to Actively Work With the Material to Produce Fluency and Transfer of Use

Of course, all the meaningful processing in the world will not be sufficient to ensure that learners will be able to use new information smoothly and efficiently. That requires practice. So the last step in designing instruction based on the cognitive model involves a much more mundane component: student active practice. Students must have multiple opportunities to put into use the information they have been learning. We want them to be able to recall and use the information effortlessly so that they can exert their mental energies not on recall, but on expanding their understanding. And we want them to be able to recognize situations that call for using that information. The literature offers several recommendations about how to accomplish this aspect of instruction.

The first requires that we revisit the notion of spaced versus massed practice that was discussed earlier. You'll recall that spaced practice is the preferred strategy to maximize retention. I'll refine that slightly now by adding that, at the point of initial learning, massed practice is useful to establish a concept. Then instruction should cycle through several iterations of practice using the information. What does this practice do for a learner's understanding? It is probably the case that you can never have exactly the same situation twice, so each slightly different situation of use makes a slightly different set of connections until more and more connections are made, thereby increasing the likelihood that something will trigger that memory. With repeated use, we are working toward what the literature calls "automaticity." This is the level at which we can use information without too much conscious effort; retrieval of the information has become automatic. The advantage of automatic information is that it takes up less cognitive processing capacity, leaving more capacity for more complex tasks. Think of it this way. When you are first learning a language, a lot of your processing time is spent translating back and forth from your native language, which doesn't leave much capacity left for appreciating what is being said or listening to more than one person talking. You have to concentrate too much on translation. As you become more fluent in a language, the words and grammar become more automatic. You eventually don't have to think so hard about what a word means because its meaning comes more easily to you. You have more capacity available for other things and so you can do more than one thing at a time. When you become fluent in a language, you spend no time in translation because the meanings of words are immediately available to you. At this point you are operating automatically. We wish the same level of fluency for our students in using the vocabulary and concepts of our discipline. We want them to understand our explanations without having to pause and reflect on what a term or phrase means. In fact, when students complain about the use of jargon in classes, they are responding to this very phenomenon; their lack of automaticity with the vocabulary slows down their ability to process and understand what's being said. Unfortunately, there is no way around this problem other than practice, practice, practice, especially in the context in which the information will ultimately be used.

There is an additional consideration at this stage of learning: the context of practice. A very frequent complaint lodged against our educational institutions is that students seem to be unable to use what they have learned in the real world after they graduate. This is the problem of transfer, which is the topic of Chapter 4. But I want to say something about it here because it is relevant when we are thinking about designing instruction. This problem arises because of the fact that all of the conditions present during the initial making of connections (i.e., learning) get connected to the new information, not just those that we intended. For example, positional cues in the textbook are learned along with the information and frequently are used to recall that information when we get stuck. ("Let's see. I remember it was on the right-hand page in the upper left-hand corner.") This phenomenon is called encoding specificity and it can both help and hinder learning. It helps when we can use those extra cues to help us remember something. It hinders when we can only recall something in the context in which it was originally learned. (For example, you can remember the words to a song only if you hear the melody at the same time.) It has been shown that students will remember information better when they're in the classroom where they first learned it. That's fairly inconvenient in terms of being able to make use of one's education.

So what are we to do? We have to break the connection between the information and any retrieval cue that is incidental to the real use of the information. This is done through variable practice with variable situations. In other words, when we design tasks to give our students practice in using the information they are learning, those tasks should not all be the same scenarios with the same cues; they should be varied as much as possible. The varied practice situations force the learners to pick out those things that are constant across situations and therefore better indicators of what constitutes an appropriate use of information.

Another good idea for designing instruction is to include a little learner reflection in the process. We want to ask the students to think about what they're saying and to learn things "mindfully," to use Ellen Langer's (1997) term. This is a slight contradiction of the idea of automaticity, but not really. Langer argues that if we respond too automatically, we can often miss the point or make simple mistakes. She says that we should encourage our students to be mindful about our content; that is, aware of how they are using it. One way to encourage this is to have students reflect on their thinking after they have attempted to use information to solve a problem. Math instructors do this when they ask students to show their work. Writing instructors do this when they have students critique their own writing. Athletes do this when they view videotapes of their performance and analyze what they were thinking and feeling at the time. Being aware of one's own thought processes is called "metacognition" in the literature, and we will be discussing that at greater length in Chapter 6. For now suffice it to say that it is useful for students to pause occasionally and reflect on their understanding before they become too practiced in possibly the wrong things.

One more interesting contradiction in the literature of cognitive psychology is the issue of how much we should scaffold students' learning. On the one hand, the research says that during initial learning we should remove as many barriers to performance as possible, we should make things as clear as possible, and so on. On the other hand, a small but growing movement (somewhat similar to Langer's mindful learning admonitions) says that learning needs to be a little bit effortful. What this boils down to is a restatement of the value of deep processing. When learning requires effort, that effort usually means mental effort and that usually equates with deep processing (Druckman & Bjork, 1991). This interpretation of the results is supported by another finding in the literature that says that this phenomenon is related to a learner's prior knowledge and experience in the area. This research comes from the area of discourse analysis, in which learners are given highly structured material to learn or loosely structured material. The former would represent a lot of scaffolding and a fairly easy task; the latter should be much more effortful because the learner has to create the structure in order to understand the material. The results showed that, for learners who had no prior knowledge of the content, the highly structured content helped their learning. For those with prior knowledge, the loosely structured content produced much better learning. The speculation is that the learners with prior knowledge had enough understanding of the area to be able to impose a structure on the loosely structured material, which would be the equivalent of deep processing it. In fact, when given highly structured material, these learners complained and did worse than learners who were given more loosely structured material. The novices, on the other hand, had no such ability because they didn't know enough to know what was important. For them, the scaffolding of structure was important to learning.

What does this say about instructional design? When you are dealing with novices in an area, you have to support their learning. But with learners who already have some background knowledge, less structure makes for better learning. It is not always appropriate to make things easy for the learner!

CONSTRUCTIVISM'S CONTRIBUTIONS

Most of the previous discussion derives from a more basic cognitive theory perspective, but constructivism also offers some insights that build or slightly modify the above suggestions. The most radical difference between a straight cognitive interpretation and a constructivist model revolves around who is doing the work. In the former, the instructor shoulders most of the burden for structuring the learning task and content organization. The instructor provides the examples and analogies, the concept maps and practice strategies. This increases the probability that the learners' conceptions of the content will be similar to the standard interpretations.

Constructivism, on the other hand, stresses the learners' part in the process. In this model it is best to have the learners create their own examples, structures, and understandings. The learners are much more actively involved than the instructor in going through the steps of learning described earlier. Here the instructor serves as a guide and facilitator rather than an orchestrator of learning. Constructivist classes are characterized by a lot more student activity and interactivity. Instructors may pose questions, but it is the students who put forth the effort to come up with their own answers. From a cognitive perspective, those answers will be more meaningful because they draw on the learners' own experiences and world views. They are more likely to be deep processed answers, because it is the learners who have put forth the effort to identify key ideas and make key connections. The disadvantage, or perhaps the paradox, of the constructivist view revolves around whether there is a right answer to the questions we pose or whether any answer the learners create is right. This is actually a misunderstanding of the constructivist philosophy, in my opinion. The constructivists do not deny that there is an objective reality (although some might come close); rather, they say that each learner's understanding of that reality is unique and derived from his or her world of experiences and probably not accessible by anyone else. Socio-constructivists assert that the reality to which we ascribe is one that we construct in conjunction with the world around us, particularly the people around us. We all share experiences and agree to think of them in a certain way.

A recent redefinition of constructivism has asserted that learners' interpretations of their experiences are influenced by three sources: the learner's own world view (a strict constructivist view), the environment (more of a behavioral view), and social interaction with other learners (a socio-constructivist view). This integrated constructivism (Chinn, 1998) is very similar to social cognitive theory, whose proponents also highlight the interaction of the learner's existing knowledge, the environmental changes that result from behavior, and the influence of others' interactions. Thinking this inclusively does offer a fairly coherent perspective on what causes learning. If there is a going to be a grand, unifying theory of psychology, this could be it.

How does such a perspective help us as instructors? We can attempt to create an environment in which the evidence of an objective reality is experienced by each learner sufficiently often to ensure that the reality he or she constructs has something in common with the reality that everyone else constructs. The important part of this philosophy is the recognition that the learner has to be, indeed will be, actively involved in drawing significant interpretations from those experiences. Learning experiences should be active and not passive, and the more perspectives represented by the learners in the group, the better and more accurate the learning will be in the end.

HOW DOES AN INSTRUCTOR USE THESE THEORIES TO BE MORE EFFECTIVE?

The ideas presented in this chapter revolve around the need for students to learn basic content: facts, principles, ideas, and how they are related to one another. The message is that this type of learning requires that the content to be learned be connected to the learners' prior knowledge and in a way that is organized and easy to retrieve from long-term memory. The best type of instructional activities for this type of learning will involve active efforts on the part of the learners to incorporate the new information into what they already know or to change what they already know to fit the new information. While the instructor can structure the learning environment to enhance the probability that key components of the content are highlighted, the learners must ultimately work with the material themselves to ensure solid initial learning and ultimate transfer to the real world.

The advantage the history professor has is that when something doesn't work, she can think about the learning going on behind the scenes and figure out what to do. The theories will suggest where to look: Are students having problems classifying examples as this or that concept? Look to see if the key features of each concept are being highlighted enough so they stand out. Or give the students more practice using those features to differentiate examples. Or look for a better first example to represent the concept in student thinking. Or all of the above. Thinking about how students are processing and learning new information provides a structure to use for organizing instruction more effectively.

3

HELPING STUDENTS UNDERSTAND

In Chapter 2 we talked about helping students learn the basics of a content area, such as vocabulary, foundational principles, and facts and figures. Many students equate this with knowing the content, and they spend a lot of time with flash cards and with highlighters to ensure that they will recognize or be able to call forth those details at test time. In Chapter 2 I also said, however, that in most disciplines this type of learning constitutes a very surface grasp of the material and is not what we're aiming for. We want students to understand the content, not just memorize it. This chapter is about that: teaching for understanding.

We really shouldn't fault the students for thinking that recognition is the same as understanding. We have been complicit in that belief by supporting the very efficient learning strategy called knowledge telling (Bereiter & Scardamalia, 1985). I know you'll recognize this strategy when I describe it. Its basic philosophy is, "If I tell as much as I know, the right answer will be in there somewhere, and I'll get at least partial credit for it." It is this last part for which we are responsible. We do give credit for effort when accuracy is past all hope of occurring. The "gentleman's C" is what it used to be called. Rather than trying to figure out what a question is asking, students tell all they know, and in many cases that works. No wonder students prefer free response tests to multiple choice. The knowledge telling strategy doesn't work in objectively scorable tests. Of course, there are ways to ensure that it doesn't work on essay tests either, but that's the subject of another book (see Walvoord and Anderson, 1998, for ideas about avoiding rewarding this strategy).

THE PROBLEM OF INERT KNOWLEDGE

The problem with the kind of surface processing of information that is implied in the knowledge telling or flash card strategies for learning is that they produce inert knowledge (Whitehead, 1929). This kind of knowledge is the kind that just sits there in long-term memory taking up space and not being useful to anyone because it can only be recalled in the specific situation in which it was learned. This is the kind of knowledge that students cram in the night before the exam and forget (lose access to) as soon as they walk out the door after the test. Students can remember it when explicitly asked for it, but can't use it for anything else. This is the ultimate evil in education. What good is it to spend all that time learning a piece of information that is going to be unavailable for any but the most specific use? I don't mean that we must always have a larger purpose in mind every time we learn. In fact, Robert Haskell (2001) asserts that useless knowledge is often useful somewhere down the road when we least expect it. But he is actually referring to building a large general knowledge base that is interconnected so that it can be accessed at that moment in the future when it is needed, so I don't see that as the response to the inert knowledge problem. The reality is that there is a lot of material that students learn in a way that makes it inert, and that's something we must overcome.

The Cognition and Technology Group at Vanderbilt University (a group of researchers who publish everything jointly) proposes that integrated knowledge structures are the solution to the inert knowledge problem. This research group says that learners need a deeper understanding of the why, how, and when of information in order to keep it from becoming inert (Sherwood, 1993). We'll discuss later how they propose we develop these knowledge structures, but they make a very convincing case for the need for integrated, well-organized knowledge.

That claim is made by several other researchers, including Lauren Resnick (1989), who asserts that "knowledge is retained only when embedded in some organizing structure" (p. 3). She goes on to point out that knowledge acquisition is actually knowledge dependent. The more you know, the easier it is to learn new information, but this is only true when what you know provides a context for new information. She calls this "cognitive bootstrapping," the idea that you can use even small amounts of knowledge to form the basis for learning new things.

IS STRUCTURAL KNOWLEDGE THE ANSWER? THE DIFFERENCE BETWEEN EXPERTS AND NOVICES

Would a well-integrated structure for our knowledge base really be the answer? Yes, most of the research points in that direction. A research area that is particularly convincing is the area of expert/novice differences. The thought was that if we could understand how someone who really understands an area (an expert) thinks, we could base instruction on what and how they know. The theory was not supported by findings, but there were some very robust and interesting findings along the way that may help us. What is it about someone that makes them an expert? Is it just that they know a lot of stuff? Certainly it's true that they do know a lot more about an area than a novice does, but what they know is not as important as how they structure what they know. The most important difference between experts and novices is that experts have a large knowledge base that is structured around foundational principles of the discipline. What does that mean? It means that rather than focusing on the surface features of a problem or bits of information, an expert relies on deep knowledge of how that problem or information fits into the big picture (Klein & Hoffman, 1993). I particularly like the way Klein and Hoffman describe how an expert thinks. They relate it to the individual's ability to visualize tasks. In fact, they say, "novices see only what is there; experts can see what is not there" (p. 203). I love this quote because what I think experts see is the structure of the content, and that allows them to see what is missing from the structure. This structuring and organization of content is what the literature on expert/novice differences seems to be pointing toward. Experts have a much more organized, structural understanding of the content, which allows them to incorporate new information quickly, search more efficiently, recognize patterns that suggest solutions to a problem, and use information much more flexibly because it is not tied to a given situation, but rather is interconnected with an array of other related information. Klein and Hoffman go on to say that experts can see typicality (what is standard about a problem), distinctions (what fine details differentiate one problem from another), and antecedents and consequents (how we got where we are and what is likely to happen next). The difficulty that the expert/novice difference research has exposed is that you can't make a novice into an expert just by teaching structure; novices need a lot of practice with the structure.

However, while a novice with structural knowledge is still not an expert, there are no experts without structural knowledge. Structuring the knowledge is probably the first step toward expertise.

Notice I didn't say getting a lot of knowledge is the first step toward expertise. This is the unfortunate path that most education today takes. Some believe that students can't think unless they know a lot of content. From our perspective as experts we can see how much there is to know to solve even simple problems in the complex fields we teach. What we don't see (because it is so automatic) is that our access to all that knowledge is driven by a really well-organized structure. In fact, when asked why they made a particular choice when faced with a problem, experts will often say it looked or felt right. Often they can't unpack their decision process because their knowledge is so tightly organized that very early on they eliminated whole branches of information from consideration because that branch dealt with the wrong foundational principle.

Another interesting way to think about expertise is offered by Robert Haskell (2001), who differentiates between routine expertise and adaptive expertise. He asserts that routine expertise is based on a more restricted knowledge base and represents something like an algorithmic application of it to routine tasks. Adaptive expertise is based on a much broader knowledge base that can be tapped in unique ways to deal with novel problems. Adaptive expertise is a much more valuable knowledge base and therefore is more desirable. In fact, Bransford, Brown, and Cocking (1999) describe several research studies on the impact of adaptive expertise on problem solving. An important component of this adaptive expertise suggested by this research is the presence of metacognitive awareness in adaptive experts. They are more aware of what they know and don't know and what to do about it. To me this implies that they are seeing the whole of a problem and identifying what's missing as well as what is there, and this overall awareness forms the basis for continued learning.

DOES UNDERSTANDING EQUAL STRUCTURAL KNOWLEDGE?

If expertise is based on well-organized structural knowledge, would it be reasonable to say that in order to understand something, one needs to develop such a structure? Let's consider whether what we mean by understanding is similar to what comes from structural knowledge. Look at the descriptions of student behavior in the list below and decide whether they would describe a student who "understands" the content.

- The student can access the information in several different ways and is not tied to one particular set of circumstances (the knowledge is not inert).
- The student can explain a situation in his or her own words more than one way.
- The student can apply information to new situations not encountered before.
- The student can see relationships between subcomponents of information or between examples that go beyond surface similarities.
- The student can reconstruct details when given a partial explanation or description.
- The student can infer effects when given causes or partial information.

Behaviors such as these do not come from having a large knowledge base if it is in isolated bits and pieces. Rather, these behaviors imply a grasp of relationships among bits of information. They deal with the connections between ideas, stated or implied, and the ability to extend those ideas to new situations and new formats. One can memorize isolated pockets of information, but understanding implies the ability to construct new pieces of information from what is known so far. This orderly network of connections is what I mean by structural knowledge, and it is the kind of knowledge that we should be encouraging our students to acquire.

To many researchers, the existence of those connections is the existence of a knowledge structure, a mental model of the information (Resnick, 1989). Resnick even points to the physical analogues that are used in abstract fields such as physics and mathematics to help experts visualize those relationships. Another researcher in the area, Edwina Rissland (1985), puts it this way: "Understanding a domain requires great familiarity with its connections" (p. 107).

HOW CAN WE HELP STUDENTS DEVELOP STRUCTURAL KNOWLEDGE?

As mentioned in the previous chapter, the first step in learning is recognizing what is important and needs to be learned. The development of structural knowledge is really no different. The first step in developing structural knowledge is for the learners to recognize that it is there. The second is using that structure as an encoding strategy. I also said in Chapter 2 that an important encoding strategy is the use of organization. Organizing content is the first phase of developing structural knowledge. Fortunately, there are several strategies, subtle and not so subtle, that help us encourage students to organize content from a structural perspective.

Helping Students Recognize the Existence of a Structure

Verbal clues. Our language is peppered with verbal cues that represent structural understanding. For example, "for example" is a way of indicating that a particular instance is a subpoint of a main idea. We also use a lot of comparative phrases, such as "on the other hand," "similarly," "the first point is," and so on. Students are very accustomed to listening for these structural cues during lectures and using them to organize their note taking. Lectures often are evaluated on how well organized they are (read that, how easy it is to follow the structure of the content). One problem with these verbal cues is that they are almost too automatically understood and therefore easily taken for granted. An interesting first step in helping students think structurally might be to discuss how these verbal cues are used to indicate relationships. You might consider having the students create a diagram from a written argument in which the words used are charted according to the relationship between points they imply. Backing up a verbal presentation with a visual analogue is a powerful way to help students think structurally.

Story grammars and text structures. A more advanced version of the verbal cueing of structure is found in the area of story grammars and text structures. Michael Pressley (1983) has studied how learners use typical plot lines to decode written text (or any other text). This means that when we listen to an explanation of something, we expect to hear a certain set of facts and sequence of events, depending on the type of content that is being conveyed. I think of them as plot lines because the content follows a given plot sequence. For example, if I am telling you a story, you expect to hear who it is about, a build-up to a climax in terms of what happened to that person, and a conclusion or resolution of the situation. If I tell you a story and violate your expectations with regard to a story plot line, you'll have trouble following me. Think, for example, about Kurt Vonnegut's *Slaughterhouse Five*, a novel in which the protagonist gets unstuck in time. The novel jumps back and forth between past, present, and future. Until the reader figures this out (and even sometimes afterward), the story is very hard to follow.

Pressley also suggests that nonfiction texts have traditional story lines as well and that these vary from discipline to discipline. For example, scientific text follows a story line that is very different from sociological text. What we expect to find in a scientific explanation (the plot) helps us understand the content. Students who are trained to use the structural schema for science to read difficult text show an increased understanding of the material and an enhanced ability to remember it later (Brooks & Dansereau, 1983). In fact, other researchers have shown that instructing students to try to create a good, coherent story out of difficult material significantly improved their ability to recall it later (Mathews, Yussen, & Evans, 1982, as qtd. in Pressley, 1983, note 1). I'll talk a little bit more about this later in the section on metastructure, but for now I'll say that teaching students the traditional plot lines for understanding content in your discipline is one way to help them develop structural knowledge. They can use those recurring plot lines as the basis for reading and understanding future text they encounter.

Concept map. An equally if not more powerful structural strategy is the use of concept maps. A concept map is simply a visual representation of the structure of the content, but laid out pictorially and nonlinearly—unlike the linear, verbal depiction typical of an outline. Figure 3.1 shows an example of a concept map of the contents of this book, for example. Web sites frequently have a site map these days, which is essentially a concept map showing the components of the site and how they fit together. Site maps help keep searchers from getting lost in the maze of links that comprise a site, a very common phenomenon with new web users. The generalization to the larger concept of getting lost in the links of a content area is very apt; sometimes learners need a concept map to help them see the big picture of the area and not get lost in the details. An instructor can provide students with a concept map based on the field's traditional structure, but it is often very helpful for students to make their own maps so that the links are meaningful to them. Of course, instruction in an area should result eventually in student maps being very similar to the experts' map structure, a finding that is supported in the literature (Naveh-Benjamin & Lin, 1994).

Figure 3.1
A Concept Map

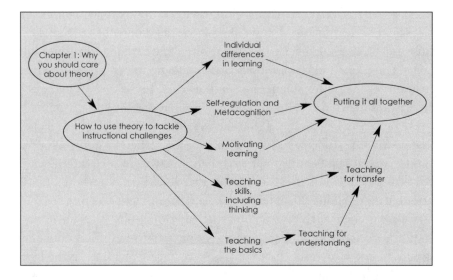

Advance organizers. Structural knowledge strategies abound in the literature on learning because they are such powerful tools. Another example of structural support is the use of various kinds of organizers. The first and most well-known organizer is the advance organizer suggested by Ausubel (1960). An advance organizer is displayed before detailed information is given and serves as a structure into which incoming information is plugged. It also helps the learners understand where they are at any point in the instruction and how that point relates to the other points being made. The most common type of advance organizer is an outline displayed on the board before the start of class. This simple technique has been shown to improve student note taking and understanding immensely (Corkill, 1992). Textbooks use advance organizers in the form of learning objectives printed at the beginning of a chapter or a chapter outline.

Comparative organizers. A more interesting structural support is the comparative organizer. This structural strategy is used during the learning to emphasize the relationships among ideas. A common comparative organizer that instructors use is the "pro-con" table (Figure 3.2). Here the visual image of two columns side by side forces the learners to consider opposing ideas directly. The table serves to stimulate learners to think in comparative terms; if there is a pro centering on a particular point, is there a corresponding con?

Figure 3.2
A Pro-Con Grid

	Pro-integration	Con-integration
Effect on kids	Learn to be tolerant	Bused away from home
Effect on parents	Social welfare cause	Makes participation difficult
Effect on school	Wider support for community	Expense of busing, public relations

The pro-con table is only one example of a comparative organizer. Some magazines like *Consumer Reports* use comparative organizers all the time to compare products in terms of critical decision variables, such as price, repair history, features, and so on. I have used this kind of organizer as a sort of algorithm for analyzing theories (Figure 3.3). Here a standard set of theory components needs to be considered for each new theory we study. As we discuss a theory, students can fill in the cells of the table until eventually they begin to think in terms of these components each time they encounter a new theory. This is a particularly useful strategy to adopt because it relieves the instructor of having to discuss every aspect of each theory in class, the content coverage issue that is the bane of every instructor's life. We all feel (however incorrectly) that we must "cover" each detail of the content area in class, and as a result we are always under time pressure. By providing students with a way to organize the material themselves, we can and should encourage them to do some of the analysis outside of class and bring to class only those aspects that they were unable to determine on their own. With such a system we not only guarantee that they understand the basics of each area, but we are helping them learn how to deal with new ideas and theories later when we are no longer there to help them.

Figure 3.3
A Comparative Organizer on Theory Analysis

	Behavior theory	Cognitive theory
Unit of analysis		
Definition of learning		
Change strategy		
Evidence of learning		

Graphic organizers. Concept maps and comparative organizers fall within the larger category of graphic organizers, an extensive area of research in learning. In her discussion of critical thinking, Diane Halpern (1996) lists several graphic organizer formats that help students understand the structure of an analysis. For example, she lists linear arrays, hierarchies, networks, matrices, and flow charts as illustrating different structural relationships among ideas. I personally have found that matrices are particularly helpful in getting students to think creatively, because they encourage students to look at intersections of ideas they might not have considered. The use of a matrix is one of the strategies often suggested in material on creative thinking.

Metaphors, analogies, and visualizations. Metaphors and analogies are based on structural similarities between sets of information. For example, to say that the glands of the body operate like thermostats invites the learners to make comparisons between what they know about thermostats and what they are learning about glands. Not only will this comparison make information that is provided clearer, but it encourages learners to speculate about whether a particular characteristic of a thermostat has an exact counterpart in glands; for example, a device for measuring the amount of something (in the thermostat, temperature; in the glands, presence of a hormone in the blood). If this piques student curiosity enough to make them want to find out if such a device exists, they have taken a first step toward independent discovery that lies at the heart of self-directed learning.

Analogical reasoning. Analogical reasoning is closely related to the work on critical thinking (Vosniadou & Ortony, 1989). Researchers in this area are exploring the degree to which learners can use structural understanding of one concept to aid their learning on a second concept or to solve problems with a similar structure. The primary purpose for studying analogical reasoning has been to explain transfer of information from one situation to another, which is the topic of Chapter 5. Theoretically, if a learner understands the underlying structure of an initial situation, he or she should be able to use that as a starting point for understanding a second situation.

Education is replete with failures of transfer, so, as you might expect, researchers would like to understand why. The literature suggests that individuals who are good at analogical reasoning are also good at transfer in general (Haskell, 2001). In fact, Robert Haskell has suggested a theory of the harmonic structure of mind, in which he asserts that we all have a general purpose perceptual learning mechanism that allows us to recognize patterns in the environment. The basis for this recognition could be analogical reasoning at ever widening circles of consideration. He gives an example of this in the levels of progression of the concept adaptation from microadaptation in genetics to adaptation in biology to learning in psychology to socialization in sociology to acculturation in anthropology.

Each concept represents the same structural understanding but at a different level.

Instructors can use analogies very productively to help students develop structural understanding of a new area. Spiro, Feltovich, Coulson, and Anderson (1989) warn against putting too much faith in a single analogy, however. They have found that no analogy is totally transferable, and that occasionally the discrepancies get wired into the learner's understanding in such a way as to cause problems later. Studying primarily medical students, Spiro et al. catalogued the kind of misdirections that poorly developed analogies produced. For example, conceiving of the circulatory system as analogous to plumbing is fine for very beginning or surface understandings, but leads to later difficulty if the learners attempt to apply all the characteristics of plumbing to the heart/blood vessel system. Blood vessels are not rigid like pipes, which allows them to deal differently with fluid pressure. A student operating only from his or her own experience with plumbing was found to have great difficulty understanding certain principles about the circulatory system that conflict with household plumbing principles. Spiro et al. recommend that instructors develop a series of analogies to help explain concepts, each successive analogy correcting any misconceptions arising from the previous one.

Sequencing examples. A similar caution can be made about the use of sequencing examples as a way of introducing new structural understanding gradually. The first example forms the nucleus of the structure of the content. Each subsequent example expands that structure by adding branches and sub-branches that represent different defining features. In fact, as new examples are introduced, it might be effective to introduce them into a comparative organizer format as a way of highlighting their commonalities and differences (see Figure 3.4 for an example). An excellent discussion of structuring example sequences has been offered by Betsy Newell Decyk (1994). She helps students develop organizational understanding by exploring the parameters of examples and nonexamples of concepts. For example, she might begin a discussion by giving an example of a paradigmatic concept—the most common example of a concept. (A paradigmatic example of a bird is a robin.) Then she begins to vary the example to clarify the understanding of bird by asking about an uncommon example. (Is an ostrich a bird?) Depending on the students' response, she picks another variation that forces discrimination along a different dimension. (Birds fly. Is an airplane a bird?) Each successive comparison builds another branch of the structure or knocks out a branch that didn't belong there. It's impossible in this brief space to give a really clear explanation of this process, but this sequencing is very typical of Socratic teaching, the back and forth of question and response between instructor and students.

Figure 3.4
Example of a Comparison Organizer

EXAMPLE	Warm blooded	Live birth	Language capacity
Dinosaurs	?	No	No
Birds	Yes	No	?
Cats	Yes	Yes	No
Humans	Yes	Yes	Yes

A more sophisticated version of the use of structural understanding as exemplified by analogies is the problem-solving model of case-based reasoning (Kolodner & Guzdial, 2000). This problem-solving method is most prevalent in areas such as medicine and law. Research on how doctors diagnose and then choose treatment for illness has shown that their expert knowledge is organized around cases. The first case of a particular condition that they encounter becomes the benchmark against which future cases are judged and is used to help retrieve details of symptoms and treatment. In law this is actually how deliberations are made, by citing case precedents. You don't have to stretch very far to see that a lot of our knowledge is organized around initial experiences. Novices are very dependent on the first example of a procedure or concept that they encounter. In case-based reasoning, an individual has a storehouse of cases that represent different significant interpretations and explanations of experiences (cases). This database of cases is then consulted when a new experience occurs. The individual has indexed all these experiences according to their relevant features. When a new experience occurs, the individual analyzes its key features and searches the database for related previous experiences and whether they worked. Finding one that is similar enough, the individual then uses that as the basis of how he or she will respond to the current experience. The key to this system is the indexing, which I would equate with the structural knowledge of the field or experiences. A good index helps the individual relate the new problem to previously encountered problems and to use their features to respond (transfer of learning to a new situation). The instructional strategy of case-based teaching exploits this type of reasoning in helping students develop structural understanding of a field and its subdivisions. The extent to which the learners understand the structure of the field is the extent to which they can respond efficiently and effectively in new situations.

Anchored instruction. An elaboration of case-based instruction is anchored instruction (Sherwood, 1993). One complaint about case-based reasoning is its close tie to a specific example or discipline. Some researchers felt that, while it was good to anchor learning in a realistic case, one did run the risk of making learning too specific. To counter this, they proposed a teaching strategy that would be more like real life learning and reflect the need to integrate knowledge across areas. Instead of having the one concept—one case method—they use a single case but approach it from multiple perspectives. Most real life cases are very messy and rich in detail and frequently contain multiple problems in the same set of data. By using the same situation to analyze from multiple perspectives, students become more flexible in their use of information. No one particular case is restricted to one type of problem, and many times multiple problems must be solved if the case is to be resolved. This is much more like real problem solving and enables a much richer structural understanding of the content.

Using Structural Knowledge in Learning and Teaching

The foregoing discussion has identified ways of highlighting the structural underpinnings of information being learned. Many of these same ideas can be continued by students themselves as a way of storing and using that information. Helping students learn how to structure informa-

tion is one of the things that teachers can do to make learning more efficient now and in the future.

Verbal clues. Making students use verbal cues would be a good way
to start students thinking about how information is structured. Showing
students how the verbal cues in written text or in lectures relate to the
nature of the information is a good idea. Having them diagram an argument or presentation to highlight the structural relationships in it is a
further step in helping them learn to use structural understanding.

Incomplete matrix. Angelo and Cross's (1993) *Classroom Assessment
Techniques* contains several exercises that are based on structural understanding, some of which I mentioned earlier. My favorite is the use of an
incomplete matrix or other graphic organizer. Providing students with an
organizer with blank cells and having them fill in those cells mimics the
process of creating structural knowledge of that content. The practice
can be taken one step further to having the students develop their own
matrices for each major concept and possibly sharing them with the rest
of the class so they can see the content from multiple perspectives. In the
earlier discussion of expert/novice differences, I said that experts can see
what's missing. This type of activity gives students a taste of this type of
reasoning.

Concept maps. In my own classes I have had students create concept
maps at various points in the course. A useful time is just before an exam,
particularly if the exam is going to contain essay questions that ask for
relationships or analysis rather than simple recitation of ideas. Comparing student maps with your own can highlight areas where students are
missing information or making incorrect assignments of ideas.

Self-explanations and self-questioning. A related idea is the use of
self-explanations and self-questioning. When students have to explain
their understanding of a concept to someone else, they must create an
organizational structure for their explanation to make any sense. A lot of
research points toward the value of having students create these explanations and questions for major concepts (Chi & Bassok, 1989; King,
1994). King was very successful in increasing student learning by teaching a series of questions for students to ask themselves in an effort to
elaborate their understanding of the content structure. She lists 23 question stems to guide student exploration of a topic. A few are listed below.

- What are the strengths and weaknesses of _____?
- What is analogous to _____?

- What is the difference between _____ and _____?
- How are _____ and _____ similar?

Case examples. Having students analyze case examples according to an agreed-upon sequence of questions or strategies will develop the habit of approaching the content in a systematic way and producing the same kinds of information for each case. That information can then be the basis of structural understanding. In the foregoing discussion, I described the use of case-based reasoning and anchored instruction as methods for helping students see structure. A particularly effective strategy in case examples is the use of speculative situations—the "what if" scenarios. What if Abraham Lincoln had been assassinated before signing the Emancipation Proclamation? What if you as a teacher were to lose your voice and had to conduct the whole class without talking? What if instead of coalescing into a solid planet, Venus had remained a set of closely spaced rings? The advantage of this type of activity is that students must really understand the cause and effect relationships within the content to be able to discuss alternative realities. The alternative structure in this type of exercise is a future oriented version in which students are asked to predict what would happen if. Remember that one of the characteristics of an expert is an ability to see antecedents and consequents. This type of activity gives students that kind of practice.

Students can benefit from being asked to generate their own examples, analogies, and metaphors. This activity also produces an artifact for you as the instructor to inspect for signs of misunderstanding. I am currently experimenting in my own classes with a variation on this strategy in order to overcome the problem of too many students and not enough me. Each student is being required to generate his or her own set of examples of concepts for each chapter. However, rather than handing those in to me, students will work in small groups online to compare their examples and come up with the best example for each concept as a group. This amalgamated list is what will be turned in to me for feedback. This strategy combines the benefits of generating examples with the benefits of questioning and explaining. It also allows students to see more examples than I can give, get more feedback than I can give, and work more intensely with the material than time allows.

WHEN UNDERSTANDING GOES AWRY: CORRECTING MISCONCEPTIONS

A very strong area of interest in both research and teaching today is the problem of prior misconceptions and the effects they have on learning. As I noted in Chapter 2 and will note again in Chapter 8, the most influential variable in learning is the learners' prior knowledge. One of the critical acts in the learning sequence is to compare incoming information with existing experience to look for a match or a relationship. When a match is found, further searching is deemed unnecessary because the category of information identified is sufficient to direct an appropriate response. I can describe this tendency in either generous or cynical terms. Speaking generously, fast decisions on matches between incoming information and existing knowledge save a lot of time and effort and could be very valuable from an evolutionary perspective if they allow us to respond quickly to changes in the environment. Individuals who spend a lot of time contemplating whether a newly encountered animal is dangerous might end up as lunch; those who respond quickly live to contemplate another day. Cynically, I could say that we are all lazy thinkers if given a choice. Why search for alternative matches once you've found one that works? So it is in our nature to use our prior knowledge to classify new things in the environment as efficiently and rapidly as possible.

Unfortunately, uncritical acceptance of our first impressions doesn't work either. It often leads us to jump to the wrong conclusions or stunts the growth of our understanding. An interesting discussion of what forces might be causing us to continue to go with our first beliefs has been offered by Thomas Gilovich (1991). He suggests that there are cognitive, motivational, and social reasons why we cling to our beliefs. For example, he says that as pattern-seeking animals, we have a tendency to see patterns even in random events and then attribute the alleged pattern to some force other than chance. My favorite example of this is the idea of the hot hand in basketball. The assertion is that a player gets on a roll and should be fed the ball when that happens because he or she has a higher probability of making a good shot at those times (he or she has a hot hand). Gilovich has very carefully analyzed this phenomenon and found that shooters were no more likely to make a shot after making the previous shot (the hot hand theory) than they were after missing the previous shot (random chance). Nevertheless, believers will argue vehemently in favor of the hot hand theory even in the face of extensive data to the contrary. I won't go any further into Gilovich's analyses of this persistence of misconceptions, but I recommend his book as an interesting argument about why it's so hard to overcome misinformation in everyday life.

Getting back to the classroom context, several researchers have found that students bring faulty prior knowledge into the classroom, and these misconceptions get in the way of learning new ideas. The phenomenon is particularly noticeable in science education. Duit (1991) argues that prior knowledge is so persistent because it is based on many years of experience and is embedded in the learners' structural understanding of the world. In fact, most researchers in this area have observed that one of the first responses to new information is to try to incorporate it into one's existing world view (Chinn & Brewer 1993)—the process that Piaget called assimilation. Duit also claims that when we confront new information we tend to remember that which is consistent with our understanding at the time rather than trying to reframe that understanding to fit the new information—the process Piaget called accommodation. Accommodation is much more effortful since more than just one piece of information must be changed; a whole structure needs to be reconfigured.

A model of conceptual change that has been very influential in trying to design instruction to overcome this conceptual inertia was suggested by Posner, Strike, Hewson, and Gertzog (1982). They suggested that to get students to change misconceptions, they had to first become dissatisfied with their current conceptualization. This is not easy, as noted above, especially in fields like physics, where many real concepts are counterintuitive, abstract, and difficult to understand in the first place. It's hard for students to go against years of personal experience and understanding. But the path to truth requires that instruction produce cognitive dissonance, the discomfort that occurs when one idea clashes with another.

In addition to experiencing cognitive dissonance, Posner et al. found that learners had to be able to understand any alternative conceptualization that was offered to replace their old familiar one. And the new conceptualization had to be plausible and good at explaining lots of data, not just the original data that produced the conflict. This is a tall order in a curriculum where the amount of content typically covered doesn't allow the luxury of repeated considerations of a concept. For most college classes, it's a one-time shot at understanding, and on to the next concept. Real conceptual change requires time and effort on everyone's part, so there's a degree of motivation needed to get over the difficulties when old ideas need to be changed.

A good summary of the recommendations derived from research in this area has been provided by Anderson and Roth (1989). They suggest that conceptual change is more likely to occur in situations where instructors concentrate on teaching a few fundamental concepts deeply rather than a lot of concepts superficially. While there is no one strategy that is right for every situation, Anderson and Roth believe that students have to be actively involved in analyzing observations and concepts in order to make the kind of change we are aiming for. Initially, students need to make predictions and overt statements of their preconceptions about a phenomenon. This makes them take a stand and allows the instructor to uncover misconceptions that need to be dealt with. Every group of students will be different, but there will be some consistency based on real world experiences that students are all likely to have had. Then the phenomenon should be explored directly with repeated reference back to original predictions. King (1992) suggests developing a series of questions that systematically bring to light inconsistencies between prior knowledge and current observations. Although King suggests that these questions be asked by students, the Socratic questioning method is an example of a teacher-led strategy to accomplish the same end. I want to emphasize, however, that most of the literature on conceptual change suggests that students themselves must be engaged in questioning ideas. To simply watch the instructor go through a clever series of theses and antitheses would produce surface understanding at best.

Another strategy that has been successful in correcting prior misconceptions is having students construct concept maps or other visualizations of their understanding of processes. Such visualizations help uncover where student thinking differs from disciplinary thinking at the process or structural level, which is where the most stubborn misconceptions reside. Creating concept maps as a group is also an effective strategy since it allows students to view one another's thinking more readily so it can be challenged or understood. Recent theories about social construction of understanding resulting from collaborative learning support the idea of having students wrestle with contradictory evidence as a group. Students derive both challenge and support in their attempts to refine their own thinking and reduce cognitive dissonance (Pressley & McCormick, 1995).

THE CHALLENGE OF STRUCTURAL THINKING

The type of learning discussed in this chapter is a real challenge to instructors because it causes us to think about our subject matter at a different level. I said earlier that we as experts find it hard to deconstruct our own thinking and return to a level at which we think consciously about all the components that make up our decisions and understandings. This is the type of activity that is called for when we try to emphasize structural understanding for our students. We ourselves have to bring to a conscious level our own structural understanding. In the process we have to tap into a lot of implicit and tacit knowledge that seems too obvious to be stated. And yet, unless we can recognize those structural details, we will have trouble leading students to see them as well. Understanding what "understanding our discipline" means is a key step toward effective teaching.

FOR THOSE WHO WANT TO GO FURTHER: METASTRUCTURAL KNOWLEDGE

I hope I made a strong point of how important I think structural knowledge is to being able to progress in an area. Now I'd like to introduce a concept of *metastructural knowledge*. I don't think this term shows up anywhere in the literature, although the concept does.

In psychology we use the prefix "meta" to imply something that is more encompassing or more of an executive function than straight whatever it is we're talking about. So, for example, we talk about "metacognition," which you will see in Chapter 6 refers to processes that control thinking or "cognition." By this we mean behaviors like monitoring understanding and making selections among alternative strategies, evaluating outcomes and revising goals. The object of all those behaviors is our thought processes. When we engage in metacognition, we are monitoring and controlling how we go about thinking a problem through.

So here I'm proposing another meta concept, this time a meta version of structural knowledge. In metastructural knowledge, the learner would understand how to structure knowledge: not a specific type of knowledge, but any knowledge. Metastructural knowledge would be like knowing the rules of the game for categorizing, comparing, correlating, and any other manipulation of information in order to understand it. Humans naturally sort things into categories, which is why we make so much use of stereotypes. Even little kids will sort things on the basis of some similarities. One of the developmental steps that children take is to move from sorting on the basis of surface features to sorting on the basis of function or relationship. But first they have to be aware that such a possibility exists. Knowing that there are multiple ways of structuring knowledge would be an example of metastructural knowledge. That concept of looking for multiple ways to structure things could be used with any information. The advantage of having metastructural knowledge is that it prevents getting stuck in only one mode of thinking. The awareness of other structures helps break the learner out of a logjam in thinking.

I will make this idea more concrete with the history example from Chapter 2. I said earlier that students tend to use a chronological structure to organize historical data. By exposing them to a different structure—say "thesis, antithesis, synthesis"—an instructor might open up new ways of thinking about historical forces. An instructor might then go back and examine the same data but from a socioeconomic structural perspective. The metamessage is that there are many different ways to consider the same data. Sometimes you get different answers depending on which way you look at them. Recognizing this would be a big developmental step for a lot of students.

Another example of metastructural knowledge might be that instances of a concept often lie on a continuum. Understanding what that continuum is allows you to make inferences about other nonobserved instances and their relationship to known instances. For example, if I maintain that learning theories lie on a continuum from strict environmental to strict individualistic, you might start to ask what theories fall in between or where does a given theory fall on that continuum. If I say it's somewhere closer to environmental but not as strict, you as the learner can speculate about how that might actually play out in the theory.

Another metastructural knowledge concept might be that things don't have to be directly correlated with one another; the relationship can be curvilinear or interactive, which might explain puzzling data trends. I remember that this was a big revelation to me in statistics a long time ago. Recognizing this opened up a whole new way to think about relationships between causes and effects.

It's possible that logic courses are designed to provide metastructural knowledge, as are statistics and other mathematics courses. But we might be able to achieve a similar, though not as rigorous, conceptualization of structural relationships in other fields that are trying to find patterns in phenomena. The advantage of figuring out what the patterns might be is that they could point us in the direction of where to look for new structural relationships in a content area. This would be a fruitful area of cross-disciplinary study.

What does this mean for you as a teacher and for your students? If you and your students explore this concept of patterns of understanding that are idiosyncratic to your discipline, you could possibly speed up students' ability to grasp the content. Earlier in this chapter I talked about the idea of story grammars and how they might facilitate understanding. At this level it might be possible for students to learn to recognize story grammars from each discipline if they know to look for them. Just as understanding the structure of the content helps students learn much of it on their own, understanding how to structure content could free them from depending on you to point the way toward things to think about. Students who learn that there are multiple ways to categorize knowledge might be inspired to attempt that categorization for themselves rather than waiting for the instructor to tell them the correct categories. This would impact their epistemological development and possibly give them more confidence about their ability to delve into a new unfamiliar area because they would have tools for making sense of new information in a different field. But this is a pretty big learning step for some students; I may be asking too much of them (and possibly of you).

4

HELPING STUDENTS DEVELOP SKILLS, INCLUDING INTELLECTUAL SKILLS

The previous two chapters dealt with some of the most fundamental tasks in learning—the acquisition and retention of knowledge to the level of understanding, the what of education. This chapter turns to the second most fundamental task in learning—the acquisition and capacity to perform skills, including using the knowledge that was the subject of Chapters 2 and 3. It would be a sad commentary on any educational system if the students learned a lot of facts and principles, but not how to use them in any meaningful way. So you might think of this chapter as being the logical extension of Chapters 2 and 3, the next step in learning.

HOW SKILLS ARE LEARNED

Although an abundance of different models purport to describe how skills are learned, they really all boil down to one very old model of learning: the apprenticeship. As Collins, Brown, and Newman (1989) explain, the apprenticeship may be the oldest and most natural form of teaching. Children learn by watching their parents and elders. Until the 19th century, most education involved being apprenticed to a master in a field and learning by observing and assisting the master as he or she went about the ordinary tasks of the profession. At home children learned the skills of everyday life by observing and assisting their parents. Even learned professions, like medicine and law, were learned through apprenticeship to a working professional. When widespread formal education was instituted, the idea of apprenticeship was relegated more to the crafts while book learning became the standard for becoming an educated person. Of course, even then, most real learning occurred after formal education when students were sent out into the world of work to learn from their employers.

The concept of the apprenticeship is experiencing a renaissance, however. The problems that formal schooling has in transferring to real life and the difficulty students often have in learning from experts have led psychologists to take a second look at learning by observing, and they have found it to be a very useful model to consider for a wide range of skills, from physical skills to intellectual skills. In the case of the latter, the method is referred to as a cognitive apprenticeship (Collins, Brown, & Newman, 1989) to emphasize that what is being learned is a set of cognitive skills, not just physical skills.

LEARNING BY OBSERVING

One foundation for the idea of the cognitive apprenticeship is the learning theory espoused in the 1970s by Albert Bandura called social learning theory or, more descriptively, observational learning. Dissatisfied with the behaviorists' insistence on trial and error learning, Bandura observed that if everything had to be learned through trial and error, no one could live long enough to have all his or her behavior shaped. If you just consider how much is learned in the first two years of life, you can see that it is illogical to assume that everything is learned by actual experience. Instead Bandura proposed that the vast majority of behaviors are learned by watching others perform those behaviors and experience the consequences of them. So children observe their parents' behaviors and try to copy them. They observe their siblings and peers. They watch television and now video games. This is a much faster and more efficient way of learning than trial and error. Of course, Bandura did not abandon behaviorist principles altogether; he retained in his theory the idea of the impact of consequences on behavior, consequences to the model and consequences to the learner. Once the learner observes a model and imitates the model's behavior, he or she is subject to the environmental consequences of that behavior, whether they be success or failure.

You can see in this theory the foundations for explaining the apprenticeship process. The learner (apprentice) watches a model (the master)

engage in the behavior to be learned. The learner is allowed to participate in the behavior to the extent possible until he or she becomes proficient, all the while receiving feedback from the master as well as experiencing the results of his or her attempts (either success or failure). What
is happening during the observational phase is that the learner is creating
a "mental model" of the behavior to be learned. This mental model is a
prototype copy of the behavior being learned and is stored in the
learner's memory and used as a benchmark against which the learner can
then craft his or her own version of the behavior later. With each successive try, the learner's behavior comes closer and closer to the mental
model until it is finally acceptable and produces the reward that comes
with proficient performance.

In Bandura's theory, the learning goes through three phases: attention, retention, and production. And the whole process is driven by motivation. Let's consider each of these in more detail and see how they
relate to instructional strategies.

Attention

In the first phase of observational learning, the learner has to pay attention to the real model's performance and pick out the key components of
the behavior that need to be included in the mental model. From an
instructional standpoint, therefore, the teacher has to make sure that the
real model can generate enough attention on the part of the learners that
they will watch it long enough to benefit from the performance—so who
is doing the modeling is an important consideration. When the real
model demonstrates the behavior, the critical components have to be
emphasized and exaggerated so that they stand out from the incidental
components and so that the learners can't miss them. It is from these
critical components that the learners form their mental models of the
behavior. You'll no doubt notice that this phase of producing a mental
model is very similar in tone and process to the cognitive model
described in Chapter 2. That is a good observation because they are
indeed linked. In fact, today the original social learning model proposed
by Bandura has been transformed into what is called the social cognitive
model in order to emphasize the cognitive nature of the modeling
process.

Retention

Once the mental models are formed, the learners must be able to remember them later when the real model is no longer present in order for the mental model to influence their behavior. For that reason the mental models need to be vivid and meaningful for the learners. They need to store those models in long-term memory just as they stored the content discussed in Chapter 2. The mental models can then be retrieved when it's time to perform the behavior, and they can be used as the basis for generating the learners' behavior.

Production

This generation of the behavior by the learners is called the production phase of the process. Here the learners perform the behaviors they are learning, observe that performance, and get feedback from their instructor about the accuracy with which they have produced the behavior. This production phase never really ends because each time learners reproduce the behavior, they strengthen their mental models.

Motivation

This is not really a phase of the process, but something that needs to permeate all phases. Learners have to be motivated to develop the mental model in the first place and to perform the behavior once they have their models in place. All of the principles of motivation that are explored in a later chapter would apply here, but perhaps the two most significant ones that apply are motivation from receiving feedback from the teacher and the learners' recognition that they are making progress. These two sources of motivation play a significant role in observational learning. I'll discuss them and some other ideas in more detail later in this chapter.

How does this process work in a concrete example? Let's take the example of Lester, who wants to learn the latest dance steps. How is he likely to go about doing this? Well, he has the option of attending a dance and sitting on the sidelines and watching the other dancers, hoping to pick out the key moves they are making until he can create a model of the dance. It would probably be more efficient, though, for Lester to enlist the help of a friend to show him the dance. That friend (the real model) would simplify the steps and talk Lester through the process, probably encouraging him to move along with her. She would probably slow the dance steps down and make them very deliberate so Lester could see what she was doing more easily and describe what she is doing to be sure he is focusing on the correct things (the attention phase). She might even count along or recite the steps ("step, slide, together; step, slide, together") to provide a verbal mnemonic to accompany the movements (for retention purposes). Lester would begin by following her movements and possibly trying to recite the steps along with her (the production phase). She might dance alongside him at first rather than in the normal reverse mode for a partner. That would make it easier for him to follow what she's doing. She would encourage him by pointing out what he is doing well and coach him on those aspects he hasn't mastered. As he becomes more confident, he would continue to recite the mnemonic, but look less and less at her movements and concentrate more and more on his own. His teacher would eventually be able to stop directing his steps altogether as he assumed control. From then on it would be a matter of practice and feedback until he became confident enough to do the dance around others. As he sees himself getting better and his instructor encourages him, Lester is motivated to continue to practice and learn (the motivation phase).

This very simple process, which is something all of us have experienced, is essentially the process for teaching a skill through observational learning as laid out by Bandura. Most of the physical skills taught in schools today involve this type of modeling and practice with feedback. A very rich literature in the area of sports and physical education describes how these instructional processes can be made maximally effective. But you might be asking yourself what this has to do with what you teach—that is, how it relates to intellectual skills such as critical thinking or process application. In fact, the cognitive apprenticeship model is the translation of the observational learning model to the area of cognitive skill learning, and it is a wonderful model for thinking about how to structure instruction to improve student thinking skills.

THE COGNITIVE APPRENTICESHIP AS A MODEL FOR LEARNING INTELLECTUAL SKILLS

The researchers and theorists who have proposed the cognitive apprenticeship model base it on social learning theory (Bandura, 1986) but expand it to include components made necessary by the nature of learning a thinking skill. In regular observational learning, such as the dance described earlier, you are learning a physical skill that can be easily observed; in the cognitive apprenticeship, you are learning a mental skill that cannot be readily observed. As a result, the instruction must be modified somewhat to make the invisible visible. The thinking processes need to be made observable by having the model think aloud. Let's look at the cognitive apprenticeship system and see how it mimics and yet expands on the observational learning model just described (Table 4.1). We'll look at a specific example alongside the series of steps, too.

Table 4.1
Steps in the Cognitive Apprenticeship Model

The cognitive apprenticeship process involves, in order:	Example: Modeling a math solution
An authentic task (motivation phase): It is important to illustrate the skill to be learned in a setting that is authentic—that is, similar to one in which it will actually be used. This motivates students because they can see the utility of the skill. Concrete examples are also easier to understand than abstractions.	The instructor chooses problems to work on that are real examples, or the instructor can begin the demonstration by showing how what is being modeled will be used in future problems or real world uses. Working a concrete example alongside the general process is helpful for students to see how the process plays out in real life (similar to my having these two columns to illustrate how the apprentice model works).
Narrated modeling (the attention and retention phases): The next step in the cognitive apprenticeship system is very similar to that of regular observational learning: The process to be learned has to be made observable. In this case, however, what needs to be observed is the thinking that the model is doing, and so in addition to engaging in any visible aspects of the behavior, the model also narrates the process. Where possible, the model allows the learners to participate in the process.	The instructor begins working the problem on the board, but as he writes each step on the board, he talks about why he is doing what he is doing, what the alternatives might be, and why he made the choices he did. This makes his thinking observable. He occasionally invites the students to suggest what to do next and engages them in a discussion of how to choose among the alternatives suggested.

Scaffolded and coached practice (the production phase): The next step in the process is to allow the learners to attempt the skill. The instructor "scaffolds" their attempts by making the situations easy at first and by providing support and encouragement. In addition, he coaches them by asking questions and giving hints and feedback on their progress.	Having completed one or two sample problems, the instructor poses another very similar problem for the students to try. He suggests that they work in pairs and help one another think through their solutions. He circulates and makes comments and observations about each pair's work. Because they are working together, they don't need constant monitoring by the instructor but, rather, can provide feedback to one another.
Articulation of the process steps by the learners (production phase): After sufficient practice with varied problems, the learners are required to describe the process steps they have learned in their own words. This articulation of the process acts to solidify their understanding of it and as a check on that understanding by the instructor.	After practicing with several problems of varying degrees of difficulty, the student pairs are instructed to write on a separate paper the sequence of steps they need to go through when they encounter a problem of this type. The steps are then read aloud by the instructor and checked against the students' lists.
Reflection on the process (an addition to the original process): When students have mastered the process, they are given an opportunity to reflect on their own learning and understanding. They write or talk about what they did while learning the process, what helped them, and what hindered their learning. They problem solve around the hindrances.	As a homework assignment, the instructor has the students write a journal entry about their experience trying to master this latest problem solution type. They are encouraged to review past journal entries in order to detect patterns in their learning.
Exploration in new venues (also an addition to the original): To encourage transfer of the learned process, the students are given a larger variety of problems in which this process can be used, or they are encouraged to think of other problems for which it would be useful. The instructor takes pains in this step to emphasize the decision rules that govern when this particular solution type should be used.	In subsequent classes, the instructor shows a variety of problems and has the students match the type of solution to the type of problem. This helps them understand when to apply each solution. Problem solutions can appear in any subsequent lesson so that students cannot use the lesson topic as the cue for which solution type to use (e.g., "This chapter is on derivatives, so the answer must involve doing a derivative.").

This is the basic design for a lesson based on the apprenticeship concept. Although I have illustrated it with a math problem-solving scenario, the same process would hold for any application or intellectual skill and any setting. For example, in writing, instructors are encouraged to share their own writing with students and to discuss what they go through in producing and editing their own work. In ethics classes, instructors can pose a problem and work through it with the class, discussing and debating each step with the students. In a biology lab, the instructor doesn't just show the students how to work the equipment, but she discusses safety procedures, possible complications, which equipment is used and why, and walks through the procedure before the students are allowed to continue. In clinical practicum, the psychology instructor demonstrates the therapy technique in a role play and keeps up a running commentary on why he is asking the questions he asks, why he probes the client further, and what the final recommendation is and why.

I have found that there are many opportunities to model this thinking process in day to day teaching when students ask interesting questions to which there are no pat answers (something that happens a lot in psychology). After acknowledging what a good question the student has asked, I take a moment to think aloud about it and how I might reason out an answer, including making false starts and backtracking. I hope that this shows them that there are no pat answers to a lot of questions and that it is possible to speculate on an answer, something I'd like my students to feel they can do.

MORE THOUGHTS ON THE COGNITIVE APPRENTICESHIP PROCESS

This method for teaching skills of all types is very rich in terms of suggestions for teaching. We've seen the basics of each component, but I'd like to expand on some of the parts in more depth to give you a feeling for what you can do with this model in terms of encouraging students to tackle higher-level skills.

Motivational Considerations

I said earlier that Bandura considered motivation to be an integral part of the modeling process of learning. For him it permeated every step. An instructor can take some specific steps to enhance motivation.

Authentic situations. An authentic situation is similar to the situation in which the skills will really be used eventually, or it can be a real situation in which the skills are needed but not necessarily one representative of the learners' future use of them. For example, writing instructors have found that basing assignments on real writing tasks, such as writing an editorial for a newspaper or developing instructional materials for elementary students, tends to produce better writing than a more abstract assignment in which students discuss a point of view without a particular audience in mind. Another example of authentic assignments are those involved in service learning. Here the students apply the skills they are learning to real projects in the community. These don't have to be projects that mimic their future careers; they usually address community needs and require general educational skills such as thinking and problem solving. One of the values of using authentic situations is that they are extremely motivating. The learners can see the value of learning this skill when it is presented in the type of situation in which they see themselves in the future or when they see an immediate benefit to the community in what they're doing. A side benefit of using authentic settings is that what is learned transfers more readily to other settings than things that are learned in sterile classroom exercises.

Evidence of progress. A second source of motivation for learners in skill learning is evidence of progress. When learners know what the target skill looks like and they see themselves making progress toward it, this reinforces their efforts. As instructors we can help students see their progress in the way we talk about their work. If our comments are directed at where they are now in comparison to where they were initially, they are more likely to see how far they've come instead of how much farther they have to go. It is particularly helpful in giving such feedback to add comments about next steps. For example, an instructor might say, "Last week you were able to take this idea only this far, but now you've gotten to this level. I think that is very good, and that a next step might be to include this new information in your analysis."

Of course, nothing is as motivating as success itself, and so it is important for students to experience and recognize their successes while learning. Instructors can aid this in two ways. First, they can structure the tasks in such a way that early success is likely. One way to do this is through the process of scaffolding mentioned earlier. In scaffolding the instructor provides support during the initial learning steps by selecting easier initial versions of the task or by doing some of the harder parts while the students do the easier parts. In our dance example, when the instructor stood beside Lester and did the steps along with him, she was scaffolding his attempts by making it easier for him to see how the steps progressed. He didn't have to watch her do them backward and then translate them to his own feet. Eventually, she would turn around and dance the way his real partner might dance, which would remove the scaffolding and see if he could maintain his level of performance without that cue. We scaffold in teaching statistics when we don't require the students to memorize the formulas, but rather allow them to create note cards with key formulas they need to be able to access quickly. We scaffold in teaching writing when we provide a series of questions that can be used to narrow a topic and make it manageable. We're scaffolding when we provide readily recognizable examples from the learners' own experience because that makes it easier for the learner to understand and remember main points; eventually, we encourage the learners to create their own examples for the same reason.

A second way to help learners recognize their own success is through the feedback we provide. Amazingly, there are some students who have a great deal of difficulty recognizing or acknowledging the things they have done right. They tend to focus on what went wrong and how bad that was. As instructors, we can encourage students to recognize their successes and to treat their mistakes as learning opportunities. This is a far healthier way of responding to one's own performance. Encouragement and focusing on progress helps learners continue to be motivated even in the face of frustration.

Narrated Modeling

Who should do the modeling? There are several ways of thinking about this issue. The literature on learning from models maintains that the most important feature of a good model is competence at the skill being modeled. That makes a lot of sense, but there is a catch. Sometimes one can be too competent, too much of an expert, because the hardest part of the cognitive apprenticeship process is being able to describe what it is you're doing. Most instructors find it difficult to think aloud while they demonstrate the intellectual skills they're trying to teach. Because instructors are experts in their fields, they often have gone far beyond the finite steps that a novice needs to understand the whole process. As a result, it is difficult for them to remember each and every step, to unpack their thinking, in order to make it visible and comprehensible to the students. Sometimes our thinking is so automatic that we can't articulate why we make the choices we make; they just look right, or worse, feel right. However, that is not going to help the students. This problem often comes up when we are trying to explain grading standards to students. Many of us have experienced the situation in which we can't describe what makes an "A" paper, but we know it when we see it. This very real phenomenon is extremely frustrating to instructor and student alike and is one manifestation of what Speck (1998) has called "the mystery of professional judgment." As instructors, we do make professional judgments and engage in professional-level decision-making that is based on a well-organized wealth of knowledge and experience that we access almost automatically when problem solving. To students it appears as though we are making huge logic leaps because they are not privy to the extremely rapid processing that we are doing almost without conscious awareness. However, with practice we can slow down and bring those intermediate steps to a conscious level, and this is what is meant by thinking aloud. This instructional skill is key to successfully modeling intellectual skills for students. It's definitely worth practicing if your students will be able to follow your thinking enough to learn the process themselves.

Of course, it is not necessary to narrate every detail all the time. The level of narration is determined by the level of the students (Figure 4.1). Beginners need a lot of help recognizing the key steps, and so with them the narration might best be confined to highlighting main points in the process. As students become more familiar with the skill, an instructor can begin to interject some ambiguous and abstract concepts in which analysis and evaluation become more important. Here narration becomes more involved but still focuses on key ideas and decision points and with an emphasis on process. Ironically, once the learners become mini-experts themselves, narration may become shorter simply because the learners are now thinking along with the instructor and filling in the gaps on their own. Figure 4.1 shows a conceptualization of this relationship. The use of technical terms and standard references becomes easier because the students are familiar with them and it is not necessary to explain them each time. This may be why teaching upper division students and graduate students is so much easier and more fun than beginning students: You don't have to unpack your thinking as much until it is challenged by a student, and then the situation is more like collegial debate than teaching. Some evidence in the literature supports this idea; one review of the literature provided by the National Academy of Sciences asserts that experienced performers might be able to get more out of watching a model than novices do because they know where to look and what to look for (Bransford, Brown, & Cocking, 1999). You may experience this yourself if there is a sport you play or follow with some degree of proficiency. Watching a football game is much more interesting when you know something about football beyond the fact that touchdowns are good, because you can actually see a lot more that's happening and infer the rest. On the whole, however, the initial modeling of a skill is probably best done by an expert who is good at breaking down the thought processes involved and making them accessible to the learners.

Figure 4.1
How Explanations May Depend on Learner Prior Knowledge

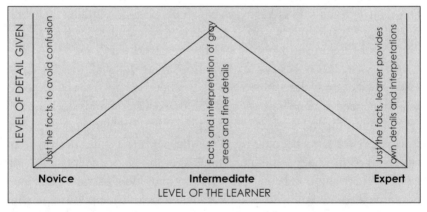

Another problem with the use of expert models is that learners can get a false sense of their own level of understanding if all they do is watch the model. How often have you heard students say, "but I understood it when you did it in class!" This illusion of understanding is a pitfall of expert modeling. Because so many of the false starts and wrong paths never get articulated during expert modeling, students don't learn what to do when things go wrong. Part of learning any skill is learning how to cope with failure. In learning a dangerous sport, like gymnastics or rock climbing, one of the first things taught is how to fall without getting hurt (admittedly not so easy in rock climbing). Students are taught how to roll with the punches. We should provide an equivalent education for those learning intellectual skills: how to fall intellectually without getting hurt.

Of perhaps several ways of doing this, two that show up in much of the literature on modeling involve less-than-competent models (known as coping models because they show how to cope with difficulties). In one version the instructor illustrates how to apply a skill by tackling a new problem in front of the class, a problem that he or she has never seen before. The process of working through this new problem in front of the class introduces students to the idea that even experts make mistakes and have to backtrack. The flawless problem-solving performance they are used to instructors displaying is actually a sham, having been worked out in detail the night before. This new strategy is a much more realistic view of how easy or difficult it is to apply the skill being learned.

Another type of coping model involves using the students themselves as models. This can be done by having some students try to apply the skill as the instructor coaches. These would not be the "A" students, but just average students. The important part of this type of instruction is empha-sizing that the student models are not expected to be able to solve the problem right away. Instead, these students are serving as surrogates for the rest of the class in a kind of one-to-one coaching session with the instructor. The rest of the class can even be invited to make suggestions to these student models as they try to work through the problem. The instructor provides hints and scaffolding just as he or she would with an individual student, but in this case the whole class is the student. Watch-ing (and helping) other students work through skill applications gets around three of the problems of expert models. First, it gives a much more realistic picture of what will be involved when one attempts the skill later alone and what to do when things don't go smoothly. Second, it helps to puncture the illusion of understanding because these coping models make the kind of mistakes that the rest of the class would make. If the whole class participates in working through the problem, students are forced to confront their own lack of understanding much more directly. A variation on this theme is to have the students work in pairs or small groups on sample problems. In the group setting, the students serve as coping models for each other and are much more likely to be confronted with their own fallacious thinking. Third, when students see another student like them working at and successfully executing a skill, their own confidence goes up. "If he can do it, so can I!" A similar phenomenon is probably occurring when we use work from a previous class. Samples of student work can serve as models as readily as the students themselves, a point that brings us to an interesting sidebar.

This expansion of the question of who should be the model is that the model doesn't have to be a live model at all. Computer animation techniques, for example, allow us to demonstrate physical skills much more clearly than we can with a live model because the sequence can be broken down to its essence, stopped, replayed, and manipulated to show different aspects. A classroom application of this is the use of trigger films to show real people solving real problems or videotapes of native language speakers in real life settings used in language classes. Although this expands our options as instructors, of course, the general rules of modeling still apply: The learners need to know how to observe and what to look for; the behavior should be simplified and the main points exaggerated; and so on, just as if the models were live.

WHAT TO MODEL IN WHAT ORDER

Deciding what to model is as important as how to model it. For example, can the skill be broken down into component parts that can be modeled and practiced independent of one another? A lot of the literature on the teaching of critical thinking discusses what those components might be and which ones can be done in isolation. For example, Halpern (1996) proposes that critical thinking is both a set of skills, such as identifying underlying assumptions, and a set of attitudes, such as willingness to consider alternatives. It is beyond the scope of this book to discuss all the alternative models of critical thinking that have been proposed. I suggest that you consult the literature in your discipline for an analysis of the critical thinking skills that seem most important for your area. Or you might want to consult Halpern's very readable book on critical thinking. However, conducting your own task analysis of what is involved whenever you try to think critically in your area is a good way to begin to

understand what has to be included in the process of modeling key intellectual skills for your students. You may not be able to include all the skill
components your students need in a single course, and so you will have
to make some difficult decisions about priorities. At this point I hope you
consider working with your colleagues to view the curriculum as a whole
and how each part contributes something to the whole picture of your
students' intellectual development. No one class can create critical
thinkers; it takes a whole department, maybe a whole institution. Maybe
that's what is meant by a liberal education.

One bright spot to the above dilemma is that most learning theorists
support the idea of practicing skills in parts and then combining them
into a whole sequence. Some more recent theories argue against this idea
and say that the whole is greater than the sum of the parts, and practicing in parts leads to a lesser understanding than practicing the entire skill
intact and in the context of its normal (consult Bransford et al. 1999, for
further analysis of this idea). While I support this assertion to some
extent, in practical terms, I find it less helpful. There is much to be
gained by breaking a complex skill into components and allowing learners to practice the parts while they build toward the whole. I will provide
one caveat, however. Practice of parts would be greatly facilitated if it followed a demonstration of the whole skill first. This initial demonstration
of the whole then becomes an advance organizer that helps learners see
how the parts eventually fit together as a whole. Constantly referring
back to the whole demonstration while introducing the parts helps learners keep in mind why they are learning each part and where it fits in the
big picture.

CREATING MENTAL MODELS THAT LAST

Recalling what I said about memory in Chapter 2, the essence of learning
something is getting it stored in long-term memory in such a way that it
can be retrieved readily when needed. The same is true with skills. The
representation of a skill in memory (usually referred to as procedural
knowledge) is the mental model described here.

As with content knowledge, mental models of skills can exist in
many forms in memory. They might be represented by a series of "if, then"
steps. They might be represented by a mnemonic, like the "stop, drop,
and roll" mnemonic that represents what to do if your clothes catch on

fire. They are often visually stored, truly a mental image of the target skill. This is particularly true of performance skills, such as in sports. Many coaches use visual mnemonics as a way of helping athletes create a good mental image of the skill they are learning. For example, in my own sport of tennis, coaches teach players how to hit overhead smashes by telling them to reach for the sky so that they'll extend their opposite hand toward the ball and drop their racquet hand shoulder, which aids in generating speed and power. We're told to hit volleys at the net by punching like a boxer instead of swinging.

Athletes in many sports can use these mental images to practice without physically moving—a practice is called cognitive rehearsal, which has been shown many times over to produce improved performance just as if the athlete had been out on the court playing. You may notice a high diver just before a dive closes his eyes and pauses—in all probability cognitively rehearsing the dive before performing it. Public speakers are encouraged to engage in a similar mental rehearsal before a big speech. They are told to close their eyes and picture themselves being successful in front of the crowd. This is a proven technique for overcoming performance anxiety of many types. We might consider encouraging our mental athletes who are learning intellectual skills to engage in similar mental practice before the actual performance.

To be most effective, these mental models need to be easy to remember and meaningful to the learners. Vivid images or simple images are usually easy to remember. Rhymes or short phrases are easy to remember. And things that are personally salient are easy to remember. Mental models that are too complex or are drawn from things with which the learner has no experience will not facilitate learning; they'll just make it more difficult.

Scaffolding and Coaching

We've already learned a little about scaffolding. The term refers to the supports that an instructor gives to learners while they are in the process of developing their skills. Scaffolding allows the learners to accomplish tasks that they would not normally be able to accomplish on their own. For example, when an instructor simplifies a problem by removing complicating factors, he is scaffolding the students' problem-solving abilities by placing less strain on their memory and reasoning processes. Once they have developed some problem-solving skills, the instructor can gradually remove the scaffolding by adding more variables that complicate the problem solution. Because the learners already have been practicing using the prescribed process for solving simpler problems, they should be able to continue its use with more complex problems.

Another important component that needs to be present during the practicing stage of skill learning is coaching with feedback (Druckman & Bjork, 1991). There is always some source of feedback when a learner is performing a skill; the environment itself will provide feedback even if the instructor/coach doesn't. For example, if I serve a tennis ball and the ball goes into the net or out of bounds, I am getting feedback on my serving skill. (It needs work!) As I practice, my skill improves and more of the balls go over the net and into my opponent's service box. This provides feedback that I am getting better. The equivalent source of feedback in academic settings is getting the correct answer. The problem with environmental feedback as the sole source is that it takes a long time before a new learner gets any positive feedback, and he or she could easily become discouraged. In addition, sources of environmental feedback (and often test grades) don't provide much coaching about how to improve. Learners are frequently left on their own to figure out what to do next.

A far better source of feedback is from a coach, real or virtual. A coach can diagnose the learner's problems and suggest what to correct and how to correct it. Although in sports instruction, most learners get this kind of individual coaching, it doesn't happen very often in academic settings. Most instructors don't have time to provide individual diagnostic feedback to each learner on each attempt to exercise a skill. Fortunately, there are now some alternatives to instructor coaching.

If individual feedback is on one end of the continuum and no feedback is on the other (Figure 4.2), some alternative points in between can be considered. For example, one way an instructor can provide feedback and diagnosis is to aggregate the comments that would be made to individual students into a class-wide feedback sheet (Figure 4.3). Here the instructor notes the most commonly occurring errors, gives specific examples, and provides remediation suggestions. Students can then compare their own papers to the common list and identify where they made similar errors. If the instructor has created a set of distinguishing editorial marks (e.g., "UC" for unclear phrasing and "support" for insufficient support for an argument), those marks can be used during paper grading to indicate to students where specific problems occur. The students can then consult the general feedback sheet to see what to do about those identified on their individual papers.

Figure 4.2
A Continuum of Feedback Possibilities

Frequent individual feedback from instructor	Rubric for ongoing self-feedback	Intelligent tutors	Feedback from peers	Aggregated class feedback	No feedback at all

Figure 4.3
An Example of an Aggregated Feedback Sheet

A Paper Analysis Guide:
Below I have listed the most commonly occurring errors in your papers. In the left column is a set of editor's marks corresponding to each error or trouble spot. Look through your own paper and find where I marked similar problems in it. Figure out why I marked it as I did and be careful to avoid the same problems in the next essay.

Th   There is no thesis for this paper/paragraph. That means I can't tell what your main point is either for the whole paper or for that particular paragraph. See handout 2 for ideas on ways to write better thesis statements.

UW   Unclear wording. This means that the way you worded this particular thought didn't make sense to me or confused me. Make sure that your sentences are not too complex with too many clauses. See the writing handbook on clarity.

UT   Unclear thinking. This mark means that your logic is faulty. Either you drew an erroneous conclusion from the data or you made an argument that wasn't supported by the information you included.

VOC   Inappropriate vocabulary. You are using terms incorrectly. Check the text-book for the correct definition and see if your word choice still makes sense.

Alternatively, many instructors have begun using the students as each other's coaches. Provided with a good rubric (a structured outline of desired qualities similar to the feedback sheet described above) for evaluation, most students are capable of reading someone else's work and reacting to it. Indeed, it is probably the case that assessing someone else's work helps a student improve his or her own work. For an especially good discussion of alternative ways of giving feedback on writing, consult Sorcinelli and Elbow's (1997) collection of strategies.

Other alternative coaching or feedback mechanisms include intelligent tutors created for computers, which help guide a learner's actions. An example is the Office Assistant built into Microsoft's products. This subroutine can monitor your writing and recognize when you are writing different types of documents, at which point it can offer help. The product also monitors spelling and grammar and signals to the writer when errors are being made. The writer can choose to ignore the messages or take the advice. Some computer tutors craft an argument in preparation for writing a paper, guiding the writer through a series of questions that help him to clarify the purpose, the audience, and the style to use.

Perhaps the best alternative is teaching the learner to be his or her own coach. This involves becoming metacognitively aware of one's actions and decisions and taking corrective steps when they go awry. To help learners with this more sophisticated intellectual skill of self-monitoring, the instructor needs to articulate the criteria for the assignment before the students begin to work on it. These criteria are given to the students, and the instructor models their use in an example, as suggested in the cognitive apprenticeship method. Students are encouraged to use the criteria as they work on the assignment and to evaluate their finished work against the criteria before they turn it in. Some instructors ask the students to turn in the checklist itself to show that they have reviewed the work against the criteria. Other instructors have students hand in a self-critique along with the finished product. Getting in the habit of using a criterion checklist prior to submission helps build good work habits. If at least some of the items on the checklist remain constant across assignments (e.g., "the paper has been checked for grammatical errors" or "the computations have been repeated at least once to check for arithmetic errors"), they will become a more automatic activity with each successive use. An instructor can even build the checklist across the semester, starting with very basic tasks like checking for spelling and factual errors and adding more and more sophisticated requirements with each assignment (e.g., beginning with "each argument has at least one piece of supporting evidence presented" and ending with "each argument considers both supporting and contradictory evidence"). This gradual increase in the level of sophistication of editing required could be considered a form of scaffolded practice. It would also be helpful to explain the sequence of editing steps at the beginning so the learners understand that they are learning a process as well as creating a product. Some instructors reinforce this notion by having students write a reflective essay on the process they went through during the semester and how it affected their work quality and how they might apply it in the future. I have found this kind of looking backward, looking forward assignment to be better than a comprehensive final in solidifying student understanding of the material they have learned.

Learner Articulation and Reflection

Having students reflect on their learning is the next logical step in the process of learning an intellectual skill. This is the step that solidifies and possibly codifies their understanding of the modeled skill so that they achieve some closure on what they have learned and how they have learned it.

In this step, the learners are required to do their own thinking aloud just as the model did originally. By describing how they solved a problem, the learners become more aware of the process and less tied to the solution. This strategy has been used for a long time in quantitative courses, in which students are required to show their work, in essence write out the steps they took to solve the problem. This narrative of the process helps both the learners and the instructor identify where problems were encountered and how the learners might have gone wrong. If all effort is focused on the answer, and that answer is incorrect, the learners are unlikely to figure out why their answer was wrong.

Writing instructors have begun to use a process similar to this when they require students to submit a writing journal and interim drafts along with the finished paper. In the journal the students describe how they selected a topic, created the argument, found the supporting evidence, and so on. They also might be encouraged to self-critique the paper, as noted earlier under the practice section of this chapter. Engaging in this activity focuses student attention more on writing as a process. It has the added benefit of making purchased papers much less attractive because they would not include all the components required in a journal and a student would have to create an imaginary paper trail to match the purchased paper. They might as well write the paper themselves; it would be less hassle.

A less formal strategy for accomplishing this kind of articulation and reflection is the use of student peers as editors or monitors. For example, in a math class, students can work in pairs in which one student is the problem solver while the other is the questioner. (Whimbey & Lochhead, 1999). The problem solver describes what he or she is doing during problem solving, while the questioner makes sure that each step is described and the reasoning behind it is logical. This is a good way for students to practice the skill of reflecting on a problem-solving skill. Eventually, however, the students should be required to synthesize what they have learned about problem solving or any other intellectual process by articulating it for themselves. This articulation then can serve as the basis for transferring the skill to a new problem situation.

Transferring Skills to New Venues

This last step brings us to the final problem with teaching intellectual skills: getting students to transfer what they have learned to new problems. If there is one universal frustration in teaching it is the failure of students to use what they've learned in new settings, even in new academic settings much less real world settings. The research on learning offers several speculations on why this is so, and they will be explored in greater detail in the next chapter. I will introduce them briefly here while this idea is fresh in your mind.

One possible reason for student failure to transfer is that the skill was not learned thoroughly in the first place. This is especially relevant in higher education. How can we think that students will learn in just 15 weeks everything they need to know about analyzing the history of civilization or evolution of life on earth or any of the other very complex subjects we teach? The problem here is that a lot of students (and a lot of faculty) equate memorizing a huge number of facts with understanding a content area. While most instructors say that they want students to understand the content area, memorization does not produce understanding of the type discussed in Chapter 3. Add to that the problem of information explosion in all fields and we are facing a Sisyphean task; that content rock is going to get way too big for us to push it up the hill, and it will eventually roll right over us and our students. It would be far better to forget about having students learn everything they need to know about an area and concentrate on teaching them a few fundamental principles and how to think about a subject instead. For example, how do psychologists decide which variables influence a given behavior? Or how do historians decide whether a given interpretation of an historical event is legitimate? Or what aspects of any virus should a microbiologist be looking at to decide if and how it is dangerous? These are the more general process-oriented questions that students can apply to any specific set of information they might encounter in the future. We all know that the specifics of our fields change, but good thinking habits are always useful. So we would be better off giving students a lot of practice on thinking skills so that they learn them well rather than making them learn a lot of information first.

A second speculation on why skills don't transfer is that students haven't learned when to use a particular skill. They fail to recognize the situation as one in which it is appropriate to apply a process. In a classic example of this (Gick & Holyoak, 1987), researchers had students study a story in which a general was trying to conquer a citadel. Initially, he tried to storm the citadel and throw everything he had against the front door, but it didn't work. Then he had the idea of dividing his forces into smaller groups that could approach the citadel from several sides unnoticed. This strategy was successful. After they discussed the story and understood it, the students were given other problems to solve, one of which involved using lethal radiation to kill a tumor without harming the surrounding tissue. The strategy of breaking the radiation down into smaller doses that would then accumulate and assemble into a lethal dose when they reached their intersection at the tumor was the correct solution, but very few of the students made the connection with the general's strategy in order to solve the problem. Even when it was pointed out to them, some students didn't see the connection. These data are held up as an example of how difficult it is to get students to transfer problem-solving strategies from one problem to a new situation.

To solve this problem of transfer, instructors need to be much more explicit about teaching when to use a solution strategy as well as how the strategy works. Fortunately, the instructional method for dealing with this problem is not overly complex and we'll look at it in the next chapter, but here are a few of the fundamentals that psychologists agree on (Druckman & Bjork, 1991). All the literature on transfer encourages us to initially provide a lot of practice on the skill in question along with emphasis on articulating the process. Then the practice should be with more and more varied examples of the type of situations in which the process would or would not be applied, along with a discussion of how to make the decision. Finally, as the learning progresses on to other problem-solving strategies, previously learned strategies should be fair game for inclusion in the practice. In this way, students don't automatically use a particular type of problem solution because "that's what we're studying this week." Instructors should think of the interconnectedness of situations that students will face as they attempt to use the skills they are learning in real life and reflect those choices when they design practice situations.

A Synthesis of Strategies

Now that you've had an opportunity to learn about all the possible components of the cognitive apprenticeship, I'll provide a synthesizing example to show how it might play out in a real class. I'll use the example of my own class that is learning the skill of critically analyzing information they get from the Internet. Table 4.2 shows the components of the cognitive apprenticeship model and how I would employ them to teach this skill.

Okay, Now We Know How, But What Skills Should We Teach?

You've probably noticed by now that the foregoing discussion has said nothing about what to teach. That is a deliberate omission on my part for three good reasons. The first involves the idiosyncratic epistemologies of the various disciplines; the second involves the research on the usefulness of training in general versus discipline-specific skills; and the third involves the wealth of other printed material that can do a much better job of providing specific suggestions.

Table 4.2

A Demonstration of the Cognitive Apprenticeship Model

Cognitive appreciation component	Applied to the skill of critically analyzing information from the Internet
Authentic situation	I want to demonstrate and teach this skill in a realistic situation, so I assign students to create a web page on a question appropriate to the course topic with links to other sites that are reliable resources.
Narrated modeling	I create a heuristic for evaluating sources on the Internet. This is the model they will be learning. For example, I might present the journalistic model of "who, what, when, where, and why" to represent the type of questions students should be asking themselves as they assess the validity of a source. "Who wrote it? What did they claim? When was it published? Where was it published? Why did this person write this?" I give an in-class, online demonstration of information searching. I talk through the heuristics and relate them to the searches the students will be conducting. I let the students choose the sample topic in order to make it meaningful to them. I use projection so that all students can see the process as we go through it, and I have a handout with the heuristics outlined. If possible, I create a mnemonic that helps them remember the sequence of steps ("who, what, when, where, why").
Coached and scaffolded practice	Part one: I have the students work in pairs to replicate the exact search I have just done, filling in a worksheet that has the heuristics on it. As they work together, they confirm with each other what is involved in each step and check any questions

	with me as I circulate around the room. After all have completed the task, the class as a whole discusses what they experienced. This is scaffolded practice because it is exactly the same search I just did so they should be able to recognize when their results differ from mine. It's also scaffolded by the use of the worksheet, which guides them through the process. It's coached to some extent because they work in pairs and because I am there to answer questions that arise. There is some preliminary reflection occurring when the class as a whole discusses their experiences. Part two: Now each pair works on a new topic of their own choosing, but applying the same heuristics. They write this up and turn it in along with a description of the process, a flow chart showing how they made their decisions. This is also the first step toward transfer since they are applying the strategy to a new topic.
Articulation and reflection	Examples from the class are discussed with the class as a whole in order to compare procedures and identify stronger versus weaker strategies. Pairs present their examples and other students question them. The purpose is to identify alternative strategies and what works and what doesn't. This step also aids in transfer because students see a wide range of topics that were tackled by the different pairs.
Transfer	In addition to the activities above, the students learn to transfer when they go on to create the web sites of the initial assignment. In addition, as an instructor, I might brainstorm with them other situations in which these heuristics might be useful (for example, in evaluating other sources). Finally, I might use this set of heuristics for other assignments involving non-Internet uses, which would also encourage transfer.

Let's begin, however, with the problem of the idiosyncrasies of intellectual skills in various disciplines. Janet Donald (Donald, 1995) and others have attempted to chart the different emphases given various intellectual skills that are used in various disciplines. For example, one possible disciplinary difference in emphasis of intellectual skills is how one goes about determining the validity of a proposed explanation. In many of the natural sciences, the strategy involves continually testing the proposal with the intention of identifying where it does not provide an adequate explanation or prediction. So, for example, in mathematics, proofs are tested by considering extreme cases, such as, "Does the proof hold for a value of zero or for extremely large values of X?" In the social sciences, a proposal is tested more by synthesis than antithesis; that is, the proposer seeks to find all the cases in which it does apply and whether it can explain all the previous cases that had been explained by a previous proposition. In another example, many natural sciences have an all-or-nothing attitude, in which something either worked or it didn't. In the social sciences, the proof of concept is much more statistically based. A single instance of success must be tested against the statistical probability of recurrence. In another characterization of disciplinary differences, Alexander (Alexander, 1992) talks about domains as being tightly versus loosely structured; hierarchical or level; algorithmic or heuristic based. These characteristics of the domain have a strong influence on the type of thinking that is done. In the end, a list of general intellectual skills would favor some disciplines and leave out important skills from other disciplines, so I have chosen not to tell you what intellectual skills to teach and instead stick to advice on how to teach skills.

Another reason I have chosen to be less specific about what to teach is the controversy in the literature on our ability to get students to learn and transfer any intellectual skills at all beyond a narrowly defined problem space. These specific skills under consideration in the literature are strong (Mayer & Wittrock, 1996), and are favored by experts in a discipline. Conversely, weak methods are general problem-solving heuristics, such as means-ends analysis or reverse engineering strategy that can be applied to any problem. The difficulty with weak methods is that they have been shown to be not very useful in most of the concrete problem-solving situations that really matter. Weak methods are most used by novices in a domain, those who don't have a lot of prior experience and are just fishing for clues on how to attack a problem. This is an active area of research and controversy, and will be examined further in the chapter on transfer. There is a lot of legitimate concern about teaching general intellectual skills outside the context of a specific discipline's needs. Rather than recommend a list of what might turn out to be relatively weak methods, I refer you to the literature in your discipline to determine what intellectual skills are most viable in your field.

That brings me to my last reason for not going into detail here about what skills to teach: There is a lot of literature that discusses intellectual skills in much greater depth than I can here. Some of the books that take an in-depth look at critical thinking as the umbrella term for intellectual skills offer very specific analyses of critical thinking in general and ways to foster it in particular. I would especially recommend Beyer (1997) or Halpern (1996) for a psychologist's perspective on what constitutes critical thinking. Each of these volumes provides an analysis of problem-solving strategies that have been researched in the context of general problem solving. Then I would send you to the literature in your own field. Many fields have attempted to identify the basics of practice and have discussed those ideas in the discipline-specific literature. This is particularly true of the sciences, math, engineering, and technology because of the infusion of support for such analysis by the National Science Foundation. It is also the case with these disciplines that the concreteness of the problems they tackle lends itself to readier identification of strategies for solution than is the case in humanities and social sciences. So a perusal of the literature in your field may turn up some key references to guide your practice.

The upshot of such disciplinary differences is that researchers in this area don't always agree on what the critical intellectual skills are. So any proposal of a set of specific skills would encounter disciplinary differences immediately. The strategies for teaching any intellectual skill can remain the same (the modeling concept just described), while the specific skills taught can be very different from field to field.

ANOTHER PERSPECTIVE ON TEACHING INTELLECTUAL SKILLS

Earlier I said that Halpern (1996) and others have often talked about critical thinking and other intellectual skills as having an attitudinal component as well as a skills components. The process I've been describing has focused on teaching the skills of intellectual life, but unless the students learn the concomitant values and attitudes of critical thinking, the skills will be a hollow exercise. Table 4.3 lists some examples of what various theories include as skills and attitudes associated with critical thinking.

Table 4.3
Skills and Attitudes Associated With Critical Thinking

Skills	Attitudes and Values
Identifying underlying assumptions	Curiosity
Clarifying the problem objective	A commitment to objectivity
Gathering information in support of a position	Willingness to delay judgment
Generating alternative solutions	Skepticism
Evaluating alternative solutions	Persistence
Selecting and implementing a solution	Desire to find a solution
Evaluating the outcome	

I assert that the same process of modeling that applies to learning the skills involved in intellectual activities applies to the development of values and attitudes. We learn those values and attitudes by watching and emulating others, specifically our instructors. When instructors model problem solving, they are also modeling the scholarly values that underlie good problem solving. To give a specific example, two of the important attitudes for students to develop in problem solving are curiosity about the subject and an acceptance of the fact that answers are sometimes not as black and white as we would like. As instructors, we model that curiosity when we react positively to students who raise questions to which we don't immediately know the answer. If we greet these instances with a desire to figure it out, we show the students that part of their success will depend on their willingness to confront new challenges. If we don't react in dismay when we don't know an answer, we communicate to our students that it is okay to not know something immediately, that the realm of the unknown is where the most learning is likely to occur. If we don't try to bluster our way through an answer to convince the students of our omniscience but rather show ourselves as not knowing everything yet, despite our advanced degrees, we are modeling that being a scholar means always being in a state of uncertainty and relishing it rather than dreading it.

The bottom line is that, along with the skills we are teaching, we should be aware of the attitudes we convey to our students, for these may be more important to them in the long run than all the facts or skills we can cram into a course.

5

HELPING STUDENTS RETAIN AND USE WHAT THEY'VE LEARNED IN OTHER SETTINGS

"I learn everything for the test, and as soon as it's done, I forget it." Have you heard students make this claim? I certainly have. I've been frustrated by what seems to be their inability to remember things from one day to the next much less one semester to the next. On the other hand, I, too, have experienced this disturbing inability to remember important information after only a short period of disuse. Obviously, an important hole in our instructional system is designing for retention of what is learned over a long period.

Even more irritating is the seeming inability of students to use what they have learned on any problem that is not an exact copy of the problem they used when they were learning it. This shows up frequently on tests, where students lament the use of tricky questions while the instructor thinks he or she is asking the students to use information in a similar type of problem. (As an aside, one of the key findings in the research on the differences between experts and novices in a field is their ability to recognize the underlying structure of a problem as a way of identifying the strategy for solving it. Experts are not easily distracted by irrelevant information in the problem statement, while novices often focus on surface features; hence, the difference between students and instructors in interpreting what constitutes a tricky problem.)

These two failures in the educational system are referred to in the psychological literature as problems of retention and transfer, and there is a great deal of research on each. The underlying learning model that drives the research and design in this area is the same cognitive model that was discussed in Chapter 2. While the initial learning of content focuses mostly on the attention and encoding steps of the cognitive model, retention and transfer focus on the encoding and retrieval steps.

The Transfer Continuum

Another way that the research literature looks at these two tasks is on a continuum. On one end of the continuum is retention, which involves responding to situations that are very similar, possibly identical to the original learning conditions. In the middle of the continuum is transfer, which involves responding to situations that differ from the original learning conditions in some way. On the far end of the continuum is what psychologists call problem solving, which involves transfer of learning to a situation so different from the original that it requires the learners to figure out what the problem is and what information they have that is applicable to it. Offering an analogy to your ability to navigate city streets, retention is like driving the same route to work every day. You are working with the same landmarks, the same directions, the same behaviors on each instance, so you just have to remember what the landmarks are and what behaviors they signal. Transfer is like going to a part of your city that you don't know very well and having to figure out how to navigate it. You know the major streets and you have a mental map of the layout of the city, so you can figure out where you need to turn and which way to drive, even though you can't respond quickly or automatically as you can on your familiar routes. Problem solving is like being in a brand new city for the first time and having to figure out which are the main streets and which way is north and what the general travel patterns are. To carry the analogy further, this continuum of familiarity describes the phases you go through in learning a new city or a new domain. To a first-time visitor, everything in a new city is a problem to be solved, and the visitor can easily be fooled by surface features and what looks familiar. As the visitor takes more and more trips around the city, he or she begins to see patterns and identify main landmarks that help in navigating unfamiliar terrain. Eventually with enough practice, the visitor (now a resident) experiences immediate recognition of landmarks to the point of not needing them to navigate. He or she is now an expert in these familiar paths.

The same path might describe how students approach learning in a new domain. Initially, everything is unfamiliar and has to be approached as a new problem. Learners look for landmarks (such as surface characteristics of a problem) that might guide their response. As they learn more and more about an area, they begin to understand its structure and the key features of ideas and problems in the area, so that their task becomes one of recognizing what kind of problem they're facing and what solution they have on file that could apply. Finally, after enough practice and experience in an area, problems are recognized as simple variations on previously encountered problems, and the strategies are applied automatically.

Using the Continuum Model to Think About Retention, Transfer, and Problem Solving

If we think about this model as the basis for what happens in learning, I can tentatively assert that retention and transfer are special instances of problem solving that are supported by slightly different thought processes. To students studying an area for the first time, everything is like a new problem. They have to try to figure out what's important and what is not, what they know that applies and what does not, what steps to take and which to skip. As they work more and more in an area, they develop a larger repertoire of associations and connections that begin to form regular patterns associated with particular problem solutions. They learn to recognize what variables are important and what variables can be ignored. Now when they encounter a new problem, they have a network of information they can search and a set of solution strategies they can apply. However, since their repertoire is still somewhat limited, they have to search through memory trying to figure out what will help them, so it still takes a while and a few false starts to transfer what they know to the new situation. Eventually with enough varied exposure to the field, they become experts (to become a real expert takes at least ten years of experience, according to the literature [Hayes, 1985]), in that what they know about the field and the kinds of problems they are likely to encounter is so well-organized and the patterns so familiar that they don't really have to consciously search for a solution; one pops up from memory almost immediately. It is only when a novel situation or an incongruity intrudes that they have to stop and back up to the transfer stage. This is a greatly simplified version of what the literature implies in this area, but it is useful for thinking about how to structure instruction.

Enhancing Retention: Remembering Beyond the Exam

Keeping our model in mind, consider what is necessary to enhance the kind of rapid responding to familiar stimuli that we would call retention. Three important components of learning for retention are 1) identification of the key memory cues and then either 2) sufficient practice with the cues that they automatically trigger the appropriate response or 3) the development of a big enough and well-organized enough network of cues in long-term memory structure that there is a wide range of cues, any one of which can retrieve the information from memory.

Focus on key features. The first of these components, the identification of key memory cues, is obvious. You have to be able to recognize key features of a situation in order to remember how to respond to it. If you're learning to categorize types of animals, you have to know what to look at: physical structure, environment, behavior patterns, etc. Therefore, an instructor's first concern during learning and testing is to make sure that the learner is focusing on and storing the key features and the test situation contains those same key features. You'll recall from Chapter 2 on the cognitive model that focusing students' attention on key features was the first task in learning. Here it becomes the first task in testing for retention, too. In order to trigger memory, the memory cues need to be present, prominent, and recognizable. A lot of forgetting is simply failure to recognize or pay attention to key memory cues that are present during testing. If during learning students have learned to identify organisms by looking only at their physical features and during the test, none of those physical features are present, students won't be able to remember or figure out which organisms are which.

Get lots of quality practice. The next factor that affects students' ability to remember information is the degree to which and the way in which they practiced it in the first place. During learning they need to have practiced pairing the characteristics with the particular type of organism. If practice in pairing is all students do, we would usually refer to that as memorization, a favorite tactic of students but the bane of most instructors. Very few things at the level of higher education need to be memorized. Nevertheless, this is a strategy that a lot of students heavily depend on. Flash cards are a common way for students to memorize the connection between a set of characteristics and a response. Enough practice with the cards will lead to an automatic triggering of the appropriate response when a particular card is shown. Present the characteristics outside the context of the flash card and many students will be stumped. I use the same flash card method for learning my students' names. I take their pictures and create flash cards with the photo on one side and the name on the other. I practice with these cards whenever I have a free moment. By the second week I'm good at naming the pictures. However, the real people are another matter. I tell them that once I take their pictures no one is allowed to change clothes or hairstyles because when the context cues change (for example, a new hairstyle), I can't recall the name!

This is the problem with memorization: Memorized links are easily disrupted by new but irrelevant features or unfamiliar contexts. For example, have you ever had the experience of running into someone in a context other than your usual context (like seeing your doctor in the grocery store or seeing a student from your class at a community event) and not being able to remember who they are even though they look familiar? You've in essence memorized that person's identity in the context of a certain set of cues (the doctor's office or the classroom) and when that context is changed, you can't remember their name; the retrieval cues are missing. However, as long as you only encounter that person in the original context, memorization is intact.

The same is true for students' studying. If they study the content in the same context in which it will be presented on the exam, memorization works; they can answer the questions as long as the questions are identical to the way they studied. Unfortunately, if they encounter the information in a different context outside the classroom, they're lost; the classroom retrieval cues are not present and they forget what they've learned. Actually, it's still there in memory: they haven't really forgotten it but it can only be retrieved with the original cues that were present during learning. In the literature this kind of information is referred to as "inert knowledge" (Bereiter & Scardamalia, 1985). It sits in memory uselessly until the appropriate cues are available.

However, if what is being learned can be practiced in the same sort of situations that will be present in the future, then remembering is more likely because the retrieval cues are present in both learning and testing. If this is the case, then time spent rehearsing information can be useful. That's why it's good to practice using situations as close as possible to the situation in which the actual information will be tested. For example, I should be learning students' names in the classroom context or in face-to-face situations. That way the test cues would be present during learning. This happens naturally in a classroom when the student's seat becomes a retrieval cue for his or her name because students always sit in the same place. "If this person is sitting in the front row, she must be Virginia." Translating this into student learning terms, if students are going to be tested using ideas in scenarios, that's how they should practice during learning.

Build an organized knowledge base. An alternative strategy for enhancing retention is the second one mentioned earlier: developing a large, well-organized, and strongly interconnected set of associations around the content being learned. Haskell (2001), in a comprehensive book on transfer, asserts that the importance of a strong, well-organized knowledge base cannot be overemphasized. Certainly, we know that knowledge base is a key distinction between novices and experts (Bransford, Brown, & Cocking, 1999). Part of this is what we discussed in Chapters 2 and 3 as structural knowledge. Here the new situation doesn't automatically trigger a learned response. Instead, the learners can figure out the appropriate response by searching for the relevant cues and building the response from those. Students would be using this idea if they were constantly testing themselves by coming up with new examples or situations in which to use the information they are learning. The more examples they've generated, the higher the probability that they'll find one similar to the new situation. Another study strategy for building this kind of structural understanding is to sort examples into categories or to generate tables that compare and contrast examples that represent different concepts. By understanding how examples relate to one another, students can figure out how a new example fits into the relationship and thus remember it or more appropriately construct it. You may recall from Chapter 2 that these two types of learning were referred to as surface processing (memorization) and deep processing (developing structural knowledge). I hope I emphasized that deep processing results in better memory than surface processing, particularly when trying to remember things for a long time.

Give lots of spaced practice (usually). Some interesting phenomena surrounding memory are significant when it comes to understanding the kinds of memory errors that students make. One is the occurrence of memory decay: the use it or lose it phenomenon. It doesn't take a deep, psychological analysis to know that information that is used on a regular basis will be more readily remembered than information that is rarely used. The method of spaced practice—that is, spreading out practice with information or skills over a longer period of time—is much more effective at producing long-term retention than massed practice—the kind of cramming in which information is studied intensively for a very short period of time (most often the night before the exam) (Druckman & Bjork, 1991). Unfortunately, in the short run usually represented by the testing schedule adopted in most courses, cramming is very effective; massed practice is good for getting a lot of material into memory in a short period of time. It just doesn't stay there unless it gets subsequent use. As an instructor, you should revisit previously studied material on a regular basis, particularly by contrasting it with information being currently learned. This repeated practice with information leads to much deeper processing and as a result better retention over the long haul. If I wanted to be really unpopular with students, I would recommend that all tests be comprehensive tests of everything studied up to that point in order to reinforce the constant revisiting of concepts. But I'd only recommend comprehensive testing if the material had a form and structure such that the comparisons across content units made sense and supported structural understanding.

Then there is the issue of how much practice is enough. The literature in this area is very interesting and the answer, as usual, is, "it depends." There are degrees of initial learning that result from different amounts of practice. In the past we have been admonished to practice, practice, practice, until you don't have to think about it any more. That's the way most athletes and musicians are taught. With that much practice, a skill or the application of an idea becomes automatic. The advantage of this is that automatic cognitive tasks take up very few cognitive processing resources. All that attention can now be diverted to more complex aspects of the skill. For example, my tennis coach advocates lots of practice hitting ground strokes over and over until the muscle memory is really solid. Then when I get into a match, I don't have to be thinking about how to hit ground strokes; I can think more about whether to hit a ground stroke or a lob or a short shot and where to aim. My playing can be more strategic because the simple task (of not hitting the ball into the net) has been relegated to cruise control. But the catch is that practicing to this level of automatic responding is not appropriate for all situations. Some situations require specific—not automatic—decision-making. Making decisions too automatically can lead to errors. I'll say more about this later, but the decision on how much to practice depends on whether the application situation is likely to vary significantly and require decisions. If the situation is always going to be the same, go for automatic responding. If there will be a lot of decisions to make, make the practice more thoughtful and analytic.

Avoid reconstruction errors. Another interesting memory phenomenon is the occurrence of reconstruction errors. In the bigger picture, all memory is reconstruction rather than direct recall. We don't store exact copies of most things; we store the gist of the information or experience. Then when we remember the information or the experience, we bring out the gist of the memory and rebuild it by adding details based on our schemas (remember those from Chapter 2?). This is why eyewitness testimony is so flawed: We remember what we think happened, not what really happened. Our previous experiences, attitudes, stereotypes, and existing schemas tend to interject details into our memories so that recent events come to fit our understanding of the world. What does this say about instruction and learning? It suggests that the kinds of errors in remembering that students make can be a window to how they think about a topic. It pays an instructor to listen to the kinds of errors students make and from them deduce the misinterpretations or misconceptions that are interfering with learning.

In fact, research indicates that it is important to understand the kinds of misconceptions that students bring to an instructional setting because those misconceptions will influence how they see and interpret what they're learning. Haskell (2001) talks about this in his concept of deep context teaching. He points out that students come to classes with a deep context consisting of all their prior knowledge and beliefs, correct and incorrect, positive and negative. This deep context influences their interpretations of what we're teaching, sometimes without us realizing that it's there. He says that in a field like psychology, there is so much pop culture to which students are exposed that it becomes almost impossible to convince them of the need for scientific thinking on the topic. On the other hand, in science education, misconceptions about the workings of the real world are rampant, and getting students to change erroneous beliefs is very difficult (Chinn & Brewer, 1993). Unless misconceptions like these are confronted directly, new learning will be very difficult and sometimes it will even be distorted to conform to those misconceptions. Instructors should understand the contexts students are bringing to the classroom. This is what Haskell means by "deep context teaching."

Transfer, the Next Step After Remembering: Using Information in New Situations

Whether they intend to or not, most instructors give unit tests that measure students' ability to remember information rather than their ability to use it. Items like lower-level multiple-choice items depend on this type of recognition memory: The answer that is correct is the one that I've seen before somewhere. At the same time, most instructors are not satisfied if students reach only that level of learning. Most instructors want students to be able to use the information in situations where they have to figure out the correct answer, not just recognize it from before. The psychological term for this level of achievement is transfer: Students should be able to transfer what they have learned to new and novel situations.

A great deal of psychological research has been conducted on this phenomenon. If you wanted to be Zen about it, you could say that every time you use a piece of previously learned information, you are engaging in transfer since you never really experience the exact same situation more than once. The river has moved on and so have you. So you can understand why learning theorists are preoccupied with what influences our ability to use previously learned information in new situations.

Many kinds of transfer are discussed in the literature, but for the purposes of this book and most instruction there are really only two useful ways to divide transfer tasks for understanding the underlying mechanisms: positive versus negative transfer and near versus far transfer.

Positive versus negative transfer. Positive transfer refers to those situations in which learning new information is helped by what was learned in the past. For example, the skills involved in catching one kind of ball are similar to those used in catching a different kind of ball. If you've learned to catch one ball, you can probably catch all balls, an instance of the positive transfer of ball catching. On the other hand, sometimes previous learning actually interferes with new learning, the situation known as negative transfer. For example, languages that are very similar sometimes interfere with one another when some words are the same and some are different. In the case of the latter, meanings from the first language can get confused with meanings from the second language, a case of negative transfer of word meaning.

Obviously, in instruction we want to maximize positive transfer and minimize negative transfer. Later in this chapter are some guidelines for instruction to accomplish that goal, but for now, let's look at the other type of transfer that plays a big role in how we design instruction.

Near versus far transfer. The best way to think about this type of transfer mechanism is to say that transfer tasks are either near transfer tasks or far transfer tasks. The behavior that the learners engage in is referred to as low road transfer or high road transfer, respectively (Perkins & Salomon, 1987). Near transfer tasks are those that look very much alike and follow the same rules for responding. For example, if you've ever driven one mid-level automatic sedan, you can drive every other mid-level automatic sedan because they all look similar inside. The steering wheel, gear shift, windshield wipers, and turn signals all look the same and are in the same position. The variations are minor annoyances, but they don't interfere with your ability to drive the second car. Therefore, driving these cars can be described as a near transfer task; they are perceptually and conceptually similar. The mechanism that supports transfer in this situation is the automatic triggering of a well-learned response by the very similar cues present in each car. You don't have to search for things; your hands automatically go to the right position on the steering wheel to find the turn signals. This is a very comforting phenomenon for people like me who travel all around the country and rent cars in other cities. As long as I always get the same kind of car, it will automatically trigger my driving responses without much thoughtful intervention on my part, the phenomenon known as low road transfer.

Once, however, I rented a Chevy Sebring convertible rather than my usual Toyota Camry. These two cars look nothing alike, so there was no automatic triggering of my driving response. Fortunately, the cars had a lot of conceptual similarity in the absence of perceptual similarity. All the parts that I used in the Camry were present in the Sebring, but I had to stop and figure out where everything was. The rules were the same; the cars just looked different. This is an example of a far transfer task: same rules but transferred to a different setting. Transferring rules requires a lot more thinking on the part of the learner. In the jargon the learner is said to abstract and transfer the rule in a far transfer situation. This is called high road transfer. Of course, I have been driving for a long time, and I have driven several kinds of cars, so I knew what to look for and what rules I needed to apply. It just took me a while to figure it all out. This kind of transfer also required me to use up a lot of working memory space just to drive the car, leaving much less available for attending to unfamiliar road signs and traffic and adverse weather conditions—all at night! This story of high road transfer demonstrates it as a much more mindful and effortful transfer than the automatic triggering made possible when situations are invariant.

Most of the transfer that we seek in classes is of the high road kind. We want our students to be able to use the information they are learning in a variety of situations for the most part. There are occasions when students confront near transfer situations—for example, in using lab equipment or doing very routine tasks. Under those conditions, the key to learning is lots of practice on equipment and in situations as similar as possible to encourage learning to the level of automatic transfer. For most other learning, especially the higher-level learning that is generally the goal of college classes, instructors should design learning and testing situations to support high road transfer—that awareness of the rules that underlies the use of responses in different settings. Being able to figure out which rules apply is a backup to use when automatic triggering is not going to occur. So what follows are suggestions that support transfer in general, but that particularly support high road transfer, since high road transfer can be applied to any situation.

Suggestions That Support Transfer

Be sure that students learn the initial responses to be transferred in the first place. Sometimes the reason students don't show any evidence of ability to use what they've learned in new situations is that they were asked to transfer before they actually learned it. The responses were too weak, or the cues that should have triggered those responses were too shaky to hold up in the new situation. We are very guilty of this rush to transfer. The rush is due to our inability to spend as much time as we would like for thorough initial learning; we have too much content to cover and so we move along before the students are ready. Students really need that initial extensive practice before we can ask them to expand beyond the original settings for learning. Yes, this will probably mean teaching less content, but why bother to teach content that will not be adequately learned in the first place and as a result can't be used? We would be much better off to pick a few key general concepts and teach them to death in a wide variety of situations in the content area. For example, when, as a graduate student, I taught introductory psychology, the primary instructors felt it was much more important that students learn how to critique psychological theories than memorizing all the specifics for each theory. After all, they reasoned, theories were going to change; what remained constant was how to decide which to keep. So they focused on only four key ideas about the scientific analysis of behavior, and every week the students applied those same four ideas to a new theory, a new reading, or a new bit of evidence. At the end of 15 weeks the students had learned how to apply those ideas to anything that might come along in psychology, and in the process they had also heard about most of the areas of psychology that were current at the time. But rather than memorizing the details of those areas, the students critiqued them, which resulted in a much deeper level of processing. Indeed, the students learned to generalize the use of these critical skills to other classes.

Make the initial learning situation more like the transfer situation to encourage positive transfer. For example, in teaching students to use a particular type of lab equipment, during the instruction and practice use equipment close in appearance and function to the equipment they will use on a regular basis. The similarity between the equipment makes it easier for students to transfer what they learn in the classroom to the laboratory or real world.

Vary the practice situation. If the problems in the learning situation are too similar, will the students know what to do if they confront a different situation? That question brings out one of the seeming paradoxes of retention versus transfer research (Druckman & Bjork, 1991). When researchers are interested in speed and ease of initial learning, studies show that making the tasks during learning as similar as possible speeds up learning and transfer as long as the transfer situation is just like the learning situation. But when students who learn under this condition are faced with a transfer situation that requires the same response but looks different, they are far less likely to be able to transfer what they know. On the other hand, researchers who expose students to a varied set of problem set-ups during initial learning find that, although initial learning is slower, transfer to a wide range of new settings improves. The students have learned how to deal with variability in the problem and are not distracted by irrelevant changes in the surface features.

Is the solution training on similar problems or exposure to multiple problem types? It depends on what the eventual real world use is going to be. If the response that you're teaching is one that will occur in the exact same form in very similar situations after learning, then it's more efficient to keep the training as similar as possible to the actual use situation and practice until the response is automatic. For example, if you're teaching students to use a particular piece of lab equipment that is found in all labs all over the world and will never change, teach them how to use that one piece of equipment and don't waste time broadening their horizons. If, however, the response that is being learned is one that could be used in a wide range of situations in the real world, then it would be best to use varied training settings even though it might slow down the initial learning. So, for example, in our lab equipment scenario, if you're teaching students to use a type of equipment that has several different manufacturers (sort of like word processing programs from different companies), but they all use the same concepts, introduce the varieties during learning and concentrate on showing how the rules transfer from one type to another. In the long run, students taught this way are more likely to be able to transfer what they've learned to the real world.

I favor the latter training strategy regardless of the use situation, because there is too much variation in real world conditions to take the chance on teaching only one set of conditions and responses. The real world doesn't operate that way. My general suggestion for transfer is that it is probably best to use varied practice at some point during learning in an effort to maximize transfer later, even though it makes initial learning more difficult. If you want to strike a balance between these two effects, you might do the very early learning using very similar situations until the learners have mastered the principle, and then gradually introduce variations in applications while still emphasizing the underlying principles. The hard part is knowing how much initial learning is enough.

Regardless of whether you use varied practice, for far transfer tasks be sure that the students can consciously describe what is being transferred—not just the specific responses but the rules behind them. The responses and rules that are to be transferred should be highlighted during learning, and learners should be directed to focus on those responses and rules when they get to a new situation.

For example, if I'm teaching several methods of analysis of variance in a statistics course, the students should be learning both the types of analysis and the rules that determine which to use when. I would want to drill into my students a list of questions that they have to ask themselves before choosing a particular form of analysis of variance: What kind of data are we looking at? Are there with-in as well as between-subject variables? How many and how independent are the individual observations? Which are the independent and which are the criterion variables? These questions determine which formula gets used in each situation, and so the first step in confronting a new situation is to run through the decision steps to decide which response to transfer. The steps constitute the key characteristics of situations that require analysis of variance, and the students should be taught to look for them right away.

In fact, the literature suggests that the best way to ensure that students are identifying the key variables in any transfer task is to have them repeat the rules before they do anything else. Students should run through these decision rules both mentally and aloud during initial training to allow the instructor to monitor what rules they are learning. This is the strategy suggested in the cognitive apprenticeship in Chapter 3. You want to have the learners articulate the transfer rules so they can receive feedback on their accuracy. It is also a good habit for the students to run through the rules before tackling each new situation.

Beyond teaching students what to transfer, a key to transfer is teaching them when to transfer a rule. Perhaps the biggest obstacle to using learned rules in a new situation is recognizing whether they apply. You'll recall from Chapter 3 that I described the classic case of students not using the divide and conquer rule they had read about in a war scenario to solve a problem using radiation and cancer treatment (Gick & Holyoak, 1987). The students did not recognize the cancer scenario as another situation in which to apply the divide and conquer rule. Even after they were prompted by questions, they had difficulty seeing the connection. It is simply not enough to know how to use a rule if you don't know when to use it. An important part of learning, therefore, should include recognition of situations in which what is learned should be used. How do we do this? The varied practice described earlier sets the stage for learning the appropriate situations in which to apply a rule. Having the students articulate the rule is also helpful. But it must be taken a step further. Students should experience a range of situations that represent when and when not to apply what has been learned, and the decision rules should be discussed. Then students should be confronted with contrasting situations that force them to make usage decisions and get feedback on the accuracy of those decisions. I said earlier that all exams should probably be comprehensive exams; I'll temper that a little bit by saying that subsequent units of instruction should refer back to previous units in an attempt to show when concepts are to be applied. Contrasting situations will help students learn to make appropriate choices.

Transfer is more likely to occur if the response to be transferred was learned just before a transfer opportunity. Here is another rule we violate repeatedly in education: We teach things in school long before they are needed in life, and as a result students regularly forget them. The classic example of this used to be medical education, in which the first two years were spent memorizing a lot of anatomy, physiology, chemistry, and microbiology—none of which ever got used on a real patient until at least two years later. Medical schools were stymied by their students' ability to forget everything they learned in the first two years and their subsequent need to go back and learn it all over again. They finally decided to teach using a problem-based learning approach, in which students don't learn something until they need it. The curriculum centers around a series of real patients who represent different important concepts and arrays of anatomical, physiological, biochemical, and microbiological information. Students are confronted with the patients' symptoms and then have to find out about the systems that could be impacting those symptoms. They learn things when they need them. Amazingly, they get enough basic information because of the care with which the cases are structured, and they are more likely to remember it because they are using it immediately and in a way that a real physician would use it. In the end, however some schools have felt uneasy about doctors who haven't been exposed to everything there is to know about human anatomy and physiology, and they have adopted a hybrid curriculum that mixes these two approaches.

However, the medical schools' initial impulse to alter the curriculum was a good one. Information and skills learned just before they are needed are much more likely to be learned, remembered, and transferred. The underlying mechanism for this has not been determined, although several options are proposed. One is motivational: Students who can see a use for information are more willing to put time and effort into learning it. Another is cognitive: The immediate use creates associations between learned information and situational cues that facilitate later retrieval. Another is based on forgetting: If information is used right after it is learned, there is less opportunity for decay or interference with the connections.

The strategies for transfer are in Table 5.1. Seeing them in this format may help you transfer them from this book to your classroom.

Table 5.1
Six Strategies to Promote Transfer

1.	Make sure the students have learned the original task well enough to transfer it.
2.	Make sure the learning situation is similar to the situation in which the learned material or skill will actually be used.
3.	Use varied practice toward the end of initial learning to prepare students for variations in the real world.
4.	Make sure the students can state the principles that have been learned and are being transferred to serve as a bridge between learning and practice.
5.	Teach students how to recognize when to use a strategy at the same time you are teaching them the strategy.
6.	Teach the skill just before students have a real opportunity to use it.

FOR THOSE WHO WANT TO GO BEYOND THE BASICS

Beyond the research on retention and transfer and suggestions to facilitate them, there are a couple of other areas of research that are currently being explored extensively.

Situated Learning

In situated learning (Resnick, 1989), the context of learning is actually part of what is being learned, and the context cannot be separated from the learners' responding. If you try to elicit from learners a particular response in a different situation, they can't do it. An example of this type of learning is involved in playing a particular musical instrument. The context of the instrument itself is necessary for learning to occur. Despite the claims made in "The Music Man," you must actually play an instrument to understand much of the information about it. A different instrument won't do; it must be that particular type of instrument because the fingerings, mouth positions, and breathing necessary for producing sounds are only possible with that type of instrument. Another example might be the skills involved in using a particular computer program. The vocabulary, key strokes, language, and capacities for that program are unique to it and can't be transferred except in the most general way.

Discussion of situated learning centers around how situated most learning is. If responding truly is situated, then transfer can occur only in a near transfer task, if at all. Teaching general rules for problem solving would be useless since each problem is unique. The recommendation for instructors is to place the learners in as authentic a situation as possible in order to allow the characteristics of the environment to become an integral part of what is learned.

It certainly seems that a lot of learning is situated in the original context and isn't transferred, but this doesn't mean it can't be transferred. Certainly, learning is generally easier when situated in a concrete context that provides its own cues and motivation for the learners. The situation suggests how and why the learners should respond. For example, if the computer keyboard has a huge red button that says "OFF," the context suggests that if the learners want to stop using the computer, they might consider pushing that button. But that response wouldn't transfer to any other keyboard unless it too has a big red button. In this case, the response is situated in the context. If you accept the tenet of situated learning, you would believe that the context of learning is critical and can't be pushed to the background. The context is being learned along with a response, so it must be present during and after learning if transfer is to occur.

That's a pretty serious limitation on education because it means that all classroom learning occurred in inauthentic environments. The classroom itself is the context and exerts a huge effect on what is learned. This can sometimes be seen in students who can perform wonderfully on typical textbook percentage problems, but can't use the very same rules to calculate the tax on a purchase. Critics of situated learning say that, while transfer may be limited by the initial environment, transfer does occur. For example, in the computer keyboard example, what might transfer is a rule that there should be a button labeled "off" somewhere on the keyboard. That more general rule is not restricted to the initial context, and it can and does transfer, especially if it is made obvious.

The area of situated learning is a difficult one in psychology right now and the discussion is far more complex than I am able to convey here. Instructional designers are trying to balance the speed of learning with the transferability of what is learned. It's the problem of single context versus varied context in practice all over again. Initial learning will be faster and will probably transfer to identical situations more rapidly if we accept situated learning as a characteristic of learning in general. However, if we don't want our learners to be tied to one particular situation/response combination, we have to fight against situated learning; the learners must eventually be invited to take that learned response out of its context and apply it elsewhere. As instructors, we have to organize the instruction to encourage that transfer, and we have to demonstrate how it should be done.

Case-Based Reasoning

Case-based reasoning (Kolodner & Guzdial, 2000) appeals to me and to a lot of instructional designers in professional fields such as law and medicine. The concept takes the idea of schemas and bases them in real instances. Instead of having a set of abstract schema as the basis for memory, learners have experienced-based cases that encompass all the integrated details that occur in real life. A friend who worked with medical students gave a very good example of case-based reasoning when she said that medical students remember diseases and conditions not by their generic descriptions but by the first patient they ever encountered with that condition. In order to recall the specifics of the disease, they first resurrect the concrete case that illustrated it. Recalling the case allowed the students to retrieve a lot of details that they would not have remembered without the concrete example to use as a retrieval cue. Becoming an expert means expanding the repertoire of cases available to help with interpretation of new instances, developing a mental case-index that organizes and files cases according to various criteria, and creating a mental case-processor that compares new instances with the case-index, looking for the base case. The case processor also helps the learners create new cases when no old ones fit the situation.

This kind of thinking has been a staple of legal education and practice for a long time. Decisions in legal matters refer to precedents, previous cases that have similar characteristics and arguments. Lawyers search for these precedents and base their own arguments on a blending of the legal thinking they represent.

This argument has a lot in common with an area of research on the importance of examples in aiding retention and transfer. I find that my students, too, depend heavily on the concrete examples I use to illustrate abstract concepts. During a recent test review, I asked about a classical conditioning concept, and the students asked, "Is that the one with the story about the vodka and Fresca?" referring to the example I used for classical conditioning in class. When I said "yes," the students were able to pull out a lot more ideas about classical conditioning than when I simply asked them about classical conditioning directly. The value of examples is discussed in Chapter 2, but here I want to make a connection between examples and cases as the way students store ideas initially and perhaps how they retain them for a long time. The more concrete, rich with detail, and familiar the example or case, the better it serves as a basis for understanding and transfer. (For a good discussion of the use of examples in teaching, see Decyk, 1994.)

Like situated learning, case-based reasoning is a theory about how learners store and retrieve information. It may not be totally accurate, but it is an interesting way to think about structuring learning for transfer. It says, in essence, that working with interesting and authentic problems results in students developing a rich repertoire of sample cases to use in making decisions and solving problems. However, an added caution is that students must also develop a case-processor, which is the ability to reflect on each individual case and identify the key elements that help group it with previous cases in order to find a solution. This is where instruction needs to be focused: Students must be engaged actively in analyzing the case and tagging those characteristics that define it. It suggests that as instructors we work with students to identify and analyze real cases that exemplify major concepts in a course. Case-based reasoning is another support for the use of an authentic learning environment as a way to increase transfer.

Anchored Instruction

A corollary to case-based reasoning and situated learning is anchored instruction (Bransford, Vye, Kinzer, & Risko, 1990). In anchored instruction, a large number and variety of skills and concepts are anchored in a situated case example that is very rich and can be revisited from many perspectives as students learn. For example, I might choose to focus my educational psychology class on a particular hypothetical classroom similar to the ones that my students will be encountering after they graduate. Within this classroom environment are students whose individual histories and actions are richly chronicled, a teacher whose strengths, weaknesses, and thought processes are available to my class for inspection, a school setting that includes the rules and policies any normal school would have, a curriculum, a set of state-mandated tests, and all the other rich detail that surrounds a real classroom environment. This is the anchoring environment. As my class studies different theories and areas of learning, we do it in the context of that hypothetical classroom. After reading about operant conditioning, for example, we may read the teacher's description of and thoughts on discipline problems and the ways she manages the classroom in light of what we have just discussed about reinforcement and punishment. While studying cognitive theory, my class would analyze the curriculum that is provided for this class to see how learning is being supported. We would come to know the teacher and students well enough to make predictions about how various recommendations for instruction might play out in real life in that classroom. As a class, we would try to design interventions to deal with problems that the hypothetical class might be having, such as the introduction of a new student who is disruptive. By having a rich, anchoring environment that is tapped for multiple purposes and under multiple scenarios, my class is operating much more authentically than if we had only a single, unrelated example for each concept we study.

The argument made by anchored instruction enthusiasts is that most real world situations are far more complex than the kinds of sterile environments we generally use in education. As a result, students are unprepared to deal with the complexity of the real world, despite having done very well on the academic tasks they encountered in school. Using complex environments to apply multiple principles is closer to what happens in reality and helps students understand the complexity of the decision-making process.

On the other hand, opponents of this approach argue that the very complexity makes initial learning far too difficult for beginners. With so many gray areas and variables to deal with, learners are easily overwhelmed by the details, fail to see the key ideas, or become paralyzed by alternatives. Better to begin simply with black and white situations and build to complexity later. But do we ever get to later? Or do our students go away from our classes with a distorted perspective on how easy it will be to function in the real world? Then when confronted with reality, they either crash and burn or become cynical and throw out all that they learned in school as useless. We certainly hear such complaints about having to learn everything all over again when they start working.

With all three of these areas of theory and research, there is one huge stumbling block to their implementation: instructor time. Very few instructional materials exist in the format required for any of these alternatives. True, case files are being developed for medical, legal, and business settings, but the time required to create detailed cases is not something most instructors can afford on a regular basis. We could just plunk the students down in real settings (like internships or service learning) and let them experience reality firsthand, but such opportunistically based instruction doesn't guarantee that every student will experience all the key situations they need for a well-rounded education. And, as any field instructor will tell you, supervising students in real settings is very difficult and time-consuming. So it is probably not practical to suggest that all education be turned into authentically anchored instruction.

Research will continue and eventually we'll find the appropriate balance between the realities of authentic environments and the realities of education. In a speculative article on experienced-based learning, a colleague and I suggested a continuum of reality along which instruction can vary and still represent different aspects of learning (Svinicki & Dixon, 1987). This continuum is shown in Figure 5.1. It implies that students can be exposed to learning experiences at levels all the way from direct experience through simulated experience to described experience. We would always favor direct experience because it would be the kind of situated learning that we have just been discussing. But with proper coaching and scaffolding from the instructor, students might be able to get as much out of simulated experiences without the difficulty, expense, inconvenience, and sometimes even danger of providing the real thing.

Figure 5.1
A Continuum of Active to Passive Learning

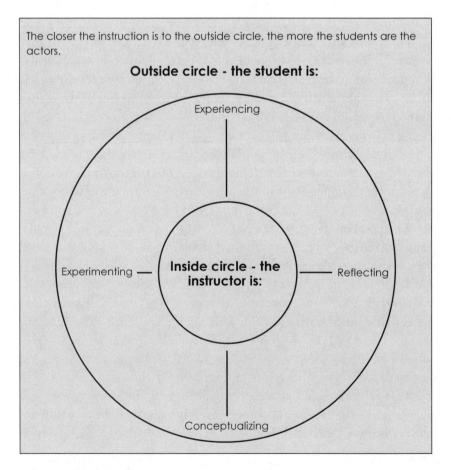

The closer the instruction is to the outside circle, the more the students are the actors.

Outside circle - the student is:

Experiencing

Experimenting — **Inside circle - the instructor is:** — Reflecting

Conceptualizing

The bottom line in all three of these next steps in the research on transfer as well as in the tried and true research-based discussion that comprises the bulk of this chapter is that retention and transfer are definitely affected by the relationship between the environment present during learning and the one present during transfer. It is worth our time as instructors to think about ways of making those two environments more similar and helping our students recognize what to do when they are not.

How Much Learning Is Enough?

I noted above that it is important for transfer that the initial skill be learned well, but that may be an oversimplification. Early in this chapter I talked about the controversy surrounding the assertion that a skill learned too well can actually hinder further learning. This particular area of discussion revolves around the opposing concepts of automaticity and mindful learning. Automaticity refers to a level of learning in which a response is so well learned that it requires very little effort on the part of the learners; it is automatic. Those who argue in favor of automaticity say that it is good to have a lot of mundane tasks learned to that level in order to free up working memory capacity for things that really require attention. That makes a lot of sense, doesn't it? For example, for most people signing their name is a skill that has reached the level of automaticity; we can do it without thinking about it—in fact, while we are thinking about something else entirely, while talking to someone, and so on. The fact that signing is automatic means there's plenty of working memory capacity available for other tasks. But what happens when our automatic response is disrupted? I once broke my right wrist in a tennis accident, and I'm right-handed. All the automatic skills that I could do so easily and without thinking had to be done with my left hand. All of them required that I think about what I was doing, thereby taking up working memory capacity. My behavior became much slower, I had to concentrate much more, my activity would be disrupted if people talked to me while I was signing my name because I couldn't talk unless I stopped writing, and so on. It was obvious that the level of automaticity I had reached with my right hand was saving me a lot of effort and time. So proponents of automaticity have a good argument; we need to have some skills so automatic that they don't require attention.

On the other hand, Judith Langer (1997) argues in her series on mindful learning that automaticity may be too much of a good thing. She asserts that responding automatically can cause real problems in some situations and in others can cause us to miss opportunities. As an example, she cites the difficulty one has driving in a country where the traffic flows in the direction opposite to the one in your country; a whole series of skills that we have learned to automaticity now become lethal, as we turn into the traffic or look the wrong way first. In the case of missed opportunities, she suggests that overlearning something might cause us to mindlessly accept something without thinking about why it might be so. My favorite story about such mindless acceptance of behavior involves a young bride who was having her mother-in-law over for dinner for the first time. She was baking a ham and before putting it in the oven she cut off the two ends. Her mother-in-law asked her why she was doing that, to which she replied that's what her mother had always done. Later, the bride called her mother and asked why she always cut off the ends of the ham before baking it. Her mother said it was because *her* mother had always done that. Intrigued, the bride called her grandmother, who said, "Well, when your mother was young, we didn't have much money for fancy pans, so I had to use the same old small pan for everything. A ham didn't quite fit in it, so I always had to cut it down to fit my pan before I could put it in the oven." A very reasonable explanation, but one that fit only her circumstances. The bride and her mother were doing something automatically rather than questioning the process.

Langer suggests that we should be careful what our students learn to automaticity. Rather, she suggests that they be encouraged to be mindful learners, who understand what they are doing and why. And they should be encouraged to question rather than accept things blindly. In this way, she asserts, they will be better able to see when things should transfer and when they shouldn't. I agree with Langer for the most part, although I also recognize that there are things that need to be at an automatic level, like vocabulary, in order not to slow down processing. The question for every instructor is determining exactly which information or tasks should be automatic. Are we looking in the wrong places?

A final area of thinking about transfer has been proposed by two of the leading researchers in cognitive theory, John Bransford and Daniel

Schwartz (1999). They propose that we have been looking in the wrong places for transfer, and as a result researchers have been disappointed in the degree to which evidence of transfer is seen in the literature. They suggest that different measures of transfer result in different interpretations about whether transfer has occurred. Most of the research on transfer uses direct applications of learning in the transfer tasks—that is, the tests are based on the same rules as the learning. But Bransford and Schwartz suggest that a better measure of transfer is preparation for future learning. In this instance, we would have to look at a much broader and longer time frame to see whether initial learning has produced an effect. What transfers in preparation for future learning is not so much the content itself but an ability to think differently based on past experiences. For example, they describe the learning of new word processing programs. Individuals who have already learned one program in general have an easier time of learning a second program, even if the programs are not similar, because learning the first facilitates learning the second. We can ask better questions and pick up on cues more rapidly because we have gone through the first learning. However, the actual improvement in learning takes a while to manifest itself, and we have to look at the learning process (not just the results) to see the benefit. Another benefit of the prior learning may not be quick assimilation of new information but more critical examination of the learner's existing beliefs. Preparation for future learning helps learners to let go of old beliefs more readily.

What does this mean for us? First, these researchers have demonstrated that students who are initially allowed to generate their own ideas about a problem before they receive a lecture on it better understand the concepts behind the problem than students who are simply told what those concepts are. It isn't the experience of working on the problem that transfers; it is the appreciation for what variables are important to consider. So, for example, if I'm teaching students about IQ tests and their problems, I might start the lesson by having them generate ideas for different types of tests that we might use. Then when I lecture on the current state of the IQ assessment, students will be able to understand the subtleties of how IQ assessments have evolved. Another recommendation from this interpretation of the literature is that being exposed to and working with contrasting cases initially is better preparation for future learning than a straight summarizing of the main ideas, even when the students do the summarizing for themselves.

An outcome of much of this new thinking is that transfer has been shown to be a much more dynamic process than originally thought. In transfer situations, learners actually transform the problem they are given based on what they already know. Being able to recognize or create a clearer picture of the problem is one of the first steps to better use of prior knowledge. As we will see in the chapter on metacognition and learning to learn, students who learn to monitor their own understanding and take steps to modify their thinking in light of that monitoring become much better problem solvers in the long run.

One of the most interesting discussions about the preparation for future learning concept is the support it lends to life experiences as a valuable aid in becoming a thinking person. Studying the humanities or going to work in the community have not yielded the direct transfer results one would hope for. However, Bransford and Schwartz argue that such experiences probably prime the pump in terms of being able to draw lessons from future experiences; they prepare students to learn from the future, especially when they are accompanied by some reflective experience directing their attention to more generalizable lessons. This certainly supports the notion of a liberal education filled with a variety of experiences rather than narrow training in a specific field, which might be more efficient in the short run but fail the test of preparation for future learning.

6

HELPING STUDENTS HELP THEMSELVES

"I studied so hard for the test. I was sure that I had it down cold. And I still got a C! How is that possible?" wailed an unhappy student in one of my undergraduate classes. You've probably had the same experience with your own students on a regular basis. We are all notoriously bad at predicting or evaluating our own performance level on a test.

THE ILLUSION OF COMPREHENSION

The research literature refers to this as the illusion of comprehension (Druckman & Bjork, 1994). Students are afflicted with this malady on a regular basis for some good reasons. First of all, students sometimes confuse familiarity with knowing. They believe they know something if they can recognize it. This is exacerbated by the kinds of tests we often give, those that are multiple choice rather than response production. The answer that looks familiar will be considered correct because they've seen it before somewhere. Unfortunately, the students are often correct using this strategy, which only strengthens their beliefs about understanding being the same as familiarity.

This particular misapprehension is probably behind the students' use of flash cards and rereading as their primary means of study. They find comfort in looking at the same material over and over, mistaking their recognition of it in familiar context with an ability to recognize it out of context. The tests, however, usually ask them to think about the content in another context simply because test questions are not usually format-ted like flash cards. Let me repeat an analogous situation in my own experience (and perhaps yours) that I described in Chapter 5. To learn my students' names, I take their photo at the beginning of the semester and create flash cards with their picture on one side and their name on the other. In a fairly short time I can name each picture with 100% accu-racy. Does that mean I know their names? No, it doesn't, because the stu-dents are not the same as their pictures. They don't wear the same clothes that they are wearing in the picture every day; their hair differs from day to day in style and sometimes in color; their expression differs from moment to moment. So I find that, although I can rattle off their names pretty rapidly in response to those pictures, the real students sometimes don't provide the right cues for me to recall their names. It takes multiple trials with both the pictures and the real students before I am comfortable with everyone's name. The point here is that I have the illusion of knowing their names if all I have to do is identify the pictures that I have taken. Take me out of that context and I'm likely not to rec-ognize them at first. Eventually, in the course of the first few weeks, I do get enough trials to learn everyone's name, but I experience a lot of mis-placed certainty about knowing their names at first. Likewise, students who depend on a recognition situation to evaluate how well they know something are likely to feel a false sense of certainty about their knowl-edge level.

Another condition that makes this illusion so powerful is the subjec-tive experience of listening to a skilled presenter or expert describe a problem solution. The fluency of the expert gives the listeners the illu-sion of understanding or the belief that the material is clear and easy to understand. This feeling that the material is easy then contributes to the false sense of security that students take away from a well-presented lec-ture. How often have you heard a complaint that, "I understood it when you worked it out in class, but when I tried to do it myself, I couldn't even start"? Perhaps you've even experienced that phenomenon yourself, pos-sibly in the context of having someone explain to you how to operate some piece of software on your computer. It looks so easy when you're doing it with an expert. Unfortunately, students probably use that false assessment of the difficulty of material to determine how much and how to study. Because they are under the illusion that the material is easy, they feel they won't need much study time.

This feeling of knowing is sometimes referred to as "general monitoring"—or a learner's ability to make accurate judgments about how well he or she will or has performed. Psychologists are interested in figuring out how general monitoring works and whether it is specific to a particular domain of knowledge (I can tell how well I'm doing in tennis, but not in math) or is a general skill that cuts across all fields. Some general findings from this literature have been summarized by Schraw, Dunkle, Bendixen, and Roedel (1995). Their findings are interesting. First they say that the learners' accuracy in judging their progress depends on when you ask them. If you ask immediately after a response, their judgment is not as accurate as it would be if you asked later. Schraw and his colleagues also found that individuals who had a lot of knowledge about an area were not necessarily good at monitoring their own accuracy. They tended to make quicker judgments that were sometimes wrong. A related finding was that monitoring ability was not related to intelligence, but it was possibly related to temperament. People who are impatient are less able to judge their own accuracy.

Of course, we contribute to inaccurate self-monitoring by the kinds of strategies we often use in teaching. Two very well-known psychologists, Carl Bereiter and Marlene Scardamalia (1985), have discussed the kinds of instructional strategies that lead students to believe that knowing something at the surface level is the same as understanding it. I list below some of the strategies they identify that explain how we might collude with students in allowing them the illusion of knowing rather than really knowing a subject.

1) When we order the items on the test in the same order that the concepts were presented in the unit itself, students can use the order of the test to interpret what is being asked for. The temporal cues signal which part of the chapter the question is dealing with. This is similar to what happens when the math problems at the end of the chapter are based on procedures from that chapter only. A student will know that if the question is at the end of Chapter 4, it's asking about reciprocals, which is the topic of Chapter 4. It could never be about any other formula.

2) When we phrase test items in a manner that is too similar to the way the material was always presented in class, students will learn to use the phrasing or special words as a way of telling what the question is about. (For example, asking "how many apples were left?" cues the learner that this is a subtraction problem because they know the word "left" as a cue.)

3) When we allow students to respond to a question with almost anything that even remotely resembles the answer and give them credit for it—the "gentleman's C" phenomenon—we may limit their deep understanding. Without a necessity to go beyond surface cues and really differentiate among concepts, students will go only so far and no farther.

Bereiter and Scardamalia point out that many of these teaching strategies are very common and have some good reasons behind them. They do not advocate abandoning them. They simply want us to realize that these could contribute to making students think they understand more than they really do.

Actually, the behaviors described by Bereiter and Scardamalia are learning strategies that students use to guide their study and learning. It just happens that these are not strategies we want them to use! Without meaning to be lazy or dishonest, students are really just using cues that seem to work in helping them remember content. When they use these cues, they have a false sense of security about how well they understand the content. What we would prefer is that they use the key characteristics that truly differentiate concepts from one another as the basis for their learning.

The Value of Feedback

Students must learn better ways to monitor their own understanding while they're learning, and we must structure our class time so that these false senses of understanding will not survive. The first step in combating students' illusions of knowing is to confront them on a regular basis with evidence of their knowing or lack of it. This is one of the best arguments for using active learning strategies and classroom assessment techniques

(Angelo & Cross, 1993). A previous chapter recommended the use of these in-class exercises to help students monitor and correct their own understanding. Until the students are forced to use information, they will rely on these perceptions of familiarity or the fluency of the presenter to tell them whether they are understanding the material. When they are asked to do something with the content themselves, their failure to understand is uncovered. At that point, the motivation to learn is increased, or at least nudged a bit.

HELPING STUDENTS LEARN TO USE LEARNING STRATEGIES AND TACTICS

Another area of psychology that is useful in overcoming student illusions of knowing is the area of learning strategies and tactics. The research in this area promises to improve student learning and help students take more control over that learning by making them more reflective about how they learn and what they can do about it.

Strategies and Tactics for Learning Content

The first step in helping students get their learning under control is to identify what kinds of strategies are useful in learning. By strategies, most theorists mean regular patterns of dealing with new information and problems. For example, the memorizing that results from the use of flash cards is a learning strategy. The flash cards themselves are a learning tactic, a specific manifestation of the more encompassing strategy of memorization. Memorization is a surface processing strategy, but it comes in handy for a lot of things that must be memorized, like multiplication tables or vocabulary in a language. If something has to be memorized, flash cards are an efficient memorization tactic for learning them.

Another strategy, one that we'd rather promote, is deeper processing through adding some sort of meaning to what is being learned, what in Chapter 2 I called elaboration. A tactic associated with elaboration is paraphrasing. Students who put concepts into their own words are processing them in a much better way than can be had with memorization. They are using their own familiar concepts and vocabulary and, as a result, are making connections between what they know and what they are learning. This adds meaning to the new information, making it easier to remember.

The learning strategies literature is interesting in that a lot of theorists talk about learning strategies without describing the specifics. One researcher who has been much more deliberate about describing strategies is Sharon Derry (1990), who has taken the cognitive model in Chapter 2 and some of its refinements and from there generated descriptions of the types of strategies that would follow from the theory.

If you review Chapter 2, you'll see that the suggestions I describe here are based on the encoding strategies discussed there. For example, Derry says that, for learning basic information (what's called in the more formal literature, declarative knowledge) you have to begin with strategies that focus attention. She cites research that shows that getting students to underline important sentences in their text resulted in more recall than simply reading the material. The key here, of course, is important sentences; students could go through underlining everything (they often do) or underlining the wrong things and learn very little of substance. In fact, Snowman (1986) did a very thorough analysis of some of the most commonly used tactics for studying and found that underlining only works if it is limited; that is, if only the most important phrases were underlined. But it's hard for a novice to know what's important. Students may be caught in a double bind: They need to underline what's important in order to learn it, but they don't know enough to know what's important.

Derry says that students can be shown how to use cues within the text itself to pick out what is important. For example, the first or last sentences in a paragraph are often the topic of the whole paragraph. Students can learn to focus on those sentences first to see if they do indeed give the gist of the paragraph. Other attention focusing cues are bold print or italics, which are often used to indicate important ideas. With more advanced text, students can learn to use figures and tables to figure out important ideas.

Derry also discusses how students can learn to use the organization of material to help them learn. For example, transitional phrases such as "on the other hand" cue a particular relationship between two pieces of information, another area that Snowman discusses (he calls it "text analysis"). One particularly interesting assertion of Derry's is the fact that disciplines have patterns for the way they organize information, and those patterns or schemas can help learners take information apart and put it back together. For example, other researchers, Larry Brooks and David Dansereau (1983), demonstrated that students could be trained to use a science theory schema to understand scientific material. I would describe this as a set of heuristics or expectations for how a scientist thinks about information. The schema for scientific text that Brooks and Dansereau used included categories into which scientists usually sort information. Using this schema, you must always look for a description of the phenomenon, a set of operational definitions, the researcher and the bias he or she brings to the situation, assertions, hypotheses, counter theories, and so on. In any discussion of scientific theory, students can be taught to look for these components. Missing components and components that contradict other theories are the areas to attack in order to understand or evaluate the theory.

Strategies and Tactics for Learning Procedures

Another type of knowledge that Derry describes is knowing how, better known in the literature as procedural knowledge. Here Derry bases the learning strategies on the two parts of procedural knowledge: the steps in the procedure and when to use the procedure. For example, Derry suggests that, in learning procedures, one strategy is to divide the procedure into parts and learn each part separately. Once the separate parts are learned, the learner can practice the whole procedure in order to become proficient and fluid in its execution.

I want to add to Derry's ideas some of my own. For example, knowing how to execute each step in a procedure is what has to be accomplished first, but just being able to do each step is not enough. You also need to create links between the steps, so that completing one step serves as the signal for the next step. The theory proposes that each step is a stimulus for the next response. The process is called "chaining" because you are creating a chain of stimulus/response pairs in sequence. This is very similar to the way comics learn their routines. They link between each joke with the one that preceded it. That way, when one joke is finished, the comic will automatically think of the next one in order. These mini-links take up very little processing space, so they don't interfere with thinking on your feet in response to the changing situation. The same holds true for most musicians and performers; they use the chain of responses to complete their performance. In fact, the chain is sometimes so strong that if it is broken somehow, the performer doesn't know where he or she is in the sequence and has to start over.

What makes these chains so strong? Lots of practice mostly. But there is a type of scaffolding that can help during initial learning: the use of a mnemonic to represent the steps in a procedure. Recalling the mnemonic then helps you remember the sequence of steps. The phrase "stop, drop, and roll" as a way of helping kids remember what to do if their clothes catch on fire is an example of a mnemonic tactic to help them remember the sequence.

Another useful tactic for procedural learning is cognitive (or mental) rehearsal. As described in Chapter 4 on skill acquisition, many behavior sequences can be practiced mentally before actually performing them.

Tying Strategies and Tactics to Other Levels of Learning

For each type of knowledge there are strategies and related tactics that facilitate learning at that level. Table 6.1 shows some learning strategies/tactics that could be helpful for students.

Table 6.1 is by no means comprehensive. It merely illustrates the kinds of strategies or (more appropriately) tactics that students could use for learning different types of information or skills. Many students have never been exposed to these different ways to approach studying or even to the idea that there are different ways to study. We can help students learn about different strategies and when to use them.

Supplemental Instruction: An Instructional Method Based on Strategy Learning

Instruction in these strategies is the basis for a lot of research and practice on improving student learning. There is a movement in some institutions to employ supplemental instruction (Martin & Arendale, 1994). Supplemental instruction was originated to help students in especially difficult courses—ones in which many otherwise able students had a lot of trouble grasping the material. Because these students were intelligent and capable, as demonstrated in other areas, researchers hypothesized that their skills were not transferring to these difficult courses. Supple-

Table 6.1
Learning Strategies

To learn at this level:	The general strategy is based on:	Here is a sample strategy to use:	Comments:
Basic definitions	Rehearsing	Use flash cards or anything that allows you to practice pairing a term with its definition.	The strategies use encoding information into long-term memory based on the cognitive model.
	Elaborating	Create a vivid mental image of the word and its definition. Think of places you've seen this term used.	
	Organizing	Group similar words together to make it easier to make connections among them. Identify examples and nonexamples.	
	Adding meaning	Generate your own example of the definition or put it in your own words.	
Structural knowledge—how concepts go together	Recognizing key ideas	Pull out all the text headings and put them in outline format.	These strategies organize the concepts in terms of their relationships to other concepts.
	Organizing key ideas	Write the concepts on index cards and sort them into related categories.	*continued on page 126*

	Recognizing relationships among key ideas	Draw a concept map that shows what is connected with what and how. Put the concepts into hierarchical categories. Draw a flow chart to show the sequence with which the concepts relate to one another.	
Application of concepts to problems	Visualizing the process	Observe someone else applying the concept and create a mental model of it.	The strategies here create a repertoire of examples or mental models in which the concepts have been used. These can form the basis of case-based reasoning (using familiar cases to solve problems).
	Developing process steps	Write down the details of how the instructor or text uses examples to illustrate concepts. Then look for common steps or characteristics. Try your steps with a new example.	
		For each example figure out why the procedure was used and what steps were taken.	This strategy has the learner figure out the steps for applying the concepts.
	Rehearsing applying the process	Look for instances of concepts in everyday use.	
	Comparing versions of the process	Compare uses with other students.	

Analysis of problem situations	Looking for relationships	Use the transition words or other text markers to identify important components or relationships.	These strategies are designed to help the learner see the components of a situation more clearly and break the problem down into manageable chunks.
	Visually representing the problem	Use a comparative organizer to contrast assumptions, ideas, and evidence.	
		Create a flow chart or concept map to identify relationships within the situation.	

mental instruction programs are designed to teach students how to succeed in a particular course by sharing with them effective strategies for learning that particular material. For example, if a course is difficult because there is so much to memorize, students can be taught to use efficient memorization strategies to help them cope with the amount of material. There may already exist strategies for accomplishing this, such as anagrams like ROY G BIV, that are well known to aficionados of the discipline, but not to outsiders. Or if a course requires a certain type of reading that is different from other courses, students can be taught to use appropriate reading strategies. For example, to use a textbook in a math course, students need to learn to work out every problem that is worked out in the text; they should not just skim through the worked out problems and concentrate on the prose as they would in a history text, because in a math textbook, the problems are the key. Students who are not math inclined are likely to glaze over when asked to read a problem solution. They need to change their tactics in order to succeed. Instructors who use supplemental instruction take any opportunity to teach their students about the kinds of learning tactics that will help them learn efficiently and effectively. By teaching these strategies within the context of the course, instructors throw their weight behind the idea that specialized tactics can be used successfully.

Some in the field contend that it is possible to teach general strategies apart from the specific course, and a lot of contradictory research compares these two alternatives. In general, it appears that it is probably best to teach learning strategies in the context of a given course, but that an instructor can help students see the broader implications of those strategies for other courses. What is hardest for students is recognizing when they should use these strategies, an assertion that brings us to consider a more interesting aspect of student study behavior—metacognition.

COMBATING THE ILLUSION OF COMPREHENSION WITH INCREASED METACOGNITION

I'll begin by saying a little about the construct, metacognition. Chapter 2 explored the process of learning—how information in the environment gets into long-term memory by being processed in working memory and encoded for storage. The question is, is this process a conscious process or does it occur without any intervention on the part of the learner? Initial theories in cognitive psychology didn't say much about the degree to which the learner was aware of and in control of those processes. In fact, in information processing theory, learning could take place without too much conscious effort on the part of the learner. The process of taking in, attending to, recognizing, and encoding new information seemed to run all the time as a matter of course. However, once psychologists started thinking about thinking, they had to face the question of what controlled that process. There had to be some sort of executive functioning that determined when to pay attention, to what, how and when to pull information out of long-term memory, which kind of encoding process to use, and so on. They called this executive function "metacognition," thinking about thinking. Just giving it a name doesn't explain it, of course, but it allowed theorists to think about what would be needed for such a function and what it would do.

Necessary Cognitive Resources

Metacognition is conceived of as the process of marshalling a learner's cognitive resources in service of learning. The best learners are those who can take control of their metacognitive processes and direct them toward a goal. The cognitive resources that learners would need to manage include knowledge about different aspects of learning:

Knowledge of strategies and tactics. In order for learners to control their learning, they need to be aware of available alternatives. Too many students come to college knowing only one or two strategies, which they use regardless of the task demands. When those strategies don't work, the students simply try to do them harder rather than changing tactics.

Knowledge about task demands. Different tasks make different demands on cognition. The structure and expectations imbedded in a math textbook are very different from those in a social science textbook or a literary text. Taking notes in a lecture is very different from taking notes in a discussion section. Students need to understand these differences in order to identify which strategies are useful when.

Knowledge about themselves as learners. Learners have different strengths and preferences that they can exploit in service of learning. But if they are unaware of those strengths or how to exploit them, they may be futilely using strategies that do not fit their abilities. For example, some students learn well from pictures while others prefer descriptions. When faced with text material that is structured in their nonpreferred style, learners have to be able to recognize the conflict and know what to do about it.

Executive process knowledge. Learners would also benefit from knowing how to monitor their own learning, how to set goals and make plans to achieve them, how to recognize when they are stuck and what to do about it. This is probably the heart of and what most theorists mean by metacognition. These processes marshal the knowledge of the other three areas and organize it into a useful plan to learn effectively and efficiently.

Characteristics of Metacognitively Aware Learners

A lot of research has been conducted on the benefits of metacognitive awareness for learners. For example, students who are high achievers seem to know more about cognitive rules and use metacognitive knowledge more often in their studying. Students with strong metacognitive knowledge are more organized and structured in the way they study. Romainville (1994), conducted a study in which he interviewed freshmen and then followed their progress through a course. Students fell into five profiles representing different levels of metacognitive awareness and use. The students with the lowest metacognitive knowledge eventually had the most poorly structured course knowledge, most of it of the surface processing variety. They associated success only with the ability to give facts, which resulted in their doing very poorly in the course. Other profiles had varying levels of metacognitive awareness, with the highest performing students being the ones with the best metacognitive awareness and ability to use it. Another study (Schraw, 1994), found that students who were efficient in monitoring their own knowledge were more confident, performed better both on the immediate task and across several tasks, and were able to improve their performance across tasks by using the feedback they derived from that monitoring.

Students who exhibit all the types of knowledge along with the metacognitive strategies just discussed plus the desire to learn are said to be strategic learners (Weinstein, 1996). This description of how students learn effectively comes from the field of self-regulated learning. Although the original discussions in this area concentrated on learning strategies and getting students to use them, subsequent research has stressed that students must be able to monitor their use and they must want to learn (called "will" in the literature). Weinstein adds to this mix that students must also have some prior content knowledge in the area if they are to be strategic. They also must be able to see present and future contexts of use for what they are learning, an ability that will form the basis for their motivation to learn. And, finally, they must have strategies that will get them through the difficult times and maintain their motivation in the face of obstacles.

GAMES: AN INSTRUCTIONAL PATHWAY TO SELF-REGULATION

Wouldn't you like to have a whole class of such self-regulating students? I would. And perhaps we can. As noted earlier, there has been a lot of research and thinking about why students will or will not use strategic learning. One of the first steps toward helping students become self-regulated learners is simply to make them aware of the possibility. I have been amazed at the lightbulbs going on in my students when I talk to them about the GAMES model that I developed to help them become more efficient learners. The letters in GAMES refer to components of good study behavior based on the research literature. Students who follow this model should be much more active in their learning and, as a result, process what they are learning at a deeper level.

"G" stands for goal-oriented study. An important aspect of self-regulation is being able to set appropriate goals and marshal the resources needed to achieve them. Too often students sit down to study without doing any planning other than, "I've got to read Chapter 2." While that is a goal (and with some students I'll settle for that), it is not as learning oriented as it needs to be. Students should learn to set goals such as, "I'm going to learn what self-regulated learning is and how to foster it in myself." The study literature suggests that students preview the reading material or the problem set and lay out some key questions they have based on that skimming. These become the goals for their studying. If they know where they want to end up, they have a much better chance of getting there.

"A" stands for active studying. By this I mean that students are doing something more than just reading the text or robotically solving homework problems. They need to be engaged in active processing of the material. Even underlining isn't active enough, because too many students have become automatic underliners rather than reflective underliners. I prefer that students do something with the material they are reading, like paraphrasing it or thinking of their own examples or even asking more questions—anything to engage their minds as well as their eyes.

"M" stands for meaningful and memorable studying. Chapter 2 made the point that material that can be related to the learners' prior knowledge and interests is much more likely to be learned. Making the important points stand out from the noise through vivid examples and activities helps information get put into long-term memory. This step in the GAMES model is intended to take the material that students are studying and make it more meaningful and memorable. Strategies to accomplish this involve creating their own examples, making connections across courses and units, and fleshing out the details of a concept with more information.

"E" stands for explaining the material in order to learn it. One of the best ways to understand what you know about a topic is to try to explain it to someone else. This in essence involves putting ideas into your own words. If you can do it, that material is yours forever; if you can't do it, that means you don't really know it yet. So I encourage students to form a study group after they have studied alone and take turns explaining the concepts to the others in the group. This is an excellent way to practice using the information.

"S" stands for self-monitoring. This is the heart of self-regulated learning. Students need to monitor their understanding and make corrections when they come up short. Monitoring can be done by comparing end results with the initial goals set for studying. Students can monitor their learning by making up and answering their own questions. They can monitor by getting together with other students and trading questions. Whatever strategy they choose, they need to implement it during learning and not wait until the night before the test.

This simple GAMES mnemonic has been pretty successful for my students. Perhaps your students will find it useful as well. I have designed a brief survey instrument (Figure 6.1) that students can complete to identify areas related to GAMES where they are not as strong. Consistently low ratings in a particular cluster of items indicate where students might want to concentrate their efforts to improve.

Figure 6.1

GAMES© Survey Instrument

How often do you do the following when you study?	Never	Sometimes			Always
Goal-oriented study					
Analyze what I have to do before beginning to study.	1	2	3	4	5
Set a specific content learning goal before beginning to study.	1	2	3	4	5
Set a specific work effort (time or amount) before beginning to study.	1	2	3	4	5
Figure out why I am learning the material I'm about to study.	1	2	3	4	5
Be sure to understand what is expected of me in terms of learning and assignments.	1	2	3	4	5
Active study					
Make notes in the margins of the text when I read.	1	2	3	4	5
Ask myself questions before, during, and after studying.	1	2	3	4	5
Pause periodically to summarize or paraphrase what I've just studied.	1	2	3	4	5
Create outlines, concept maps, or organizational charts of how the ideas fit together.	1	2	3	4	5

Look for connections between what I'm studying right now and what I've studied in the past or heard in class.	1	2	3	4	5
Write down questions I want to ask the instructor.	1	2	3	4	5
Reorganize and fill in the notes I took in class.	1	2	3	4	5
Work through any problems that are illustrated in the text or in my class notes.	1	2	3	4	5
Create vocabulary lists with definitions and my own examples.	1	2	3	4	5
Take breaks periodically to keep from getting too tired.	1	2	3	4	5

Meaningful and memorable

Make up my own examples for concepts I am learning.	1	2	3	4	5
Put things in my own words.	1	2	3	4	5
Make vivid images of concepts and relationships among them.	1	2	3	4	5
Make connections between what I am studying and past classes or units.	1	2	3	4	5
Be sure I understand any example the instructor gave me.	1	2	3	4	5
Create concept maps and diagrams that show relationships among concepts.	1	2	3	4	5
Ask the instructor for more concrete examples and picture them in my mind.	1	2	3	4	5
Look for practical applications and real life settings for the things I'm learning.	1	2	3	4	5

Explain to understand

After studying, meet with a partner to trade questions and explanations.	1	2	3	4	5
Write out my own descriptions of the main concepts.	1	2	3	4	5
Discuss the course content with anyone willing to listen.	1	2	3	4	5
Answer questions in class.	1	2	3	4	5
Make a class presentation.	1	2	3	4	5
Help another student who is behind in progress.	1	2	3	4	5

Self-monitor

Make sure I can answer my own questions during studying.	1	2	3	4	5
Work with another student to quiz each other on main ideas.	1	2	3	4	5
Keep track of things I don't understand and note when they finally become clear and what made that happen.	1	2	3	4	5
Have a range of strategies for learning so that if one isn't working I can try another.	1	2	3	4	5
Remain aware of mood and energy levels during study and respond appropriately if either gets problematic.	1	2	3	4	5

WHY DON'T LEARNERS USE STRATEGIES MORE REGULARLY?

Unfortunately, all of the studies on learning strategies found that, although students could learn the strategies readily enough, they were less likely to use them in practice. Some of the reasons for this tendency and guidelines for overcoming them were identified by Borkowski, Carr, Rellinger, and Pressley (1990):

1) Strategies should be appropriately challenging to learn—not too hard or too easy—so that students respect them as worth learning.

2) Strategies should be directed at learning what students think is worth learning; they won't bother with strategies that will help them learn something trivial.

3) Students need to experience success during the initial phases of strategy learning, so they will be motivated to keep going.

4) There should be clear goals for their learning so they can see the degree to which the strategy is helping them meet those goals.

5) Students should receive constructive feedback while they are learning, both to avoid learning the wrong things and to encourage them to be aware of what they are doing.

6) Students should be encouraged to recognize that it is normal to make mistakes and have problems initially but that in the long run learning new strategies will pay off.

Most of these suggestions revolve around the fact that students are being asked to give up using tried and true methods that are inefficient from our perspective but have always worked from theirs. The new strategies that are being learned will feel awkward in comparison. It is also human nature when under stress to regress to well-honed strategies, which only reinforces the students' trust in the old ways. To achieve such a conceptual change, as in any change situation, the individuals must become dissatisfied with the old ways, they must understand the new ways being offered, and they must believe that the new ways are indeed better than the old even if they feel uncomfortable at first. To get a sense of what we are asking students to do, think of a time when you were asked to change an old, comfortable habit in the interests of future gains. It wasn't easy, and you were very likely to abandon the effort at the first sign of difficulty. However, if you managed to hang in there for long enough, your skill with the new habit increased and you became more self-confident about using it. This is what the research shows happens with students as they learn new learning strategies. They need a lot of support and incentives initially until they can develop some minimal level of proficiency (Borkowski et al., 1990).

TEACHING STUDENTS TO USE STRATEGIES

How do we teach students to use new learning strategies? As I noted earlier, there is a lot of work going on in this area, especially revolving around the question of whether learning strategies should be taught independently from content or whether they should be folded into each and every course. I favor the latter position, primarily because I believe it has higher motivational possibilities and because concrete skills are easier to learn than abstract, disembodied skills. Some general similarities from the literature about teaching strategies might be useful to consider.

1) It appears to be best to teach strategies just a few at a time rather than laying out the entire buffet.

2) It is important to teach students to monitor their understanding in order to avoid the illusion of knowing. This involves teaching them to ask themselves questions and check their answers against the material rather than simply relying on how it feels. Mimi Steadman and I examined using the classroom assessment techniques discussed earlier to help students learn how to improve their learning in general by making them better self-monitors (Steadman & Svinicki, 1998).

3) It is important to teach both the strategies and when to use the strategies. The hardest part seems to be transferring from the learning situation to the implementation phase. This is one reason why learning strategies in the context of their use is preferred; it minimizes transfer problems.

4) Most successful programs include feedback on the success of using strategies all along. As noted above, students must be convinced that what they are doing is working and will help.

5) Most successful programs also have a lot of give and take between the students and the instructor. The instructor demonstrates the skills, supports the early stages of learning, and gradually shifts responsibility for learning over to the students.

6) It is important to teach strategies over the long term rather than looking at them as quick fixes. It takes a while for such skills to become solid enough to stand alone, so we and the students must be patient (Symons, Snyder, Cariglia-Bull, & Pressley, 1989).

Most programs recommend the direct instruction of metacognitive skills in a content context, followed by constant dialogue between the instructor and the students. The instructor initially constrains and directs the students' behaviors to ensure the success of their attempts, but gradually allows the students to take over their own monitoring. Like the critical thinking skills discussed in Chapter 4, the skills involved in self-regulation are probably best taught by this combination of cognitive apprenticeship strategies, coached practice, and a development of motivation, which will be discussed in Chapter 7 (Paris & Winograd, 1990).

FOR THOSE WHO WANT TO GO FURTHER

The Interaction Between Motivation and Learning Strategy Use

An interesting aspect of the research in this area is the interaction between motivation and learning strategies use. Researchers have been making a distinction among the kinds of goals students have for their learning and the impact that those goals have on their learning behavior (Dweck & Leggett, 1988). Specifically (and as discussed in Chapter 7), sometimes students have goals that are aimed at truly learning something; these are called learning goals. At other times, students are more focused on appearances and comparison with other students; goals of this type are called performance goals. The latter have been broken down further into performance approach, in which the goal is to be successful or better than others, and performance avoid, in which the goal is to avoid failing. In both cases, however, the students are focused on their performance rather than on learning.

What is interesting about this research is the impact that these different types of goals have on student learning strategies. They result in two very different arrays of behaviors, particularly when considered in light of a third variable, the students' beliefs about whether abilities are inborn or learned. First let's look at the different learning strategies that accompany the major division of goals into learning versus performance. Jean Ormrod (1999) provides a wonderful compilation of the research findings in this area. Individuals who are focused on learning goals direct their energy toward strategies that are going to ensure that they learn something new. They are more interested in challenging themselves and trying something they don't already know how to do. They tend to use learning strategies that require more effort and deep processing of the material. When they make a mistake, they analyze what happened in order to learn something from the experience. On the other hand, students who are operating under performance goals select those tasks that are most within their capacity to perform. They want to avoid failing/not succeeding and so they stick to things they have been able to do in the past. Their learning strategies focus more on confirming what they know than on expanding their understanding.

On the other side of the argument, we can speculate that, as students expand their knowledge of learning strategies and their ability to self-regulate, they may change their goal orientation. With enhanced strategies and better monitoring, they should find that they can handle minor setbacks better because they have more alternatives. The expanded repertoire of strategies also should enhance their self-efficacy as they discover that they have more and more ways of achieving their goals. It should become a happy cycle of expanded success breeding greater openness to learning new strategies, which in turn enhances future chances for success, and on and on. If the pragmatic argument of increased efficiency in studying didn't encourage you to consider teaching your students new strategies, perhaps this argument will.

Is it difficult to teach strategies? Yes, but mostly because most of us have been using strategies so long that we have become unaware of them. That level of expertise makes it harder to recognize when we are using a strategy that is not obvious to others. This is very similar to the discussion on the cognitive apprenticeship in Chapter 4. Experts have problems being complete enough in their descriptions of what they are doing. However, this is probably another argument for the apprenticeship model; having the apprentices there to ask questions and attempt the skill keeps the instructor from leaping too far from one step to the next.

Another strategy for better communication on these tacit knowledge issues is the idea of learning communities. This involves groups of learners, one of whom is the instructor, working together on a real problem of interest to everyone in the group. Because the problem is an authentic one challenging the instructor as well as the students, the behavior will be more natural and the communication more constant. This is one of the arguments in favor of authentic learning environments and learning communities, and seems to be working fairly well so far.

Self-Regulation and Volition

As we'll see in Chapter 7, an area of self-regulation that concerns researchers more recently is the concept of volition, a companion to the concept of motivation (Corno, 1993). Motivation is what causes students to set a goal and volition is what sustains them as they try to implement their plan to achieve the goal. Researchers and theorists in the area of self-regulation are looking more closely at what they believe is a dynamic relationship between cognition and affect (emotions), motivation, and volition. I suggested one such relationship above: as cognitive strategies prove useful to students, the motivation of the students to use them and learn more about them increases, which then gives the students more options, which might lead to more success, and so on.

It's not so hard to think about the motivational aspects of learning—how to convince students to adopt goals that are academically appropriate—but it's more difficult to know what to do when students fail to achieve those goals or procrastinate in completing a goal. This is the purview of volitional researchers, who are interested in the strategies that students use to pursue goals. They are the strategies that a lay person might call persistence or focus or nondistractability. How does a student maintain focus while working on a task and not get pulled off task? How does the student manage to keep focusing only on the relevant information while working?

One interesting research program (DeWitte & Lens, 2000) looking at these questions in the context of procrastinators versus non-procrastinators in college is studying the difference of volitional strategies and goal setting between these two groups. They found no difference in the initial level of motivation for procrastinators and non-procrastinators, nor any difference in their general ability level. They found that having a good road map to follow in accomplishing a goal will help non-procrastinators when the going gets rough, but it doesn't help procrastinators. Instead, it appeared that procrastinators couldn't keep going in the face of boredom, so they had to be reminded of the overall broader goals they were striving for in order to get past the immediate difficulty.

Another research program (Oettingen, Honig, & Gollwitzer, 2000) is studying "goal implementation behavior," which is essentially the volitional strategies that students use to keep working toward a goal. They have found that, while it is important initially to establish the value of a goal, value alone will not sustain the behavior. They found that it was necessary for a lot of students to have a clear idea about what they would do at various points while pursuing their goal. The students had identified specific actions they would take if this or that situation got in their way. Students with this level of specificity were able to make the designated responses when they ran into trouble, while students who simply relied on setting the initial goal often reverted back to examining the goal instead of making progress. Oettingen and her colleagues infer that, by setting up the sequence of if/then recipes for action, the learners were turning control over to the environment, and they knew beforehand just what to do to get out of trouble. Students with vague plans would get stuck and give up.

Oettingen's group also found that students could use mental simulations to prepare them for problems they might face in trying to carry out their plans. They would in essence carry out a series of what-if scenarios and plan and practice for them. When the actual situation arose, they were prepared. Of course, there has to be a balance between preparing and actually attacking the goal. But the implication here is that some students might fail or give up because they don't have a ready plan for dealing with obstacles that might arise. As instructors, we might want to help students play out some initial what-ifs to inoculate them before they begin their task.

7

MOTIVATING STUDENTS TO LEARN

Great teachers are often said to be those who can motivate their students to do their best work. Certainly that's what the students think, because when I ask groups of students to talk about their best teachers, motivation is almost always the number one quality listed. I find this a bit mystifying because I've certainly seen a lot of highly motivated students who didn't seem to learn very much, and I've been able to learn in the absence of any apparent motivation. Perhaps motivation is half the battle; if you've got that, learning at least becomes less onerous. But what is it about motivation that influences learning?

There is much of speculation in the literature about what motivation does for learning. Here are some of the ideas that have been offered:

1) Motivation directs the learners' attention to the task at hand and makes them less distractible. We know from the cognitive model that attention to the key variables is the first step to learning, so anything that focuses learner attention is bound to help learning.

2) Maybe motivation changes what learners pay attention to. As in item 1, attention is the focus here, but rather than dealing with the vigilance aspect of attention, here motivation influences what the learners focus on rather than that they simply pay more attention in general.

3) Motivation helps the learners persist when they encounter obstacles. This particular set of qualities is often referred to in the literature as volition rather than motivation, but they go together. Volition keeps the behavior going after motivation has gotten it started (Corno, 2000). Learning cannot occur unless learners are willing to engage the task.

4) Motivation in the form of goals may serve as benchmarks that the learners can use to monitor their own learning and recognize when they're making progress and when they've finished a task. So motivation may support the kind of metacognition controlling learning that was discussed in Chapter 5.

These different interpretations of what motivation is and does can help us think about what we do to support or frustrate those effects.

ALTERNATIVE THEORIES OF MOTIVATION

There is no grand unifying theory of motivation in the psychological literature. Instead, bits and pieces of a theory have accumulated over the years. The recent ascendance of cognitive theory in the learning realm is being accompanied by a similar focus on thinking in the motivational realm.

Early Theories

Early theories of motivation depicted it as an inner force driving external behavior. Motivation was increased when some type of imbalance or deficit in needs was felt by the learners. Subsequent behaviors were then directed at rebalancing the system without much conscious action on the part of the learners. One early theory of motivation known as drive theory asserted that organisms were motivated to maintain a physiological balance. So for example, if something in their bodies was out of whack, such as a lack of water or food, the organisms would direct their behavior toward actions that would correct the imbalance. Initially, the deficits were focused on physical needs, but eventually the scope was expanded to include psychological needs, such as needs for approval, achievement, and affiliation. There was even a theory that held that humans had a need to keep their thinking and behavior in balance. When the two were at odds with one another, the condition was called "cognitive dissonance," and the behavior of the individual experiencing it was directed toward realigning thoughts and behaviors. Although the original theory is no longer around, the cognitive dissonance concept is a useful one and has remained in the repertoire of most psychologists and educators.

Behaviorally Based Theories

Most of us are more familiar with what passes for motivation in behavior theories. A strict behaviorist would not acknowledge the existence of motivation because the very idea implies some sort of cognitive planning or interpretation. Motivation comes before behavior. But a behaviorist would say that what influences behavior is what comes after it, not before it. A behaviorist would say that reinforcement and punishment cause behavior. We motivate an individual by reinforcing or punishing the target behaviors.

This strategy certainly is found in education at all levels. We praise students for their efforts, reward them with points and grades, scholarships and honors, and punish them with bad grades or points taken off when they don't learn fast enough or thoroughly enough. It would be foolish to think that these policies and practices would or should ever be abandoned, but things are never as simple and straightforward as these strategies would imply. What reinforces or punishes one student is not always reinforcing or punishing to another. We will continue to use these strategies because they work, but we will use them more effectively if we understand why they work or don't work and when, which brings us to cognitive theory.

Cognitive Theory

The advent of cognitive theory in the last part of the twentieth century spilled over into motivation theory. Psychologists began to shift the focus away from internal, pre-existing, semi-autonomous drives and needs, and started talking about motivation being a function of how learners interpret a situation. This was an important shift in focus because it placed motivation into the minds and hands of the learners. It was the learners' interpretation of a situation that determined whether they would be motivated by it. As an example, think about two children who receive new computers at Christmas. One of the children is happy with the gift. The other looks glum and depressed. What happened? It's the same computer; shouldn't the effects be the same? The difference here is in the perception of the computer by the child. The first child thinks of the computer as something to be used for fun, to play games, and surf the Internet. For the other child, the computer represents another tool for doing more schoolwork, thus not nearly as exciting. The perceptions of the two children make the computer a success or a failure at motivation. Paradoxically, this cognitive interpretation of motivation may make it seem like influencing motivation is beyond the reach of the instructor; it's the learner's interpretation that affects motivation. In a way that's true, but if we have a useful model about what influences learner perception, we also may be able to see how the environment influences those perceptions. In a sense, the source of motivation resides in both the learner and the environment; each influences the other. This is the basis of social cognitive theory, the latest and probably most complete theory about the sources and effects of motivation.

An Amalgamated Theory

For our purposes as instructors, the models of motivation that focus on learner perceptions are more interesting and more likely to suggest ways for us to intervene to enhance learner motivation than the old deficit models. To make your life a little easier, I have assembled into one diagram all the motivational theories currently being researched, based loosely on the model of motivation that I think is most useful (see Figure 7.1). The various components of this amalgamated model can suggest factors for instructors to consider in designing instructional methods to motivate students. The amalgamated model is based on three of the most prominent theories about motivation in use today. The first is the expectancy value model as refined by Wigfield and Eccles (2000), the second is Bandura's (1997) social cognitive model, and the third is the goal orientation model (Dweck & Leggett, 1988). A lot of the other models of motivation can be woven into this one amalgamated model.

As shown in the figure, the best way to think about motivation is to think about it as aiming at a specific goal, because much recent work approaches motivation through this avenue (Wentzel, 2000). The strength of the motivation is then a function of the type of goal selected, the value of the goal being pursued in relationship to other goals, and the learners' beliefs in their own ability to achieve the goal. These three aspects work together in a compounding fashion to create the motivational effectiveness and direction of a given goal.

To put that in everyday language, let's say that I am being asked to chair a departmental committee on academic integrity. How motivated would I be to accept this assignment? The theory says that part of the strength of my motivation would come from my orientation toward this goal. Am I thinking that this is a good way to develop myself and to make some change in the department? Or am I concerned about how competent I will appear to my colleagues and others in influential positions? Then I will factor in my perceptions of the value of chairing this committee. Is it something that I'm interested in? Will it be sufficiently challenging to be interesting? Or will it be too challenging and frustrating? Is it something that is needed by the department? Will the people on the committee be fun to work with? Will this add to my own value in the department, thus making tenure more secure? How much control will I have over the committee and its findings? Will my colleagues thank me for doing this and breathe a sigh of relief that the assignment wasn't given to them, or will they resent not being chosen? How would this goal compare with other goals I'm currently working on, either professional, personal or social? These are the kinds of questions that would assess the value of chairing this committee. Obviously the answers will influence my motivation.

But there is another set of considerations: How likely is it that I will be able to succeed with this committee? Are the people on the committee dedicated workers who will contribute to the task? Do I have enough time in my already crowded schedule to give it the attention it needs? If the committee issues recommendations, will they be accepted by the chair or the dean? And will they have any real impact on the students? No matter how valuable the committee's work might be, if there's no chance of getting it done or of it having any effect, I am less likely to be willing to spend my time on it. If I think that it is a good area to explore and that I can do it successfully such that the college benefits, my motivation to be the chair is increased.

Motivation involves a constant balancing of these two factors of value and expectations for success. Both must be present for motivation to occur, but their relative contributions will vary from situation to situation. Students perform this same balancing act as they approach the task of studying. They weigh the value of coming to class with estimates of whether they'll learn anything once they get there. They are constantly evaluating their chances for an A and making studying choices accordingly. Is there anything we as instructors can do to influence those choices? I believe so and now turn the discussion to each of the components of the amalgamated model shown in Figure 7.1 and how we as instructors might use this model to think of interventions to keep student motivation high.

Figure 7.1
An Amalgamated Model of Motivation

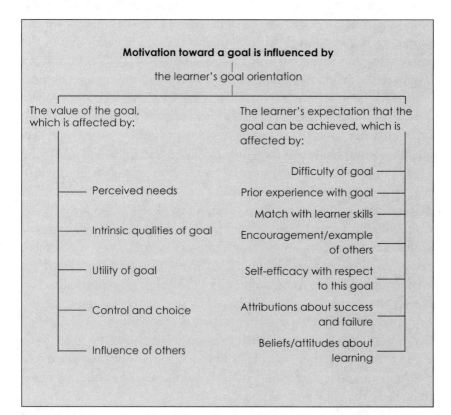

The Value of the Goal

Let's begin on the side of value. We obviously think our course is the most valuable one that any student is taking, but we may have to convince the students. There are many factors that influence how valuable a course is perceived to be by the students.

Value from expected outcome. The most obvious value of a goal comes from the outcomes of achieving it. What does the learner get if he or she is successful? The outcome might be a good grade, a higher salary, tenure, the satisfaction of a job well done. Actually this is what most people think of when we talk about motivation: the reward at the end of the line. Certainly this was how behaviorists interpreted motivation; it was the manipulation of rewards and punishments. And these are the easiest things for teachers to control. We give grades, we give praise, we give privileges, or we take them away. Most of the things that we can control, however, fall under the category of extrinsic motivators, things that exist outside the learner and the task. Extrinsic motivators are pretty good at getting a behavior going and keeping it going as long as they are in effect, but over the long haul, some intrinsic motivators are needed to keep learning strong and fresh. Intrinsic motivation also frees the instructor from having to constantly supervise and reinforce the learners. Students eventually need to be on their own.

There is an argument in the literature about the detrimental effects of extrinsic motivators on intrinsically motivated behavior (Pintrich & Schunk, 1996). The argument asserts that if you provide extrinsic motivation for a behavior that was initially already intrinsically motivating, you kill the intrinsic motivation and leave the learner dependent on the extrinsic motivator. Let me give an example. Let's imagine that you have a student who loves to study and enjoys working in the lab. Since his enthusiasm is so obvious, he would make a perfect lab assistant. So you hire him to work in the lab and help everyone else with their problems. Initially, this is a good thing for him, and he enjoys coming to work and helping others. Over time, however, the lab becomes a job rather than the fun activity that it used to be. He has to be there at specific times and he has to accomplish specific tasks whether he wants to or not. His enjoyment turns to annoyance and resentment. Theory says that what is happening has to do with perceptions of control. Once an extrinsic motivator (pay for the job) is in place, control over the behavior shifts from the learner to the person who is providing the extrinsic motivator, and that is a bad thing for motivation.

Extrinsic motivation has long been the staple of education, even though we say we want students to learn for the love of learning. Some students do love to learn; we professors were probably like that at least for courses in our majors. It's hard for us, then, when students aren't as fascinated by our subject as we are. However, reverting too strongly to a dependence on points, extra credit, or threats only compounds the problem. Those (minus the threats, please) can form a foundation of motivation to get learning started, but it is the intrinsic motivators that will keep it going over the long haul.

As instructors, we should find ways to enhance students' intrinsic motivation for the course by showing them the connection between the course and their own interests. Bringing things from their outside life into the course has many uses, only one of which is building on the intrinsic motivation of the students. Of course, we have to give grades, but the best way to lessen the influence of grades per se on student behavior is to have such clear expectations for grading that control over the grade is essentially in the hands of each individual student. They know what they have to do and if they do it, they get the grade. In the meantime, you make the rest of the course as intrinsically motivating as possible in hopes of successfully competing with their concerns about a grade.

Value from satisfying a need. Harkening back to the discussion of early models of motivation, we can glean from them some useful thoughts along these lines. Although it is unlikely that student physical needs (like food, water, and shelter) are being met by our courses, there is an association between a college degree and the eventual ability of students to purchase these necessities. Helping students understand how your course will give them an edge in the world of work increases the value of the course content in their eyes.

In terms of affiliative needs (the need to be accepted by a group), one thing that can influence motivation in a course is the degree to which the class becomes a community of learners. When students feel they are part of the social group of the class and are working with others in the class to achieve similar ends, their motivation to participate is enhanced. There is a lot of social psychological literature about the importance of others in shaping our behavior both on a daily basis and over time. Establishing rapport with the students and using that rapport to make them feel part of a bigger community can increase their willingness to come to class and participate in learning.

A related need that we might consider is the impact of approval (or lack of it) on behavior. Early theorists asserted that people had an inborn need for approval and would work to get it. I can give you a lot of other, simpler possible explanations for this phenomenon, but it can be useful to remember that approval is a powerful incentive. Extrinsic approval, such as praise from the instructor or other students, is something we can easily interject into our teaching. There is also a sense of something like internalized approval that most adults have developed. We have internalized the values of our social group, and we can assess our behavior in light of those values, even if no one else is around. This kind of self-approval based on internalized values is a powerful tool. To an instructor, it suggests that we should be overt in modeling and communicating the values of our classroom to the students: appropriate behavior, attitudes and behaviors we value in students or in thinking adults in general. Students who then adopt those values can provide self-reinforcement beyond the classroom.

Also dominant in the literature both in early theory and more recent cognitive theory is the need for achievement. Being successful at a task or in general appears to be something that motivates us. Actually, the basic value of need for achievement has been modified to say that, for some individuals, this is manifested as the need to succeed, while for others it is the need to avoid failing (Atkinson & Raynor, 1978). These two goals result in very different behaviors. I'll discuss this very interesting area later in the chapter when we talk about learning versus performance goals. As teachers, we can influence the possibilities for success by the way we set up and respond to the assignments we give students. Students will factor in our influence with that from other sources—their peers, their parents, and society—in determining what achievement means to them.

A broader need to feel competent or to have high self-worth can also influence motivation. We need to believe that what we do is valued by others and that our success at it reflects well on all aspects of our self, not just this particular instance. In this area, we are not simply trying to maintain an image of self-worth; we are also driven to enhance that self-image whenever possible. Instructors who help students see their strengths and how those fit into the larger picture of learning are making it easier for students to build a sense of self-worth based on important characteristics rather than shallow, immediately obvious qualities. For example, some students may be seduced by the idea that being able to do things quickly is the mark of worth in a field. While this might work for some situations (like game shows), in many cases a more valuable quality is an ability to do things accurately on the first try (like brain surgery). Instructors can help students focus on qualities that are valued in a particular setting or show how those qualities that a student already has have a place in the field. The most obvious instance of this misplaced source for self-worth in our society is appearance. Especially with girls and women, the equating of worth with standards of beauty does great harm. Turning their attention to other qualities as a source of worth is a wonderful way to counteract society's messages.

An interesting corollary to the work on students' need to protect or enhance their image of self-worth is research done on maladaptive strategies that some students use. Remember that the goal is to be considered competent. One inappropriate way that a lot of students do this is "self-handicapping" (Covington, 1992), in which learners sabotage their own chances for success by engaging in counterproductive behavior. For example, students who stay out all night before a big test can laugh off their poor showing as a result of their being such "party animals." If under these conditions they fail the test, they can protect their image by attributing that failure to their lack of preparation rather than their ability or understanding. And in the unlikely event that they do the same thing and pass the test, they can enhance their image as being so smart that they don't need to study. Either way their self-image is intact. Self-handicapping has been shown to take many forms. The one just described might be thought of as the reckless model of handicapping. Some students accomplish the same ends through procrastination. Putting things off and then rushing at the end provides an excuse for not doing your best work. Others take on too much responsibility and give themselves an excuse for failing by having too much to do. Whether this handicapping is deliberate or conscious is hard to say, but the effect is the same.

Another version of these attempts to protect self-worth is called "defensive pessimism." A defensive pessimist spends a lot of time worrying about and predicting failure, even when they have no history of failure to support their concerns. This can have two positive outcomes. For some students, the excess worry spurs them to study harder and therefore increases the probability of succeeding in the long run. For others, it protects them in case they do fail, for they have already prepared themselves for the pain of failure and can console themselves because their prediction was accurate.

A final motivational need is cognitive in nature but not in process. It is associated with some theories that have since given way to other more powerful explanations of behavior. Yet a kernel of this "need" remains in other forms in other theories and I think it has some useful implications for teaching. This is the need for cognitive balance mentioned earlier. The original notion was that individuals need their beliefs and behaviors to be consistent with one another. An imbalance leads to cognitive dissonance (in cognitive consistency theory). This is similar to the disequilibrium proposed as the mechanism for growth in Piagetian and other developmental theories. Individuals who run into situations they can't explain using their current world views or behavior systems engage in behaviors to bring perceptions and behavior back into balance. This is an important idea in explaining how students develop new world views, the conceptual change process.

The implications for instruction are obvious. When learners hold beliefs or misconceptions about a field, one of the best ways to get them to change is to confront them with the inconsistency between their views and reality. While this dissonance may not be totally capable of changing an individual's behavior or beliefs (there are some other factors operating as well), it can start the process of getting the individual to question his or her existing beliefs that the dissonance created.

As mentioned earlier, the concept of motivation as arising from the need to undo an imbalance or fill a need is a fairly old way of thinking about motivation. Yet, I believe it has some value in helping us think about ways to influence how students look at and react to the learning situation. We can make it physically pleasant and comfortable, a social group to which our students want to belong, a source of approval and achievement in a safe environment, a way to build their feelings of self-worth. And we can disrupt those feelings of safety and balance as a way of encouraging them to develop cognitively.

Value from intrinsic qualities of the task. This may sound simplistic, but some things are just more interesting than others. For example, I used to teach introductory psychology in the days when introductory psychology texts were completely text based—no pictures, no sidebars with interesting details, no biographies of the psychologists. They were, to put it mildly, capable of making a very interesting topic very boring. Then along came the textbook put out by *Psychology Today*. It was full of interesting details, pictures, graphs, stories, and so on. Students actually enjoyed reading it. Although students had learned from the old texts, the new models were much more likely to be read. Psychology textbooks haven't been the same since, thank heaven. So the presentation of material can be manipulated to enhance its motivational value by making it more interesting.

This particular source of value is one half of what we normally think of as intrinsic versus extrinsic sources of motivation. Richard Ryan and Edward Deci (2000) provide an updated look at this type of motivation. What is interesting about their discussion is that they propose that there is almost a continuum of motivation states, from totally intrinsic based on the type of enjoyment and inherent satisfaction that we usually associate with intrinsic motivation to what they call amotivation, or no motivation. In between are degrees of internality/externality of motivation. For example, external motivation in their system is what we normally think of as external, something imposed from the outside. Next is motivation that is internal to the learner but imposed from the outside. So when we do things to obtain the approval of others or to avoid censure, we are experiencing what they call introjected motivation. At the next level, the individual still is reacting to outside norms but has accepted those as important for him or her and so to some degree the individual identifies with the principle on which the motivation is based. Students who study content that might be relevant for their future are experiencing identification motivation. And one step beyond that is what Ryan and Deci call "integrated regulation," when the individual has fully accepted the principles that originated from the outside and no longer sees them as imposed on him or her. Most of our beginning students are still responding to outside pressure and are therefore extrinsically motivated to a degree. Majors and graduate students have probably integrated the motivation of learning the discipline into their value system and don't see it as imposed from the outside, so they'll work more autonomously. For a few, the activity of studying the discipline itself is motivating and we can experience that intense intrinsic motivation that comes from it.

Another source of intrinsic motivation derives from novelty and variety of the materials. Curiosity that arises from incongruity or change is an example of this type of motivational source. Posing questions and citing paradoxes are two ways for instructors to invoke the curiosity that is a natural characteristic of most learners. It is a mistake to hide the incongruities of our fields from students. The most interesting things are those that happen in the cracks between disciplines or those that turn out differently than predicted. That's where real learning occurs. Exposing students to the questions that still remain in the field is also a way to help them develop epistemologically. They move beyond what is safe and sure to what is still under development, and as a result they can vicariously participate in that development.

Another characteristic of the task that appeals to intrinsic sources of motivation is challenge. In fact, a whole area of research is devoted to the kind of motivation that arises from pitting the challenge of the task against the skill of the individual. When these two qualities are high and in balance, the individual will frequently experience "flow," the ultimate state of intrinsic motivation. This phenomenon was first studied in individuals who engaged willingly in very dangerous sports like sky diving and rock climbing. The researcher (Csikszentmihalyi, 1990) found that these individuals described their experiences in similar terms. They spoke of losing touch with their surroundings as they focused totally on their task. Time seemed to both shrink and expand because they lost track of it. They felt some danger, but a lot of control. The whole experience was a highly motivating one. Csikszentmihalyi went on to study other instances in which extremely intense focus was a characteristic of the condition and found the same sort of descriptions applied across situations and individuals. This area of intense intrinsic motivation is being studied for clues about how to produce it in more mundane circumstances. Although sometimes students almost seem to be in flow during a really stimulating class discussion, a fascinating experiment, or a difficult but doable assignment, I don't think we can produce it regularly. I'm not sure we'd even want that kind of intense experience on a regular basis, but it would be nice to be able to induce it when we want to.

What we can do to take advantage of this branch of the motivation model is to organize activities that challenge our students within their capacity to respond. We can use interesting examples and materials that relate to the interests that the students have or are experiencing outside the classroom. We can use a range of instructional methods and materials to keep the learning fresh. And we can help our students recognize and pursue their own interests as they relate to the course content.

Value derived from utility. A lament of many students is that they don't see any reason for learning important concepts. It's hard for novices to appreciate the value of foundational concepts unless they have a way of relating to them in a more concrete way. Two of the most useful ideas about influencing motivation revolve around this idea of giving students a reason to care about the concepts. They both deal with the functionality of the material, but one is immediate and the other is long range.

The immediate functionality arises when students learn things just in time, that is, right before they need the information or skill. In Chapter 4 I noted that this disconnect between what students are learning and when they are going to use the information is a possible source of failure to transfer ideas from the classroom to the real world. Lack of motivation is another reason why we should be better at timing when students are asked to learn things. In my experience as a psychology undergraduate and graduate student, I had to take a lot of statistics courses, something that is not my forte. I studied hard and learned what I needed to pass the tests but forgot most of it until I was working on my dissertation. Then, I had a functional need for statistics. I learned more statistics in the year I was working on my dissertation than I had in all the formal courses I had taken. My motivation to learn statistics was very high; I couldn't be distracted or discouraged. I had to do it. This is a cautionary tale for all of us who teach: Students who have an immediate need for something are more likely to learn it. As you think about when and how to introduce different skills and concepts, think about the natural flow of interdependence of topics and skills and design your curriculum accordingly. If you are going to have a guest speaker from the writing center talk about the process of writing, schedule that talk when students are about to start writing their papers. The same is true for presentations on library research or practical considerations in laboratories. There may be a similar interdependence of topics in your course. Juxtapose those that will best be learned in contrast to one another so that the immediate need to understand is underscored.

The second use issue has to do with longer range goals. It is difficult for novices in an area to understand how the minutiae of the immediate relate to their overall goals. They simply do not have the bigger picture to help them make the connections between what they are learning now and where they intend to be in five to ten years. You, on the other hand, may recognize this relationship. If so, you should make a point of drawing the connections for the students. In the undergraduate class I teach, I have education majors, nutrition majors, and speech therapist majors. Throughout the semester, whenever I get the chance I talk in terms of what they will be doing in later life and how it is supported by what we're doing in class. I try to give examples from all the fields often in class so the students can make the connection between now and the future. In fact, the final assignment is a "future uses" paper, in which students must select two or three ideas from the class and relate them to their future careers. I have had many papers begin with the statement, "when I started in this course, I didn't realize how many connections there would be for me as a . . . " Other colleagues have the students start the semester with a reflection on why they might be required to take this class. By example and content we instructors need to help students start thinking about the course content as a natural component of their future plans.

Value from choice and control. A strong source of motivation, negative or positive, comes from learner perceptions of self-determination and control (Deci & Ryan, 1987). The desire to be in control of our lives and fates is a strong source of motivation for most individuals. Students in classes in which there is little freedom of choice can easily abdicate responsibility for their own behavior; they're not in charge. When students have the opportunity to make decisions for themselves, they are most vested in the outcomes of those decisions and therefore more likely to invest the effort necessary to make the outcomes happen. Students who have made choices are also more likely to make the connection between their own behavior and the environmental consequences. This is an important developmental step toward adulthood. In fact, in some programs that work with juvenile offenders, the most common failure of these young people is an inability (not a reluctance) to make the connection between their choices and the outcomes. Some of the most successful programs for these individuals are those that force them to see that connection.

In a different part of the population, self-determination opportunities allow learners to develop more self-confidence and feelings of competence. If they are given a chance to determine either the process or product of their efforts, they take more ownership of the outcome, and when it's a success they experience it as affirmation of their self-worth. Research has shown that self-determination results in more creativity on the part of students and a willingness to take greater risk. This makes sense in terms of feeling in control; if you feel you are in control, you will be able to decide how much risk to take and when to get out. If you have that control, you are more willing to accept a challenge.

How do instructors allow students choice and control? There are almost always alternatives from which students can choose. They might not be able to choose the type of paper they need to write, but they can choose the topic and the schedule. Or if the topic is decided for them, perhaps they could choose the medium in which to express the learning. Instructors also can avoid excessive rules that seem to regiment or supervise student behaviors too closely. It is best to keep the rules to a few really important ones. It is even better to involve the students in determining the rules, which gives them much more control over what happens to them. If you as the instructor must make rules for safety or ethical reasons, explain the reasoning to the students. They'll usually understand and feel less like they are being controlled and more like they are being respected as thinking adults. And speaking of respect, respecting student opinions and questions is another way of giving them some control over their own fate. They know they can express those feelings without fear of ridicule or censure. Obviously, students can't control all that happens in a course, but to the degree that you can share control with them, you will have a more compliant audience.

Value that derives from the influence or opinion of others. When others appear to value a goal, learners will often adopt that value as their own, even in the absence of the qualities just listed. Something that everyone wants is something that we want, too. This probably works because of a combination of affiliation and approval, but it means simply that what society values will be valued by our students. Unfortunately, this sometimes leads to placing value on some fairly superficial things, like possessions or surface cleverness. This also can work against us as teachers when our students yield to social pressure and place value on counterproductive behaviors, such as binge drinking or slacker-type attitudes about work.

How do we overcome this? Fortunately, learners are also susceptible to influence by us as models and the things we value. When we show enthusiasm about a subject or a task, students will look at it in a different light. "If she thinks this is interesting, maybe it is," they might think to themselves. Certainly if it appears that we place no value on a particular behavior or outcome, students are likely to follow our lead. As noted in the chapter on modeling, teachers are models of much more than knowledge of the subject. Through our behavior we indicate what we value, and our students will take that into consideration as they are deciding on the value of various things we ask them to do. For example, I place a high premium on students coming to class prepared to work. That means that they will have read the assignment and thought about the questions in the textbook and possibly some of their own. I always come to class prepared to work with them, and what happens in class is always based on what they were to have read. This consistent behavior on my part speaks to them about what I value and what I think they should value. They can hardly be expected to put a premium on preparedness if I don't.

In summary on value. Helping to increase the value of a goal for students is the easier part of motivating them. As instructors we can intervene at just about every point as they decide how valuable a goal is and how much they're willing to do to obtain it. If you're having trouble with unmotivated students, trying to determine if and how they value what you're asking of them is the first step in motivating their best work.

The Expectancy That a Goal Can Be Achieved

Now that we've explored half of the motivation equation, increasing the value of the goal in the students' eyes, we can turn to the other half, increasing their belief that they will be successful at reaching the goal. This half is a little more difficult because we have less access to and ability to manipulate the bases for student expectations for success. These are internally generated by the learners rather than responses to qualities of the goal. Nevertheless, we can know something about why and how students think about their chances for success, and possibly help them develop healthy attitudes and strategies for building their self-efficacy with respect to our content.

Expectations based on learner self-efficacy. Self-efficacy refers to learners' beliefs that they have and can engage in the skills necessary to be successful at a task (Bandura, 1997). This doesn't necessarily mean they will be successful, but rather that they believe they have the capacity to be successful. In research on student achievement, self-efficacy is one of the strongest contributors to success (Zimmerman, 2000). In addition to influencing motivation, self-efficacy is itself influenced by most of the qualities below, but it would not be appropriate to equate self-efficacy with expectations of success. Research on self-efficacy and its influence on achievement has been growing lately as social cognitive theory has become more influential in psychology (Snow, Corno, & Jackson, 1996; Zimmerman, 2000). An implication of its importance is that, as instructors, we should adopt instructional strategies that help students make accurate estimates of their potential for success. A sample teaching strategy to enhance student self-efficacy would be to provide clear prerequisite statements that students could use to assess what they know and can do with regard to the content. This paired with information on ways to remediate one's skills or knowledge would help students plan their work and make them more confident about their ability to succeed at it.

Expectations based on difficulty of the goal. I said earlier that challenging goals are more motivating than easy goals. There is a balance here that has to be considered, however. Challenge is good, but too much challenge and you bump up against the learners' expectations for success. Let me give an example. I play tennis and because I am an average player, it is very motivating for me to be scheduled to play someone who is better than I am (high task value due to challenge). In that match I will have an opportunity to test myself, to try things that I haven't done before, and to evaluate my level of play. But suppose the person I'm scheduled to play is Venus Williams. In this case, my expectancy for success in the match is less than zero. I'd be lucky to get off the court without hurting myself. So, while playing Venus would be really exciting, I have no motivation to do so because I know I'd fail miserably. I'd be far more motivated to play someone who is slightly better than I am; that challenge would be doable. It would represent the best combination of challenge and expectations for success. (Think back to flow.) As instructors, we need to make our assignments challenging but doable if we want to motivate students to attempt them honestly.

Expectancy based on prior experience. One of the yardsticks learners use to decide on the probability of success at a task is their prior experience with it or related tasks. If students have been successful at math in the past, their estimates about success in a new math goal are likely to be high and therefore their motivation to pursue the goal is high as well.

Prior experience doesn't necessarily have to be with the exact task that is being considered at the moment. Expectations can be influenced by similar tasks. The problem is that a lot of students don't make the connection between what they have done before and their current task. It may fall to the instructor to point out those similar experiences to the students. Sometimes we even have to point out that they were successful in the past in addition to pointing out successful at what.

As instructors we can manipulate this aspect of expectancy for success by the way we structure the learning sequence. If goals early in the sequence are structured to produce student successes, later goals can be made more difficult without losing student enthusiasm. If we start the learning sequence with success, student motivation to continue will increase. Of course, it is important not to cultivate unreal expectations, so you want to quickly get the students to the right challenge level.

Expectancy based on skill matching. Sometimes the tasks we have for students are ones that they have not done before as a whole. But it is seldom that we ask our students to take on a totally new task. Most of the skills in education are built on previous skills, and there is the expectation that students will transfer what they have learned before to this new situation. Once again, however, students may not be able to recognize how a new skill derives from what they already know. It may be necessary for the instructor to help them analyze the requirements of the new task and find the component skills that they already have. Let me give an example. I frequently work with non-profit organizations in their training divisions. On one occasion I was charged with helping a group of mid-level managers develop teaching skills. The group members were very skeptical about their own abilities to take on this new set of skills, and they were quite nervous about it. I could see the link between their managerial skills and their teaching skills, but they didn't. So I first asked them to imagine that they had just been promoted and they had to hire their replacement. They had to analyze what skills they would look for in that applicant. There was a lot of consensus about what skills would be paramount. Then I had them think about a training session that they had attended that was really successful. I asked them to think about the person who led the session and what qualities that person had. When we compared the two sets of lists, we discovered that most of the skills that they already had as successful managers were closely related to the skills of a successful trainer. It was a definite "aha" experience for them. Their concerns about their abilities to succeed as trainers lessened considerably in light of the evidence that they already had many of the key skills.

The same might be true for your students. They might be approaching every class, every content area, as a brand new situation with nothing they can transfer in. You can help them see the connection between the skills and knowledge that they have and the kinds of goals that are going to be pursued in your course. This could dramatically increase their expectancy for success and therefore their motivation.

Expectancy based on the encouragement and modeling of others. A theme running through the previous discussion is that what you say to students influences their expectations for success. There is a wonderfully telling and famous piece of research that demonstrated that teacher expectations for students were more influential in the level of achievement reached than most other factors (Rosenthal & Jacobson, 1968). In this study teachers were led to believe that students were either about to bloom or not, even though students were chosen at random to be identified as bloomers. In subsequent classes, those students who had been randomly identified as bloomers did much better than the rest of the students. The researchers attributed the difference to the expectations of the teachers and how that influenced their treatment of the students. While this is a controversial study and replicating it has been a problem, it certainly makes sense that what you believe your students can do and how you communicate those beliefs to them will influence their motivation.

Usually the influence is a positive one. If you say, "This is a good class, and I know that you have the capacity to excel on this test," the students will respond positively. Of course, we have all heard and maybe even experienced a case where an instructor has motivated a group by telling them that there was no way they were going to succeed. The students then band together to show the instructor that he was wrong. I suppose this is the stuff of entertaining drama, but it is not the stuff of good teaching. You will get a far more motivated class when you set them a challenge and then tell them that you believe they have the ability to meet it.

There is another, less direct form of expectations based on the influence of others. It derives from the social learning theory discussed in Chapter 3 and deals with the influence of models. Learners' beliefs about success are strongly influenced when they see someone like themselves succeed. It's the case of, "if he can do it, then so can I." From an instructional perspective, this suggests that having other students demonstrate their own successes or their attempts at reaching the goal will influence all the students' beliefs about their own success probabilities. Alternatively, instructors can talk about their experiences of working toward similar goals, including the failures, false starts and attitudes they experienced. This is one strategy that may serve as a basis for the success of group learning methods. The opportunity to see other students in the group working with the same problems and succeeding serves as a source of motivation for everyone.

Expectancy as influenced by learner beliefs. One thing about expectancy beliefs is that they are strongly influenced by learners' other beliefs. This notion is less useful for teachers as designers of instruction, but more useful for teachers as interpreters of student behavior. Although there are ways to intervene with student beliefs, it's very difficult for any one instructor to have a large impact on a single student's deeply held beliefs. Nevertheless, understanding what some of them might be and how they might influence learner behavior is worthwhile.

A student's general self-confidence as a learner: Rightly or wrongly, some students are very confident about their own abilities to cope with anything we can throw at them. Students who have such high self-confidence are likely to believe that they can be successful at almost anything. Such students are also often fairly resilient and able to bounce back from failure. In the literature, a distinction is made between general self-esteem as a global trait and situation specific-confidence, which is the self-efficacy I described earlier (Ormrod, 1999). I can think that in general I am a good student, but have doubts about my ability to do well on high stakes tests, for example. The latter would be an indication of lower self-efficacy with regard to testing.

There isn't much you can do about most students' self-esteem, but you can help them make accurate appraisals of their abilities with regard to a specific task—that is, their self-efficacy. This won't hurt or help those with high general self-confidence, but it could help localize the confidence of those who have low general self-confidence. You can help them to see that, just because they haven't been successful overall, they have the possibility of being successful in this instance.

A student's beliefs about the nature of ability: There is a very interesting area of research that studies how student beliefs about the nature of intelligence and ability can influence their reactions to learning situations (Dweck & Leggett, 1988). The essence of the research revolves around whether an individual believes that ability is fixed or malleable. Students who hold the fixed perspective believe that one is born with a certain level of ability in an area and it cannot be changed. They are likely to say things like, "I'm just not good at math and never will be." These individuals will accept their failure at a goal or even their having to expend effort on a goal as evidence of the hopelessness of their situation. Why try if you are destined to fail? The flip side are the students who think they don't have to try because they've "always been an A student."

Students who hold the malleable perspective on ability believe that you may start out with a given level of some ability, but you're not stuck with that level for the rest of your life. Through hard work and effort, you can improve. You may not ever be the best at something, but you can always be better. These students interpret failure as a local phenomenon, something that indicates where they need to focus, and not as a condemnation of them personally.

Obviously, we would like our students to adopt the malleable attitude. Can we change student beliefs about ability? Yes, through modeling and through the way that we talk about student effort. If we focus on what can be done and on effort rather than focusing on some inborn ability, we are both modeling an appropriate belief and encouraging students to reframe their thinking.

A student's beliefs about the origins of success and failure is a very rich and growing area of theory and research. The theory associated with this area is called attribution theory, and it deals with how individuals explain what happens to them. Each individual has an "explanatory style," a way of thinking about why things happen. Of the several manifestations of this style, one primary manifestation is whether individuals believe that they are responsible for what happens to them (an "internal locus of control") or that forces outside their control are responsible (an "external locus of control"). Students who have an internal locus of control believe that it is something about them that determines the outcome of their effort. So, for example, a healthy internal locus of control statement is, "I can succeed if I am willing to put in a sufficient amount of effort." Students with an external locus of control place the responsibility for outcomes outside themselves. Someone with an external locus of control might say, "I got a good grade because I was lucky" or "I got a bad grade because the test was too tricky."

In most cases, it might seem that we would want students to develop an internal locus of control, to take responsibility for their own fate. But in reality, that is not always the case. What we really want is for students to make appropriate attributions about locus of control. Sometimes the test really is too hard, and no one is able to succeed at it. If that is the case, students shouldn't be blaming themselves and lowering their self-efficacy. However, when they do something or fail to do something and it results in their failure, they should be able and willing to accept that responsibility and make a change for the next time.

Can we as instructors influence student attributions for success and failure? Yes, at least within the context of our courses. The best strategy for attribution retraining (the technical name for it) is to put the learners in a situation in which they have to make choices and experience the consequences of those choices. If the instructor or some other force outside the students is always calling the shots and telling them what to do and how to do it, when things go wrong, students are very justified in pointing the finger at the instructor. "I was only following orders." If, however, the students make some of the choices about how to accomplish a goal and then monitor their progress (as in journaling), they are more likely to be able to recognize when their action leads to a particular outcome. This might help students make appropriate attributions, at least in that situation. For example, I have been very successful at getting students to think about the connection between their study behavior and the outcomes on their tests by having them write a learning analysis paper right after the first exam. In the paper, they describe how they studied for the exam and then analyze the exam performance itself. They look for commonly occurring errors, both in content and in the way they thought about and responded to the questions. For example, they sometimes discover on reflection that the questions they made the most mistakes on were those that called for application of concepts. Tying that back to their study strategies might show that they need to generate more of their own examples during studying. It doesn't work for everyone or for every kind of error, but for some of the students it's the first time they've ever analyzed what happened on an exam beyond just looking at the grade.

An interesting area of research related to attributions is the study of learned helplessness (Peterson, Maier, & Seligman, 1993). This phenomenon is characterized by a learner's belief that there is nothing he or she can do to affect the outcome of any situation, and as a result he or she simply stops trying. The literature in this area suggests that this is a learned response (as opposed to a personality trait) that came about by some past experiences in which the learner indeed had no control and could not predict the outcome of any behavior. They "learned" that they were helpless, and that situation then expanded to the rest of their functioning. Individuals who display learned helplessness are generally apathetic, indecisive, passive, and very susceptible to control by others. Some of these same characteristics are also common in people with depression, leading some researchers to speculate on the interrelatedness of the two phenomena. We may be seeing a learned helplessness syndrome in students who have a long history of failure in the school system. Because nothing they have done in the past has been successful, they simply stop trying and start believing that they never will be able to succeed. Working with students like this is particularly difficult, but some success can be achieved by starting with small goals that are achievable in a short span of time. If students see themselves as successful with these small goals, they might break out of the belief that they cannot do anything to help themselves. Certainly this is something we hope for any students caught in that downward spiral.

A Hybrid Source of Influence: Goal Orientation

Another interesting area of research on motivation is the idea of goal orientation (Dweck & Leggett, 1988; Pintrich, 2000). It's hard to say whether this concept is related more to value or expectancy, but it appears to be very influential in determining learner behavior, so I'm putting it here by itself to emphasize its importance and unique nature. This research says that there are different general types of goals that lead to different learner behaviors. When originally proposed, this theory divided goal orientations into two types: learning goals and performance goals. (There are actually several different manifestations of this theory using different terms, but these are my preferences.) When an individual is oriented toward learning goals, he or she wants to learn a new skill or content no matter what has to be done to reach the goal. The purpose is to master the skill eventually, even if there are wrong turns on the road. When an individual is oriented toward performance goals, he or she is interested in demonstrating competency in comparison to others. The purpose is to show how well you can perform the skill rather than how much more you can learn about it. These two orientations have been shown to lead to very different behavior patterns.

Individuals who are operating with learning goals are focused on improvement. They are willing to take risks and try new strategies if there is a chance that those changes will lead to better learning. They interpret mistakes as learning opportunities, and they are interested in getting as much feedback as possible so they can improve. On the other hand, individuals who are operating with performance goals are focused on demonstrating competence. They are not willing to take risks because risk taking could lead to failure, which they want to avoid. They will practice in private so that others don't see their mistakes and only make their performance public when they know it will be better than everyone else's. They are interested in monitoring what others are doing, but not sharing what they themselves are doing.

When this theory was initially suggested, these two types of orientations were essentially thought to be related to some personality variables and somewhat particular to the individual. That proved not to be a good representation of the data. Instead, the theory has changed to say that individuals can have both learning and performance goals even within the same task. For example, back to the tennis court. I can have two goals when I step on to the court. I can want to get better (a learning goal), and I can want to avoid looking foolish (a performance goal). The former would encourage me to try new shots and to be adventurous. The latter would encourage me to stick to what I know best. These warring tendencies will be balanced against one another and go more to one side or the other probably depending on how the match is going. If I'm winning or doing well, I might be encouraged to try new things. If I'm struggling, it's back to basics—just get the ball over the net and into the court. This is probably a realistic description of what learners do all the time. But in classes, where learning is supposed to be key, we should be encouraging students to adopt learning goals because that's what they need to do in order to learn.

How do we as instructors encourage students to adopt learning goals? Carol and Richard Ames (1991), two prominent researchers, have studied this question with younger students, but I think their ideas hold for college-level students as well. The first admonition is to make the classroom a safe place to take risks. If students know that they will be supported if they try new things, they are more likely to do so. Instructors who berate students for making mistakes are pushing them toward performance goals; instructors who accept mistakes as a part of learning are making it possible for students to adopt learning goals. One way to decrease risk is to provide alternative ways of achieving the same goal and allowing or even assisting students to choose the alternative that best fits their strengths.

Instructors also can make a class less risky by not pitting students against one another in terms of performance. Rather than competing with the other students in the class for the highest grade, students should be competing with themselves, with their previous performance, or with an absolute standard that is achievable. Researchers recommend downplaying public comparisons and emphasizing self-reflection as ways of encouraging learning goal orientation.

The instructor can model the kinds of behaviors that are associated with learning goals. For example, if instructors welcome new ideas and are open to working problems out in front of the class, mistakes and all, they show the students the kind of attitude that supports a learning orientation.

Synthesis

To guide your thinking, I've summarized below the ideas about motivation presented in this chapter. I'm not guaranteeing that if you follow them all your students will never experience a lagging motivation again, but I think these suggestions have a sound basis in the literature and are not difficult to implement.

Svinicki's Seven Strategies for Enhancing Student Motivation

1) Be a good role model of appropriate motivation.

2) Choose learning tasks with utility, challenge, and interest value.

3) Encourage accurate student self-efficacy about the course.

4) Base evaluation on progress or absolute level achieved to produce a mastery goal orientation.

5) Encourage attributing success to effort and interpreting mistakes as learning opportunities.

6) Provide choice and/or control over goals or strategies to the learner.

7) Communicate high expectations that are in line with student capabilities.

Other Attempts at Theory Synthesis

The above discussion has been focused very tightly on cognitive models of motivation, which I think are most useful for faculty in higher education. They offer fairly straightforward ways for instructors to look at their students' motivation and do something about it. There are, however, other really excellent syntheses of the literature that are aimed at higher education environments. I mention them here to point you toward further reading on this very complex topic.

One motivational model that has found much of support in the realm of technology-enhanced learning is the ARCS model proposed by John Keller (1999). In this model, instructors are encouraged to consider four aspects of learning represented by the four letters in ARCS: 1) attention, 2) relevance, 3) confidence, and 4) satisfaction. Note the relationship between this model and the amalgamated model described in this chapter. Both deal with value (attention, relevance, and satisfaction) and expectancy (confidence). Keller has primarily worked in distance learning and other technology areas, but the principles are very much the same across the board. An interesting tangent in the research using this model was the development of a motivationally adaptive approach to instruction (Song as reported in Keller, 1999), in which learners' motivation levels were sampled periodically during learning, and the amount of motivational intervention by the instruction varied according to their current levels. The theory was that if you already had a motivated learner, it would be either unnecessary or even counterproductive to interrupt learning to motivate them further. Instead, learners received motivational intervention during learning only when their intrinsic motivation appeared to be diminishing. Keller reported that, under these adaptive conditions, learners' levels of motivation and performance were much higher than those who received continuous motivational support and those who received none. This one study fits with the notions of self-determination and the negative influence of outside interference.

Wlodkowski and Ginsberg (1995) have proposed the Motivational Framework for Culturally Responsive Teaching as a synthesis of theory and research on motivation across cultures. Their model lists four motivation-enhancing conditions that need to be present to enable students to do their best work:

1) Inclusion—students and teachers must feel respected and connected.

2) Favorable attitude toward learning—students experience personal relevance and choice.

3) Meaningfulness—learning experiences are challenging and thought provoking and are based on learners' perspectives and values.

4) Competence—students feel they can succeed.

As you can see, these elements are very consistent with the model proposed in this chapter.

A synthesis of motivational models was presented by Michael Theall and Jennifer Franklin (1999). This contribution summarizes the ideas of 13 authors writing about motivation in higher education. When all the terms, constructs, and research results were compared, Theall and Franklin settled on six key motivation terms that all the theories had in common:

1) Inclusion
2) Attitude
3) Meaning
4) Competence
5) Leadership
6) Satisfaction

The first four terms came primarily from an initial model of motivated learning proposed by Wlodkowski and Ginsberg, and the meanings attributed to them were similar to those proposed by Wlodkowski and Ginsberg. The other two terms were drawn from the remaining theorists represented in the book and are described as follows:

1) Leadership—high expectations (from the authority), structure, feedback, and support
2) Satisfaction—rewards

These terms also seem to be in tune with the amalgamated model proposed in this chapter, although the additional aspect of inclusion goes somewhat beyond self-determination to include others, and leadership speaks to the role of the instructor more than the learner. Nevertheless, the synthesis presented by Theall and Franklin affirms the importance of value and efficacy in motivating learners.

The theory you choose to make motivational decisions is a matter of personal conviction, because so many of the same constructs occur in each version. The important point of this chapter is to recognize that, in cooperation with your learners, you can create an environment in which students will value what they are learning and believe that they can be successful at it, which will be the cornerstones of their motivation.

FOR THOSE WHO WANT TO GO BEYOND THE BASICS

As I have in other chapters, I'll devote the last part of the chapter to some of the more speculative or less well documented ideas that may play an interesting role in instructional concerns in the future.

The first of these is emotion or affect and its relationship to learning. This is not a new area, but it has revived recently as new findings from physiology are raising interesting possibilities in explaining some previous findings. First, however, I should say that the more standard discussions of the role of emotions in learning center around anxiety. This is a fairly well-researched area (Ormrod, 1999), and so some pretty safe statements can be made about how anxiety and performance are related. Although there's some question about the way a particularly prominent description of this phenomenon, called the Yerkes-Dodson curve, has been expanded beyond its origins, it does have a lot of face validity for anyone in education. The Yerkes-Dodson curve (Figure 7.2) relates an individual's level of arousal by a situation to his or her measured level of performance. In general, at low levels of stimulation or arousal, an individual will not perform well in terms of quantity or quality. As the level of arousal increases, the quality and quantity of the performance increases until it hits an optimum. From then on, increases in arousal or stimulation are accompanied by a decrease in performance. The hypothesized cause for this bell curve is interference with performance at high levels of arousal. This essentially means that some tension or arousal is good, but too much is bad. For example, this is frequently seen in students in the form of test anxiety. Students who under practice conditions (which are not especially anxiety arousing) perform quite well will fall apart when the actual test is given. Their minds go blank and they have trouble concentrating. One proposed explanation is that they use up working memory and attention capacity by dwelling more on what is going wrong than on actually addressing the task at hand. Eventually, their capacity is exceeded and they shut down. Allegedly, this relationship would hold with positive arousal as well, but I expect that we will seldom see that level of arousal in the classroom.

Can we as instructors do anything about this problem? Most institutions that have student study help centers have programs to teach students how to cope with test anxiety. Although we're often not capable of intervening with an individual student, there are things we can do for a

Figure 7.2
The Yerkes-Dodson Curve Relating Arousal to Performance

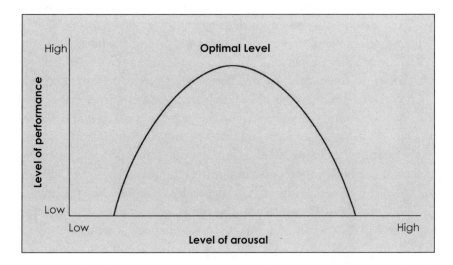

class in general. For example, providing a lot of information about the test situation, its format, the type of questions, the time limits, acceptable behavior, and so on well before the test can alleviate some of the unknowns that are often sources of the anxiety. Practice tests which make the question formats familiar are really appreciated by students. Try to avoid high stakes testing in which the students' grades depend on only one or two test scores. More measures of student learning are not only better for their test anxiety, but also make for more accurate measurement. Students especially appreciate the opportunity to drop a low test score, and I appreciate it because I don't have to allow and arrange make-up tests or listen to all the reasons why a student couldn't take the test.

During the test itself, keeping interruptions or disruptions to a minimum is important so as not to damage student concentration. Be sure that you've proofread the test and had someone else do it as well, so you don't have to make corrections during the exam. If you can, give students a lifeline in case they get confused. For example, with my multiple choice tests, students are allowed to write an explanation of their answer on a special page if they are struggling over a particular question. Not all students take advantage of this, but it does make them feel less anxious. Another similar anxiety reducing strategy that also influences learning is to allow students to earn back a portion of the points they have missed on a test by redoing or reflecting on those items. The first time I instituted this practice, a student said to me afterward, "Gosh, I guess you really do care whether we learn this or not." I was pleased to be able to tell her that I did and to have my policies and procedures back it up.

There are other aspects of emotion and learning that are a little bit farther out on the cutting edge. There is a lot of speculation and some research being conducted around the impact on memory of emotion at the time of learning (Haskell, 2001). One proposal is that memories have an emotional tag attached to them reflecting their importance at the time of learning (LeDoux, 2002). During recall, that emotional tag serves as part of the retrieval process along with the memories. This had been suggested earlier in the form of state-dependent learning. The research at the time indicated that returning to the state you were in when first experiencing some event will increase your chances of remembering its details. I like to think of an example of this in the context of having a fight with your significant other. As tempers flair, all the things that that person has ever done to irritate you come flooding back and are interjected into the argument, thereby escalating it further. What does this say to us as instructors? It might be telling us that emotion in the classroom has a positive function and can support learning and memory. For example, humor evokes emotion, thereby possibly tagging the content of the joke as something worth remembering. Conversely, negative emotions could be tagged to particularly painful learning episodes, causing them to be avoided and repressed. There is some indication in the literature that "happy" or positive emotions facilitate interconnections and integration of material, a strong component of learning (Isen & Daubman, 1984).

Recent advances in our ability to understand brain structure and function have given a tantalizing hint about a physical reason for the close tie between emotion and memory. The structures in the brain associated with emotion lie very close to those associated with the formation of memories (LeDoux, 2002). And the neural processes connecting these two areas suggest that information passes through the emotion center before going on to the site of long-term memory, the neocortex. It is safe to say that the emotional tone present during learning and performance have a definite impact on the learning that takes place.

A related area has been explored by Antonio Damasio (1994) in *Descartes' Error: Emotion, Reason, and the Human Brain*. This time emotion is related to decision-making. Damasio gives some very convincing evidence about the importance of emotion in the rational decision-making process by showing how individuals with damage to emotional centers of the brain frequently have difficulty making decisions.

This is also related to the area of conceptual change and hot cognition. A lot of original theories about concept formation and change portrayed the learner as a cool and rational evaluator of the evidence—like a scientist who takes in new information, evaluates it carefully, and makes changes based on the evidence. This implies that when we are trying to change a student's mind about some misconception he or she has, all we need do is produce the facts, and the student will adopt the new ideas. However, plenty of research evidence and personal anecdotes say that people frequently hold on to misconceptions in the face of data. I recommend *How We Know What Isn't So* by Thomas Gilovich (1991) or Carl Sagan's *The Demon-Haunted World* (1995) for wonderful discussions of why even intelligent people persist in their beliefs.

This impact of motivation on cognition and conceptual change suggests to instructors that we need to be aware of how different aspects of motivation might assist or inhibit learning. A comprehensive article by Pintrich, Marx, and Boyle (1993) lists seven areas of motivation that have been shown to impact conceptual change. We've discussed many of them already, but they include such things as whether a learner has mastery goals versus performance goals. Obviously, mastery goals make a learner more open to conceptual change. The sources of task value such as personal interest and utility influence the degree to which a learner will expose himself or herself to data that might cause conceptual change. Self-efficacy beliefs and epistemic beliefs about the nature of knowing influence a learner's assessment of the difficulty of changing. And from the conceptual change literature, Pintrich et al. point to the need for a learner to experience disaffection with his or her current beliefs before change is considered.

Another area of advanced interest is the differentiation between motivational behaviors, like goal setting, and volitional behaviors, like persisting in the face of difficulty. One of the first to suggest the multiple nature of motivation was Kuhl (1985), who proposed two distinct stages of motivation. The first was predecisional and was involved in making the decision to engage in some action. This is what we generally think of as motivation, the force that impels us forward toward a goal. The second was post-decisional and was focused on keeping the momentum in the face of obstacles. This is now what we generally think of as volition. Once the learner has crossed the Rubicon between decision and action, the behaviors required are different; this is now thought of as the Rubicon model of motivation/volition (Heckhausen & Kuhl, 1985). On the decision side are such things as the intrinsic motivation or extrinsic motivation associated with the goal plus the tendencies for action. These are the kinds of things that I've been discussing in this chapter. On the implementation side are things like those discussed in the chapter on self-regulation. They have more to do with actions that allocate resources, adaptive strategy use, and emotional control. There is some evidence that learners are susceptible to different influences depending on which side of the decision they're currently on (Corno, 1993). For example, prior to making the decision to engage in a task, learners can be easily influenced by arguments about its usefulness. Once they cross over to implementation, they become much more focused and less susceptible to arguments from others. However, they are susceptible to the conditions they find on the other side, like unanticipated difficulties.

Corno (1993) provides interesting examples of the kinds of volitional control strategies that students use. For example, under motivational control she lists things like setting contingencies for performance, meaning establishing rewards and punishments to implement depending on how the learning goes. She also lists "visualize doing the work successfully," a sort of mental cheerleading for yourself. Under emotional control, she lists "count to ten in your head," a common technique to avoid reacting too quickly in an emotional situation. She also lists "visualize doing the work successfully and feeling good about that." Notice how this differs from the motivational version; here the point is the feeling/emotion associated with success.

Why is volition important? For one thing, procrastination is a major problem in academic life, and the desire to find a solution for it impels a lot of research. Some researchers have pointed to volition as the source of procrastination for a lot of students (DeWitte & Lens, 2000). In studying procrastinators and non-procrastinators, these researchers have found no differences in intentions or abilities, but they do show a difference in the strategies associated with volition. For example, procrastinators have difficulties remembering their initial intentions to achieve a certain goal (Oettingen, Honig, & Gollwitzer, 2000). If the learner formulated a plan for a goal, fantasized himself or herself following that plan and achieving that goal, and, perhaps most important, having contingency plans in case something went wrong, the learner was more likely to follow through on the plan later. Oettingen and her colleagues said this was particularly true for naïve students, although more advanced students also benefited from imagining future successes. The skill here seems to be the ability to mentally contrast the current situation with future possibilities. This ability to imagine a possible future self may be one of the important developmental steps in moving toward better volitional strategies.

This issue of volitional strategy use is an important step forward in helping students progress. I've made quite a point of saying that we have to help students over the initial hump of making the decision to learn our content, and I still think that's crucial. If they never make that step (over the Rubicon), they won't need anything else. But once we do convince them to tackle the learning involved in our course, we should perhaps help them develop some strategies for coping with the obstacles they might face.

I said earlier that one possible strategy for helping students learn is to provide a coping model, an example of someone who runs into difficulty and overcomes it. This is one of the ways we can teach volitional strategies to our students. When they see how we cope with uncertainty or how other students react to failure, they are being exposed to volitional control ideas. However, just seeing the model may not be enough. Just as I suggested in Chapter 4 that learning a skill by watching a master needs to be accompanied by an articulation of the thought processes behind the skill, I believe the same applies here. When modeling coping or volitional strategies, an instructor should be very explicit about what he or she is doing. Including comments about affective states in the midst of a cognitive demonstration might help students see that it is normal to feel frustrated or irritated when things go wrong. It doesn't mean that they are inadequate to the task; everyone feels that way now and again. It's what they do in the face of those feelings that counts. The combination of being told that it's normal to feel frustrated (or excited or angry or whatever) and suggestions about how to deal with those feelings (take a deep breath, count to ten) and obstacles (take a break, take a different perspective, brainstorm without editing) could be just as valuable to the learners as specific suggestions about learning the content itself.

This area of volition is very close in feeling to the self-regulation strategies that I discussed in Chapter 6. The research and theories in these two areas overlap, as you might have noticed. In general we might think about these two areas as metacognition dealing with content learning and metaconation (conation is the technical term for the affective aspects of learning) as dealing with motivation/emotion. They are almost inseparable in terms of producing success in learning. But as instructors we tend to favor working only with the cognitive issues and leaving the conative issues to the touchy-feely disciplines. That would be a very short sighted and unproductive stance to take. Perhaps this discussion about helping students take strategic control of the conative side of their learning will inspire you to move from the decision/planning side of the Rubicon of motivational teaching to the implementation side.

8

WHAT TO DO ABOUT INDIVIDUAL DIFFERENCES IN LEARNING

Sometimes I wonder if the students in my class all come from different planets. I can conduct the same class for the entire group and get a dozen different reactions, different interpretations, and different levels of understanding from different students. Of course, psychology has known this for a long time. In fact, it's one of the biggest impediments to progress that research in the area faces: Humans are very complex organisms with lots of variables impacting their behavior, which makes it very difficult to get any semblance of order out of the data.

Obstinately, we try our best to create some order out of this chaos, to identify patterns of responding and types of students so we can tailor our teaching to their needs. It's only logical, right? Yes, it's logical, it's appealing, and it's impossible. To try to reduce the complexity of human responding into two, three, or even 16 neat categories can't be done. Psychologists have tried and failed (if you read the research critically). But I can testify as an experienced faculty developer that whenever we talk with faculty about students, the desire to type students comes up. If we could just understand what type of students we're dealing with, maybe we could figure out why they are or are not learning and do something about it. But it is just not that simple. We can't identify X types of students and if even if we could, what would that really tell us? What could we do with the information?

The purpose of this chapter is to discuss this concept of individual differences among students. I want to dispel some of the misconceptions that instructors have about this source of complexity in teaching and identify the individual difference variables that have some support in the literature and about which you might be able to do something. But I need to state up front that I am not an advocate of "typing" individuals, so everything I say is colored by that bias.

THE PROBLEM WITH CLASSIFICATION SYSTEMS

Description Versus Explanation

I'll begin with the general idea of finding individual types as a way to simplify teaching. One common misconception about the value of typing individuals is the confusion between description and explanation. In most cases, even well-founded systems of placing individuals into categories are primarily descriptive systems; that is, the categories are clusters of individuals who are characterized by similar behavior patterns. For example, in terms of student patterns of class participation, some students are thinker-talkers and some are talker-thinkers. The former like to think about what they are going to say before they talk, while the latter use talking as a way of thinking aloud. The category name talker-thinker describes their behavior patterns, but it doesn't explain the pattern. There may be many causes for that pattern represented in a single group of students. Some students might talk first because that's how they get instant feedback to modify their thinking; some students might talk first because they are looking for attention; some might talk first because they see themselves in competition with the others so that the first one to talk wins. These are three very different causes of the same behavior pattern. To assume that labeling someone a talker-thinker means we understand that behavior is wrong. To then try to prescribe instruction that will presumably fit everyone in the group is also misguided. And yet it is very common for instructors to assume that the label used to describe a group also explains the cause of their behavior. For example, the Myers-Briggs Type Indicator (MBTI) is widely used to classify individuals according to their responses to a set of questions. As a result of their responses, individuals are classified according to a four-letter scheme. I, for example, fall into the ENTJ category. Each letter represents a subset of behavior descriptors. The problem is that once they've done the MBTI, individuals start to talk about themselves as being "an ENTJ" and they'll make statements like, "Oh well, she's an ENTJ; no wonder she acts that way." This phrasing has subtly changed the purpose of a system meant to be descriptive of the way a person responds into one that now explains why she responds that way. In reality, classifying someone as an ENTJ doesn't give us any additional information about the causes of her behavior. Maybe I am an "E" (which stands for extroversion) because I find all that attention reinforcing; maybe it's because I am afraid of being left out of things; maybe it's a symptom of an underlying hormonal imbalance that raises my ability to tolerate stimulation. What often happens when a classification system is transformed into an explanation system is that we stop looking for the underlying causes and start assuming that the same treatment fits everyone in a given category. It's convenient and less work, but probably not very accurate.

Correlation Versus Causation

Another aspect of systems that type individuals is the assumption of causation when all we really have is a correlation. The statistics used in different classification systems tend to be based on correlations among variables. As we all know (but often forget), high correlations do not equal causation. For example, there is a correlation between the number that a football player wears on his jersey and the number of points he is likely to score in a game. Both low numbers and high numbers result in higher number of points scored. Does this mean that if all my players dress in numbers over 100 the team will be a high scoring one? Of course not. This is an example of the fallacy of correlation/causation. That would be as silly as thinking that if a player starts scoring a lot of points, the number on his jersey will go up (or down). After all, if we're going to make cause and effect assumptions, which measure (jersey number or points scored) is the cause and which is the effect? In reality, both measures are a result of a third variable, the player's position the team. For example, most points are scored by the offensive backfield (like the running backs) or the field goal kickers because that's their job. They run down the field and catch the ball in the end zone or they kick field goals. Players in those positions are generally given jersey numbers that are higher than the rest of the team (running backs) or lower than the rest (kickers) to make their identification easier. Linemen (who rarely score points) are given middle jersey numbers. This assignment system creates an artificial correlation between jersey number and points scored but does not cause any particular behavior. If we didn't realize this, we might fall prey to the fallacious reasoning of increasing or decreasing everyone's jersey number to score more points.

To bring this argument closer to the classroom, the research literature contains several studies that show a correlation between the amount a student talks in class and his or her grade. If we wanted to type students, then, we might classify them as talkers and nontalkers and say that the talking explained their grades. But have we really explained it? If we figured out a way to get everyone into the talker group, would their grades all go up? Maybe. If the instructor gave points each time a student talked, then, yes, getting everyone to talk would actually be the cause of higher grades. But maybe talking and grades are both caused by a third variable, say, class preparation. Students who prepare for class are 1) more likely to talk in class and 2) more likely to do well on measures of achievement that result in higher grades. So here the intervention would be to get students to better prepare for class. Or maybe that talking in class results in better learning because of the talking itself, in which case, getting students to talk more in class would improve their learning, which would then improve their grades. This is one interpretation of the success of group work and one reason why psychologists encourage instructors to get students to talk in class.

What's the bottom line here? Be careful about the way you interpret classification systems. Don't confuse a high correlation with an understanding of cause and effect.

Traits Versus States

Another problem with the interpretation of classification systems is the difference between what psychologists call a "trait" variable and a "state" variable. The former is a global characteristic that is evidenced across multiple situations and multiple occasions. We say that an individual is characterized by a trait variable. State variables are susceptible to the immediate situation and can vary widely across situations. For example, for some individuals anxiety is a trait variable; they are almost always anxious regardless of the situation in which they find themselves. We classify them as neurotic, which as we just learned doesn't explain the behavior but simply describes it in one word. Other individuals, in fact most of us, are anxious sometimes. At those times we are exhibiting the state variable of anxiety. The anxiety is a function of the particular situation and not an over-riding characteristic.

Many individuals look on classification systems as reflecting trait variables. Once you are an ENTJ, that's it. It is related to everything you do in every situation. In reality, most research finds that individuals' behaviors are more situation driven. In fact, a leading researcher and theorist in the area of individual differences, Richard Snow (1998), talked about an "aptitude by person in situation" effect, by which a given "aptitude" or behavior measure was a function of an individual's situation. This was an extension of his Aptitude by Treatment Interaction model, which cautioned researchers to recognize that treatment outcomes would vary by individual aptitudes. Snow expanded that original caution to say that even individuals with similar aptitudes might vary in their response to a given situation based on how they experienced it. A student who one day does really well on a test might do poorly under different conditions (a different state), even though the test itself doesn't change.

This caution about assuming trait status for individual differences is really a variant of the caution about assuming too much about underlying causes. Most categorization schemes are misinterpreted as trait categories and as a result are generalized beyond their original purpose. A very frequent reaction to style inventories is to want to rush home and have your significant other fill out the inventory so you can find out what's wrong with him or her. Individual difference measures should come with a warning about not extending their interpretation beyond the situation for which they have been created.

Inborn Characteristic Versus Preference

Another closely related misuse of many classification schemes is to confuse a preference for a trait. Most valid style instruments will caution users that the categories or behavior patterns they expose represent response tendencies or preferences, not some inborn drive to behave in a given way. For example, the VARK learning styles inventory was developed to describe how different individuals take in and process information (visually, aurally, through reading, or kinesthetically) (Fleming, 1995). However, most agree that learners can vary their use of these different modes and can learn to use all of them effectively. One may be preferred over the others, but good learners can adapt to whatever the situation demands. In fact, there is some debate in the field about whether learners should be taught with their preferred mode or taught to adapt to other modes.

In addition to the categories being fluid across situations, researchers in the area of individual difference believe that characteristics of learning vary across time. The most recent compilation of work on individual differences proposes a very complex PPIK model that reflects almost all of these considerations. The editor and compiler, Phillip Ackerman (1999), includes in those individual differences measures of intelligence as a process (the first P), personality characteristics (the second P), manifestations of interest and motivation (the I), and the level of knowledge the person has about the situation (the K), all varying across the characteristics of the task (the situation) and age. To paraphrase and summarize his conclusion, although individual differences start with basic physical differences in ability to process information, as the individual grows, his or her unique experiences start interacting with those differences to create a unique knowledge structure. By the time that individual reaches adulthood, the individual differences in capability have come to be more a function of life experiences and knowledge than the initial physical differences (Ackerman, 1999).

Qualities to Look for in a Category System

The foregoing discussion may have scared you off using any categorization system, and that might be a good thing. But instruments and models that help differentiate individual differences are available in abundance and have some practical value, which I'll discuss later in this chapter. The key is to be aware of the qualities to look for when using a model and temper your conclusions based on the degree to which a given instrument provides you with information about its underlying structure. Although instrument developers should provide validity and reliability data on their instruments, they often don't (Mayer, 1995; Stellwagen, 2001). Here are some intuitive factors to consider when assessing the usefulness of an instrument or even a theory of individual differences:

1) Are the items on the inventory clustered into groups that are distinct from one another and that fit the model of learning behavior on which the system rests? For example, are the items in group A consistent with one another and obviously different from those in group B? The supporting material should provide you with information about the statistical basis for the division of the items into different groups representing underlying variables.

2) Scores on the different groups should be able to predict performance on everyday tasks that are related to the underlying measure. There should be a correlation between these scores and other measures of the same thing. Using the thinker-talker example, those students who scored high in the talker category should also come out on top if we went into the classroom and actually observed how much they talked during class. A lot of times a sort of posthoc analysis is used as evidence of the validity of a measure, like reporting that there is a high incidence of talkers in the sales population. Such analysis frequently uses only positive cases as evidence and fails to account for the large number of nonexamples that exist in a population. How many of all talkers are not in sales, for example? Do all talkers become salespeople?

3) Individuals in a given group should be more different from members of other groups than they are from members of their own groups. (Technically, the variance between groups should be larger than the variance within a group.) So talkers as a whole should behave more like other talkers than like nontalkers.

4) The assignment to groups should account for a large enough portion of the variance between individuals in comparison to other differences that group assignment is actually worth doing. So, for example, in the "thinker-talker" group, being in the "talker" group should account for more of your unique behavior than things like gender or age or where you sit in the classroom.

5) The score that an individual makes on the instrument should be fairly reliable. For example, if you take the instrument today and a week from today, your scores should be fairly similar. If there are significant changes in scores, they should occur only after some relevant situational change. In our thinker-talker example, the talker group would fall consistently within that group every week until we intervened and gave them some training on how to let others talk first. Then their scores might shift to the thinker group cluster. Or an individual student's score might shift over the course of the semester as he or she developed more confidence in his or her grasp of the material. (This would be evidence that talking is not an inborn trait, by the way.)

6) The supplier of an instrument should provide some data on the instrument's factor structure, reliability, and validity based on a sample of people similar to the ones to whom you're administering the instrument. Most instruments that have been statistically tested can be found in various indexes of measurement instruments, like the *Mental Measurements Yearbook* published by Rutgers University. Another good discussion of instruments is found in Riding and Rayner's (1998) book on cognitive styles.

INDIVIDUAL DIFFERENCES THAT MATTER

How do you reconcile all these flawed or false classification schemes with the differences you see among your students? There are some real differences among learners that have good support in the research literature, but they're not as flashy or appealing as the usual set. This next section discusses some of the real individual differences that impact student learning.

The individual difference areas that have the best support in the literature are similar to those mentioned earlier as cited by Ackerman (1999). They are 1) an individual's prior knowledge and experience, 2) the learning strategies the individual has and uses plus the individual's tendency to process information in certain ways, 3) aspects of the individual's motivations for learning, and 4) the individual's self-efficacy in the topic. These are mostly malleable conditions that can be changed with instruction and situation, which is good news for education. If we were dealing only with "traits," we would be a lot less successful at our jobs.

Prior Knowledge and Experience

Chapter 2 introduced the cognitive model of learning and talked about the important role that prior knowledge plays in learning. Prior knowledge impacts what learners pay attention to, how they perceive and interpret what they are experiencing, and how they store new information based on what they already know. I'm bringing up the concept of prior knowledge and experience again because of the important role it plays in explaining the impact of individual differences on learning.

Virtually all psychologists will agree with the statement that past experience influences present behavior. That goes for learning behavior as well. Because each learner has had unique experiences, he or she brings to the learning situation an idiosyncratic understanding of the world, which then colors how he or she responds to new situations. Every instructor is faced with learners who vary tremendously in how much and what they know about a topic. Research has clearly shown that students who have extensive and well-organized prior knowledge about a topic will outperform novices (Alexander & Murphy, 1998), especially if they combine that knowledge with a strong interest in the content and are able to marshal learning strategies that help them build on that prior knowledge. In fact, one of the biggest differences between experts and novices in a field is the amount and structure of the knowledge they have about a field (Alexander, 1992). This literature on differences in knowledge encourages us to think about three types of knowledge differences that impact student learning: depth, breadth, and accuracy.

Depth of knowledge differences. The most obvious individual differences in knowledge that faculty grapple with is difference in the depth of knowledge about the topic. Students who know more about the topic find it easier to learn more and more quickly than those whose knowledge is superficial. The former are easier to teach because they can fill in the blanks and follow a complex analysis more readily. Course prerequisites are supposed to narrow the differences among students, but in most cases a student only needs to have passed a course to move on to the next course, and the difference between a student who earned an A and one who earned a C is pretty large. All faculty know that simply having the prerequisite courses is not enough for students to enter a new course on an even playing field. (We also know that students are very good at getting around prerequisites.) As a result, instructors are faced with students entering with widely differing prior knowledge, which makes it very hard to teach efficiently and effectively.

When I work with faculty members who are dealing with a knowledge depth issue, I usually advise them to begin the semester with some data gathering to establish what will be needed in the course. First, it is important to analyze the course requirements carefully and pick out the half dozen most important prerequisites that students need. There are usually more than that, but you can't repeat previous courses so you have to draw the line somewhere. Students must be able to work in these six areas before they can make any progress in the current course. Consider consulting with your colleagues who teach the prerequisite courses to make sure everyone is working from the same agenda. It would be unfair to blame the students for something their previous instructors failed to emphasize. Then I recommend pretesting the students on those areas. This can be a real test with questions or problems, or it can be a checklist. I use the latter in graduate courses (Figure 8.1). The checklist contains the key ideas, areas of understanding, or experiences that I want to be sure the students have mastered. For the checklist, I identify a concept and then have students indicate where they fall along a continuum from "I don't know anything about this" to "I am well versed in this area and could analyze situations using this concept." I trust the students to be honest with me, but the checklist is anonymous in case they don't feel comfortable confessing their knowledge gaps. For a test, I would construct a couple of questions at different levels for each concept and administer it early in the semester (probably not the first day, however). The test can be corrected in class and the students will see immediately how they fared. Then the test results can be compiled in order to make the next key decision about prior knowledge differences.

Figure 8.1
Pre-Semester Prior Knowledge Inventory

The following are topics we are likely to study in this class. Indicate the degree to which you already know about each topic using the following scale:

1   I don't know anything about this topic.
2   I have heard about this topic, but only superficially.
3   I have studied this topic in the past and remember it fairly well.
4   I know this topic very well (could probably teach it!)

Basic cognitive theory of learning	1	2	3	4
More advanced topics in cognitive theory				
Cognitive apprenticeship model	1	2	3	4
Situated cognition	1	2	3	4
The role of emotion in learning	1	2	3	4
Application of cognitive theory to education design	1	2	3	4
Basic social cognitive theory of learning	1	2	3	4
Application of social cognitive to educational design	1	2	3	4
Motivational theories				
Expectancy value theory	1	2	3	4
Attribution theory	1	2	3	4
Social cognitive theory	1	2	3	4
Self-determination theory	1	2	3	4
More advanced topics in motivation theory				
Goal orientation theory	1	2	3	4
Volition theory	1	2	3	4
Situated motivation theory	1	2	3	4

If, using either method, I find that less than a third of the class scores below what I consider to be an acceptable level of understanding, it is probably not necessary to take class time to remediate that group. I would provide them with remedial materials or direct them to resources to shore up what they are missing. If I find that more than two thirds of the class are performing below par, there would be no sense in ignoring that lack and trying to push ahead with the course. I would recommend instead that some initial class time be devoted to working with the most crucial knowledge or skills. If the results fall somewhere in between one third and two thirds, I would refer students to the support materials and at the same time spend a little class time throughout the semester touching on those areas that are needed for the next unit.

In a class of some advanced students mixed in with some who are at just the right level for the class, I have seen instructors do some interesting mixing of content in a single class. For example, one astronomy professor was teaching a general astronomy course for nonmajors, some of whom had had advanced math and some of whom had not. To keep the interest of the former, he would occasionally pause in the class and say, "For the next five minutes, I'm going to go into some of the higher level math that is used to think about this phenomenon. Those of you that haven't had advanced math can just kick back for a while or read over your notes. On the other hand, you might find it interesting and challenging to see if you can follow the discussion. For those of you with advanced math, this will help you understand the topic better." Then he would spend five minutes with the math, after which he would announce that he was returning to the main stream of the day's content. Far fewer students than you might expect relished the opportunity to tune out for a while. Students don't mind being challenged in their thinking as long as it's in a safe way, and this was a safe situation. They didn't have to know this particular derivation for the test, but it was interesting and challenging, and a lot of them accepted the challenge and tried to see what they could understand. I felt that this was an effective strategy for dealing with the advanced students in the class while not losing the rest.

One final set of recommendations about differences in knowledge depth have to do with what type of knowledge you help the novices develop. As mentioned earlier, the research on differences between experts and novices focuses not only on how much the experts know in comparison to novices, but also on how they structure what they know and go about using it. Experts structure their knowledge around higher-order principles like major classes of problems commonly found in the field. This structure then points toward problem-solving procedures for dealing with new information and when to use them. Experts spend most of their time setting up a problem and classifying it according to one of the higher-order principles around which their knowledge is organized. Novices tend to focus on the concrete details of a problem and miss the bigger picture. Experts also mentally test out a plan for problem solving before proceeding so they can see whether their solution will make sense (Rohwer & Thomas, 1989). Unfortunately, we can't simply create experts out of novices just because we know these characteristics. The development of expertise takes a lot of time. However, we should help students build efficient structural knowledge organized around the types of problems common to a field and flexible problem-solving strategies to attack those problems instead of concentrating on details or memorizing specific procedures (Rohwer & Thomas, 1989).

Breadth of knowledge differences. Another type of individual difference in prior knowledge is breadth. Differences in knowledge breadth refer to the fact that students often have different types of prior knowledge. Some may have approached the concept from one perspective while others have looked at it from a different perspective. Even in graduate classes that are highly specialized, you still encounter differences in the emphasis that a given student has had. There are two ways to deal with this phenomenon. The first acknowledges it directly and the second takes advantage of it.

My first recommendation about dealing with breadth issues is to become more broadly educated yourself. If you know that you have students from three different majors taking your course, you need to think about the ways they might approach the topic and the uses to which they will put the content in their future. For example, in my own undergraduate class I have students who are education majors, nutrition majors, communication disorders majors, and a sprinkling of business and liberal arts majors. I go out of my way to use examples and situations that represent the different majors.

Similarly in my graduate classes, I have a diverse group of students from different specialties, and I use them as resources to the whole class. For example, if we are discussing a topic that is not central to my own training but is to one of the student's, I will turn to that person for expert advice or to provide an alternative interpretation to mine. I have found that by recognizing the students' expertise, I learn a lot in class, and the other students come to rely more on one another for consultation on issues surrounding their specialties.

The same sharing of expertise can be done with undergraduate classes but in a more structured way. For example, one of the most widely used collaborative learning models is called the "jigsaw" strategy, in which students form groups with each group member representing a specialty area. That person is responsible for learning a particular part of the content and teaching it to the others in the group. Everyone is eventually tested on all the material, so it is important that each student do a good job of representing his or her area to the rest of the group. This can be done by using pre-existing differences in content knowledge, or it can be artificially induced by having students designated to study a particular perspective and bring it to the group.

This idea of individual differences in prior knowledge can become the basis of a kind of typing. In other words, if you are going to type students, do it on the basis of something useful, like what they already know about the topic and could contribute to the class or on the basis of skills they have that will be needed by the group. For example, if the students are going to work in groups on projects that require an array of skills, administer a pretest on those skills and create groups with representatives who have different skills. In that way each individual's contribution to the group effort is necessary and each can be a leader at some point or around some task. Likewise, you can create groups that have different patterns of content understanding. You can put all the advanced students into one group and give them particularly difficult problems to work on while another group works on catching up. This is somewhat like tracking in the lower grades, which has a lot of problems, but can be handled more graciously with older students. On the other hand, the literature on the zone of proximal development concept (Vygotsky, 1978) supports the idea of having heterogeneous grouping. Students at slightly different levels of expertise should be put into the same group to learn from one another. Some students with higher levels of expertise will complain that they always end up doing all the work in these groups. I tell them that they are lucky if that's the case because the literature also shows that the person doing the most explaining is actually learning the most as well.

Accuracy of knowledge differences. The research literature in science education points to this area of difference as one of the most difficult to overcome. Students come to classes with a range of misconceptions about the topics that are very hard to dislodge, and yet they must be corrected directly or they will undermine new learning. (Refer to Chapter 3 about conceptual change for a more extensive discussion on this.) Pressley and McCormick (1995) discuss some of the research on the existence of misconceptions in science by college students. For example, they describe an experiment in which students were to decide whether each item on a list was alive. The list contained items like a burning match and an unlighted match. All the items on the list should have been identified as not alive, and yet the researchers report that at least one-quarter of the class indicate that one or more items on the list were alive. We might assume that taking the appropriate course would dispel the students' misconceptions and change their ideas to be more in line with scientific facts, but this is not the case. Study after study reports that students frequently do not change their misconceptions even in the face of instruction about the correct concept. What many students do instead is incorporate the new information into their existing conceptual framework without recognizing the contradictions that result. Another researcher (Duit, 1991) discusses the effect as an example of seeing what you want to see. Students will see a demonstration in a way that is consistent with their existing beliefs. In fact, this tendency has been documented by Thomas Gilovich (1991) in a wonderful book on the persistence of inaccurate beliefs. Gilovich discusses the role of beliefs in altering our interpretation and even observation of events.

If it is true that students come out with the same misconceptions that they entered a class with, it's a pretty depressing state of affairs. What can be done about it? Faced with this situation, instructors need to do more than just present the correct concept; they must induce conceptual change in the student. Fortunately for us teachers, students who are confronted with information that is different from their own conceptions are temporarily in a state of conflict, which they will attempt to resolve. It is, as they say, a teachable moment. Unfortunately, one exposure is not enough to induce conceptual change. Without deeper reflection students will figure out a way to explain conflicting evidence using whatever current conceptions they have unless the instruction persists. Pintrich, Marx, and Boyle (1993) have laid out what they call "hot cognition," which is cognition colored by motivation and emotion. The idea is that students don't necessarily adopt a rational approach to conceptual change; there are other motivational factors operating. They have to have a reason to change. Posner, Strike, Hewson, and Gertzog (1982) describe a four-stage model for conceptual change. First, the individual has to be dissatisfied with his or her old concept. This often happens when the individual is confronted with contradictory data. In fact, there are seven forms of response that a learner can make at this point (Chinn & Brewer, 1993). The learner can 1) ignore the discrepancy, 2) reject the new data, 3) reinterpret the data to be consistent with existing concepts, 4) hold on to the new data for a while, but not deal with them, 5) reinterpret the data and change existing concepts slightly to accommodate them, 6) say that the data don't belong to the question at hand, or 7) change the existing theory to be more in line with the data. Only the last of these is real conceptual change.

However, let's say that the data are convincing enough to merit consideration. Then when a new explanation is proposed, it has to be understandable, believable, and what the authors call fruitful, that is, it has to appear to be useful in explaining not only that discrepancy but others as well as new data. Probably where we fall down in most classes is that we either allow one of the other reactions to anomalous data to stand or we present a new interpretation in a way that is not understandable to the novice.

Posner et al. (1982) suggest six strategies to help instructors overcome prior misconceptions. They suggest (and I have embellished their ideas):

1) Producing the kind of cognitive conflict we've been considering by confronting students with conflicting data, but in a way to make it hard to ignore. One good strategy is forcing students to make a prediction before they see the real data. This makes it hard for them to hide their misconceptions.

2) Monitoring student thinking so that if they do try to use one of the six fallacious strategies, you'll know right away. One of the advantages of collaborative learning is that it makes student thinking public and therefore possible to evaluate.

3) Asking students probing questions as they struggle to accommodate the new information. Don't give them the answer right away.

4) Modeling scientific thinking as a way of dealing with conflicting data. Show the students how to process conflicting evidence more deeply in order to identify key areas of conflict and its causes.

5) Using multiple modes to present content so that various approaches to explaining the data are explored (e.g., mathematical, pictorial, experiential, analogical).

6) Using ongoing assessments that will expose students' thinking so inaccuracy or failure to change can be observed and countered. For example, when you provide incorrect choices on a multiple choice exam, make them reflect what would result from fallacious thinking. That way if a student chooses one of those options, the probable cause of his or her incorrect thinking will be exposed.

Have students generate and attempt to answer questions that involve making use of their prior knowledge. Pressley et al. (1992) have shown that having students answers questions that ask for explanations based on prior knowledge produces better learning.

What do I recommend as an instructor based on these ideas? First, find out what and how much your students know about the prerequisite skills and content for your course. Decide based on those data where to start, how fast to go, and what to offer remedially. Second, based on who is in the class, try to connect the content to their experiences and interests. This may require extra work on your part to learn about different disciplines and how they relate to yours. At the same time, don't hesitate to invite students to teach you and other students from their own areas of expertise. Finally, be aware of inaccuracy in student understanding and bring those beliefs and ideas out in the open for examination.

Learning Strategies and Styles

Although prior knowledge forms the foundation for learning, there are many ways to go about learning and students vary almost as much here as they do in how much and what they know. I'd like to emphasize that the strategies and styles that I'm about to discuss are empirically based differences in the way learners go about mastering new information. They are not based on personality differences or inborn traits. They are learned responses and attitudes, and they can be unlearned or relearned. They also can be used strategically—that is, truly flexible students can learn an array of strategies that allow them to cope with all the different kinds of situations they encounter.

A lot of models have been proposed to describe different learning strategies, and you really don't need to know them all, so I've picked out the three approaches that I think are best supported in the literature and make the most sense in terms of differences among learners. They are all derived from the cognitive processing model that was discussed in Chapter 2 and are based on the three steps of information processing: attention, encoding, and metacognitive (executive) processing.

Differences in attentional processing. I'm going to collapse a whole area of research here because it fits into the idea of how students initially take in information from the environment. This synthesis is based on an analysis by Schmeck (1988b). The various models differentiate between individuals who prefer to take in the big picture first as opposed to those who prefer to take in information one piece at a time.

Individuals who prefer the one-piece-at-a-time strategy are described by Schmeck (1988b) as follows:

> People with an extreme *analytic* style are field independent and have focused attention, noticing and remembering details. They have an interest in operations and procedures, or the proper ways of doing things and prefer step-by-step, sequential organizational schemes. Their thinking, like their attention, is more controlled and consciously directed than that of individuals with a global style. This control and focus of attention allows them to divorce feelings from objective facts. They are gifted at critical and logical thinking. They are also gifted at seeing differences between apparently similar experiences. (p. 328)

The other strategy, also known in the literature as "global" or "holistic" processing, focuses first on the overall structure of information, how it all fits together. Here's how Schmeck (1988b) describes this strategy:

> Individuals with a *global* style are field dependent with attention tending toward scanning, leading to the formation of global impressions rather than more precisely articulated codes. Rather than lin-

ear and sequential, their organizational schemes involve more random or multiple accessibility of components, allowing numerous and varied associations between coded experiences. Their thinking is more intuitive than that of an analytic person, including entry of feelings into decisions. Their emphasis on conscious control and directing of thoughts is less evident, and global individuals are likely to be more impulsive than analytic thinkers. Also, as noted above, they are more gifted at seeing similarities than differences. (p. 328)

Note the reference in these two descriptions to the concept of field dependence versus independence. Sometimes this quality is associated with personality differences, but here Schmeck is using a narrower definition of the concept, one that focuses on the ability of the individual to pick out details from a background (field independence). Those who tend to process information as a whole would be referred to as field dependent or field sensitive because they tend to analyze information only in relation to its surroundings.

Another possible way to think about these tendencies is in terms of how focused they are in attention as well as what they focus on. Individuals who display global processing tendencies are more likely to focus broadly, a sort of forest perspective, looking for overall patterns. Individuals who display analytical processing tendencies are more tightly focused, a sort of trees perspective. Another researcher, Pask (1976), describes the difference as being between simultaneous versus successive processing of information. Global style involves considering a lot of variables at the same time (simultaneously), while the analytical style moves more systematically from one variable to the next (successively). Pask also describes the excessive use of the styles as globetrotting and improvidence respectively.

Looking at the basic research on learning (particularly Ausubel's [1960] idea about advance organizers discussed in Chapter 2), I believe the better strategy is to present a global view first. It will certainly help the global people, and no one will be hurt if the instructor gives an overall picture of what is being learned before giving the details.

Another set of attentional preferences is frequently discussed in the literature. These are preferences based on modality of stimulus presentation. In general, they focus on information presented visually, aurally, or kinesthetically (in an activity) (Jonassen & Grabowski, 1993). A good example of an instrument based on these differences is the VARK (Fleming, 1995), which adds a reading mode (the R) to the list. They are also called visual/haptic styles or visualizer/verbalizer styles. These differences probably have the most face validity of all the posited individual difference variables, but the research that backs them up is mixed (Fromme & Daniell, 1984; Jaspers, 1994; Jonassen & Grabowski, 1993). There might be a confounding variable that is making these attempts at verification difficult. It is possible that what appears to be preference for visual stimuli is really a preference for holistic presentation and processing. Likewise, aural presentation may be confounded by a preference for sequential or analytical presentation and processing. Riding (1997), one of the leaders in this area of theory and research, suggests something of this confounding as well with his cognitive style model. The aural versus visual preference might be the same as his verbal versus imagery dimension, but rather than being a preference for the actual visual stimulation or an attentional process, it is based on the fact that visual stimuli also are usually presented all at once (holistically) while verbal stimuli, particularly aurally presented stimuli, are more sequential and analytical.

Regardless of what the actual functional mechanism is for this modality preference, there is a lot to be said in its favor. For example, Fleming (1995) has developed a very extensive set of teaching materials that help students to learn under different conditions. Let's say that you are identified as a strong visualizer. He suggests that if you are trying to study material that is very sequential in nature, you should make diagrams and concept maps that will allow you to use your visualization strengths in learning the material. Likewise, if you are very aural, you might find it better to read a particularly confusing passage aloud to engage your aural learning preference. In addition, administering an instrument like the VARK is an opening into the discussion of differences in learning strategies and how to make them work for you rather than against you.

Riding also has developed a way to help individuals assess their preferences, but it is quite different from most instruments. While other instruments are usually self-report inventories, Riding's Cognitive Styles Analysis is a computer-administered test (Riding & Cheema, 1991). The theory is that the dimensions that Riding is testing will be manifested in the way and speed of responding to an array of items that should favor one preference over the other. For example, if you are a visualizer, then statements in which something is presented descriptively will be processed more rapidly than if the statement is in the abstract. Test takers are divided according to their response patterns. This approach has the potential of being less prone to test-taking bias, but it has the difficulty of making inferences about the cognitive processes underlying the items. Nevertheless, it is a good step toward being able to differentiate learners' cognitive processes.

Differences in encoding strategies. Another way to look at the holistic versus analytical dimensions is as ways of processing information once you've attended to it. Riding (2001) agrees with Schmeck about the holistic/analytic dimension, but he talks about it as being related more to processing information and he calls this "cognitive style." Here holistic processing refers to organizing information in terms of the whole picture, while analytical processing refers to dealing with the parts sequentially. As I noted above, Riding also adds a second broad category around the dimension of verbal versus imagery thinking. Some learners process new information in words or descriptions, while others create images as their storage strategy. If you recall the chapter on cognitive theory, the dual code model says we store both ways. Riding's analysis suggests a greater facility or preference for using one or the other as the main way information is processed or encoded.

A second strategy/style difference that has a lot of support in the literature is the difference between learners who have a surface processing approach and those with a deep processing approach. From our earlier discussion about cognitive theory, we know that research supports the use of deep processing as the best way to learn material. And yet students do show a difference in their tendencies toward these two styles. The difference might be based on motivational variables, which we'll discuss later, but there are different learning tactics associated with each that could possibly be taught. The two most common categories of learning strategies revolve around the idea of the depth at which the learner processes new information (Marton, 1988).

Students with a surface processing approach to learning tend to use learning strategies that emphasize repetition and practice. They also tend to manipulate new information to make it more meaningful by changing its surface structure rather than probing further. For example, the use of vivid or humorous imagery is an example of a surface processing strategy. The learner will be able to remember the information, but may not be able to place it in a usable context. A variation on imagery is the use of mnemonics, which was discussed in Chapter 2. Creating mnemonics as a memory aid really only substitutes one surface feature (the rhyme, acronym, or nonsense sentence) for another surface feature (the features that represent the categories). Mnemonics can easily be substituted for understanding when it comes to remembering unrelated bits of information and give the learner the illusion of knowing something. In fact, for some types of information, surface processing is perfectly acceptable—for example, memorizing the capitals of the states or the order of the presidents of the United States. There may be no other way to learn the information if there is indeed no real structural relationship tying the parts together.

Of course, recalling the cognitive model discussion in Chapter 2, surface processing makes for shaky memories. Deep processing is a much better long-term memory strategy. Deep processing strategies include creating a graphic organizer (like an outline or a concept map) that relates the parts of the concept to one another; organizing the information into a meaningful pattern that reflects its underlying structure, and elaborating on it by adding details and information that connects new information to prior knowledge. In all the deep processing strategies the learner is focusing on the inter-relationships among the different parts of new information.

Surface versus deep processing strategies refer to how learners are encoding the information into long-term memory. The strategies used for such encoding are learned behaviors, and therefore they can be modified by further learning. The hard thing about doing that is that most learners have developed their learning strategies to a finely tuned edge such that they are almost automatic. Convincing a learner to abandon a well-oiled strategy in favor of a new one that will initially be very time-consuming and clumsy is an uphill battle. In the long run, learning new strategies will pay off in efficiency and effectiveness, but try telling that to a student who has put off studying until the night before the test and now has eight hours to learn as much as possible in order to pass. So perhaps the best strategy of all is to learn how not to procrastinate!

This surface/deep processing approach categorization has been expanded in recent research to include a third one called achieving by Biggs (2001) or strategic by Entwhistle, McCune, and Walker (2001). Biggs describes the students who take an achieving approach as seeking to maximize recognition and achievement for the purposes of being recognized by the instructor or other students, but without learning as the goal. Students with this perspective will pull together all their resources strategically to obtain the best possible outcome with the most efficiency. This approach differs from the other two in that it doesn't really address the outcome of learning (deep versus surface understanding), only how students go about it. Biggs concludes by exhorting instructors to encourage the deep approach to learning and discouraging the surface approach by the way they structure instruction. He also points out that the surface approach is less work for students in the short run, so there will be some inertia to overcome.

Differences in self-regulation of learning. The third aspect of learning strategies and styles that differs greatly among individuals is their ability to martial those strategies in the face of a given task. Learners need to be in control of their own learning (as explored in Chapter 6), which requires that they have a good background in at least four areas.

First, learners need to have a background in how tasks differ from one another. For example, they need to know that reading one type of textbook is not the same as reading a text from a different discipline. This is known in the literature as task knowledge. Second, learners need to understand their own strengths and weaknesses as learners. This is known as self-knowledge. For example, they need to know that they have a tendency to get distracted easily in the face of very repetitious tasks. Third, they need to have at their disposal an array of strategies. This is known as strategy knowledge, and it includes using different ways to mark important concepts (e.g., highlighting, underlining, writing in the margins) or using different ways to create study notes (e.g., recopying them in chronological order, creating a concept map that relates ideas to one another, creating a series of questions and answers about key concepts). Unfortunately, it is often the case that our students have one or two strategies that they use regardless of the situation. When faced with a new type of situation, they just repeat those strategies harder.

A fourth type of knowledge that falls into the self-regulation literature is conditional knowledge. This is the kind of knowledge that helps learners decide which strategy to use in which situation. Students with this kind of knowledge are often thought of as flexible learners because they can vary their learning according to the demands of the situation. Obviously, this is the level of understanding toward which we should push our students because in the long run it will benefit them the most.

Some very interesting research about the interactions among prior knowledge, interest, and strategic behavior has been conducted (Alexander & Murphy, 1998), in which it was found very consistently that successful students had to bring to bear a combination of knowledge, interest, and strategic processing. No one characteristic alone was sufficient to help students with ill-structured learning situations. Absence of any of these qualities resulted in less effective learning.

In light of this discussion, what do I recommend to you as an instructor? Several self-assessment instruments are available for helping you and your students identify their strengths, weaknesses, and preferences with regard to learning strategies and styles. Two of these are the Motivated Strategies for Learning Questionnaire (MSLQ) developed by researchers at the University of Michigan (Pintrich, Smith, Garcia, & McKeachie, 1993) and the Learning and Study Strategies Inventory (LASSI) developed by researchers at the University of Texas-Austin (Weinstein, Palmer, & Schulte, 1987). Both of these inventories are derived from the cognitive model of learning and have items that ask students about specific learning strategies and motivational behaviors. Students complete the inventories and then score them to see where in their study repertoires they are strong and where they are weak in comparison to norms. I have used the MSLQ in my own classes as a way of stimulating the discussion about student study behavior, and I find that it helps my students think more objectively about what they do when they study. By looking at strengths and weaknesses, they can spot places where they are using inefficient strategies, which will hopefully motivate them to change their behaviors. Just having the discussion about different strategies is worthwhile. Also available are several other more global inventories, such as the Kolb Learning Styles Inventory (Kolb, 1981), the Schmeck Learning

Styles Inventory (Schmeck, Ribich, & Ramanaiah, 1977), the Approaches to Study Inventory (Entwhistle & Ramsden, 1983), and the VARK (Fleming, 1995). Having your students complete one of these inventories helps you initiate a conversation about differences in learning and how strengths and weaknesses can be used to advantage. It is important, however, to stress that such instruments do not reflect basic abilities or personality differences; they are merely inventories of what students do. Their usefulness is more in stimulating thinking than offering answers.

Another caution about introducing your students and yourself to these different inventories is in order, too. As is usually the case in psychology, the picture about learning strategies and styles is more complex than it appears on the surface. Researchers are beginning to take note of the interaction between the learners and their instructional situations—the "person-situation perspective" (Renzulli & Dai, 2001). These researchers recognize that both the inner environment (such as prior knowledge, abilities, attitudes, motivations, etc.) and the outer environment (the subject, instruction used, instructor skills, etc.) interact positively or negatively. If the interaction is complementary and in harmony, positive learning experiences are the outcome. But because each student is unique, an instructor cannot predict how a given method will work all the time. We must be flexible enough to provide multiple opportunities and venues for learning to take place.

In terms of your actions as the instructor, I've already noted that the use of advance organizers is helpful to students who process information globally rather than sequentially. In general, providing students with an overview or a big picture prior to learning should be helpful even to those for whom that is not a preferred strategy. These kinds of overall organizers are tied to deep processing of information. When the big picture focuses on relationships among main ideas, students are encouraged to process information at a deeper level, which is better in the long run. Whatever an instructor can do to encourage deep processing in all the students will pay off with longer retention and better understanding. Sometimes it is hard to convince students who prefer surface processing strategies to put in the effort needed for deep processing. However, activities that ask them to elaborate on an idea or apply it to new settings or compare it with similar ideas will force students to go beyond surface features and memorization. In essence, we're asking some students to go against their well-learned preferences; others will already be leaning in this direction and won't need much encouragement.

There is some disagreement in the literature about this issue of forcing students to go against their preferences. Some researchers suggest that we should compensate for differences by attempting to match learner preferences—for example, provide information both aurally and visually. This would be a form of scaffolding, that is, modifying the instruction to make it easier for the learner to learn. The decision to match learning preferences and instruction is tempered by two factors: the purpose of the instruction and whether there is a difference in the effectiveness of learning under the various preference conditions. In the case of the former, each instructor must decide whether the main purpose of the instruction is to teach the content or to teach learners to become more effective in learning. This is similar to the argument often made about developing student writing skills. Is a math instructor responsible for teaching math and helping students learn to write? I don't think there's a right answer for this one. On one hand, we should model (and expect) good, high-level communication for students all the time as a way of indoctrinating them into the culture of scholarship. In that case, math instructors are as responsible for enforcing writing standards as rhetoric instructors are. On the other hand, trying to accomplish too many instructional goals in a class runs the risk of diluting all of them. Each instructor and each institution must decide what is best in their situation.

With regard to the other point about requiring students to go against their tendencies, I believe that if we really know that one type of strategy is going to result in better learning, then we should force students to learn the new method. There is enough research to say that deep processing results in better learning, and therefore we should help students develop their abilities to use deep processing strategies, even if that is not their initial preference. It's hard to get them to change in the course of a single semester, but if all instructors emphasized this point, then over the course of their college tenure, students might be persuaded to change.

As to the differences in self-regulation propensities, this is another area where helping students expand their options will benefit them in the long run. It is hard to get students, even those who have learned about better strategies, to employ them. Perhaps the best instructional strategy is to model those self-regulation behaviors yourself at any opportunity and design class assignments that support them. For example, early in the semester a discussion about how you go about reading materials in the field might help some students see that there are differences between disciplines in the ways they are structured. Developing a template for solving problems in your field and then making that template very overt through repetition when you solve problems in front of the class is also a good strategy for helping students develop self-regulation. Making assignments that require students to explain how they solved a problem rather than just carrying out the solution strategy brings their self-regulation strategies to light so they can become conscious and be critiqued, which will encourage student self-reflection. When students come to you for help, weave the self-regulation strategies into the discussion by asking them about the strategies they used and offering alternatives when theirs are less than optimal. Make sure that the evaluation of their learning is based on something that requires more than just memorization or surface learning. Give them choices about how they demonstrate their competence as opportunities to engage in self-regulation and provide feedback on their choices.

Differences in Motivational Factors

Next to differences in prior knowledge, differences in motivation are probably the most recognized individual difference variable among learners. It is easy for most instructors to see how differences in motivation influence student behavior. In fact, one of the most frequent questions I get as a faculty support person is about how to motivate students. A lot of instructors find it easy to blame instructional failures on their students' apparent lack of motivation. In reality, some of the differences among students is indeed a difference in motivation. As noted earlier, student interest (one version of motivation) is one of the key factors in producing the best learning (Alexander & Murphy, 1998).

I'm sure I don't have to convince you of how differences in motivation influence learning, and I've already discussed motivational strategies in an earlier chapter. What I'd like to emphasize here are some specific aspects of the individual differences part of motivation and how they influence student behavior. Three very interesting and well-documented areas of research have focused on some key differences in student motivation, aside from amount of it. They deal more with 1) the direction that motivation takes, 2) how students interpret what is happening to them, and 3) how those two influence what students will do.

Goal orientation. The first of these three areas of research is the area of goal orientation (Dweck & Leggett, 1988). Because no one is totally unmotivated, what we see in students' behavior is different types of motivation, some of which are positive and some negative. Researchers have categorized one dimension of motivation as the learners' orientation toward different goals or task completion. Individuals with a mastery orientation are intent on learning or completing whatever it is they are working on. They are focused on mastering the task, no matter what it takes. Instructors love these students because they seem highly motivated. It would probably be more accurate to say that they are correctly motivated, that is, their motivation is based on a goal that we approve of, learning the material. Students with a performance orientation are not as interested in learning for its own sake, but are more focused on appearing competent. This orientation has subsequently been broken down into two types: approach (the goal is to succeed) and avoidance (the goal is to avoid failure). Some students with this orientation are seen as too grade conscious or too focused on extrinsic goals. They want to learn, but not because they see an inherent value in the material. Rather they are more focused on success. These students are the students who constantly ask, "Will that be on the test?"

Individuals with these different orientations have been shown to have very different behaviors with regard to approaching a task (Ormond, 1999). For example, students who are working toward mastery goals are willing to take risks and invest effort in a task. They're not afraid to make mistakes. They persist in the face of failure and are willing to seek help. Students who are working toward performance goals will take the safer path to avoid making mistakes. They balance the effort they are willing to expend with the probabilities of success or failure and respond accordingly. They will often interpret having to exert effort as a sign of low ability and give up easily. They seem to use surface processing strategies more often than deep processing ones.

Students with mastery goals are the kind we would prefer as instructors. When this theory was originally proposed, these different goal orientations were considered to be much closer to personality traits than temporary states. If that were the case, we might despair. But more recently, researchers have come to believe that the kind of goal orientation that students adopt is more based on their immediate situation. Researchers have also concluded that students can be working toward both mastery and performance goals in the same task. This is a much more hopeful interpretation of these differences in students, because it means that, (as with other differences), goal orientation can be influenced from the outside. Instructors can encourage students to adopt mastery goals where appropriate. For example, focusing assignments and evaluation on the improvement of skills rather than comparison with other students is more likely to encourage mastery goals. Having students work on topics they are inherently interested in is more likely to result in mastery goals. Taking a diagnostic perspective on feedback, focusing on how to improve rather than on what was wrong, tells students that an instructor is more interested in their learning than in evaluating their abilities. More suggestions about structuring a learning environment that encourages mastery goals can be found in the chapter on motivation. Just recognize that these goal orientations are mutable and they reflect the situation as much as the student.

Student interpretation. Another area of individual difference in motivation is based on how students interpret what is happening to them. Again, this is discussed in the chapter on motivation with attribution theory, but I'll link it here to individual differences. The same situation can easily produce two different levels of motivation depending on how students see what influences it. For example, when students succeed, they could attribute that success to their effort, their ability, luck, or ease of the task. Of these, attributions to ability enhance self-perceptions, which can increase motivation. Attributions to effort also increase motivation, since the link between effort and success should encourage effort expenditure in the future. Attributions to luck or the ease of the task should decrease motivation because these are things that the students have no control over. Why try harder if your success is based on luck?

On the other side of the coin, failure can be motivating as long as the cause for failure is seen as something that one can change. Of the four causes listed earlier, only effort is something that students can do any-thing about. So if they attribute failure to their lack of effort, they'll be more motivated to try harder in the future. If they attribute failure to luck or task difficulty, their motivation would probably be unaffected or lowered because, again, these are things over which they have no con-trol.

The interesting attribution conundrum is what happens when suc-cess or failure is attributed to ability. Here an additional variable is thrown into the mix: whether ability is fixed or changeable. Students who believe in the entity perspective on ability—that ability is something that is fixed and cannot change—will be adversely affected by failure. If they fail and believe that failure is a function of their lack of ability, some-thing that cannot change, they are more likely to give up. If they fail and believe that ability is malleable, that it can be changed, they will con-tinue to try since increased effort is what might change ability (Dweck & Leggett, 1988).

The hopeful aspect to this interpretation of individual differences is that we believe these attributions can be changed. We can get students to focus on the impact of effort so that failures will result in renewed or improved effort. And we can get students to believe in their own ability and that they can improve it. The same strategies that encourage adop-tion of mastery goals are thought to influence attribution (Ames & Ames, 1991). When we focus on effort, give students choices so that they see how their choice affects the outcome, and base evaluation on improvement rather than comparison, students will begin to accept the idea that they can affect the outcome, which is what we mean by a change in attribution patterns. That belief also leads to the next individ-ual difference in motivation, self-efficacy.

Self-efficacy. Self-efficacy refers to an individual's belief that he or she is capable of succeeding in a given task or area (Bandura, 1997). I have a lot of self-efficacy with regard to teaching because I have a deep and broad knowledge base about it and a lot of positive feedback over the years from a wide range of students about my abilities in that area. I have very low self-efficacy with regard to sports (except tennis) because over the years I have not been very successful in sports or physical activities. My self-efficacy in tennis is so-so; sometimes I win, sometimes I lose.

What is important about the concept of self-efficacy is that it produces different behaviors in learners. Students seem to be more likely to adopt mastery goals when they set about a task in the area in which they have high self-efficacy. The behavior patterns are very similar. If you are self-efficacious, you are more willing to try new things, less concerned about making errors, more willing to assume that a little additional effort is all that you need to succeed. As a result of this attitude, you are probably more likely to persist, experiment, change strategies, and get more exposure time to a task. You are probably more likely to initiate a task and get into it rather than standing around trying to decide what to do.

The other good thing about self-efficacy is that it can change. As instructors, we can encourage student self-efficacy with regard to our class. When we plan in some initial successes, focus our feedback on progress made, give the students some control over their activities, and communicate high expectations and our confidence in the students' abilities to reach them, we are encouraging students to believe in their own ability to accomplish whatever we set before them. The belief might not last beyond the confines of the course, but it will help them until then.

One area that you might not relate to motivation but which psychology does is anxiety, and this is a big determiner of individual differences in performance. Every teacher is familiar with the effects of test anxiety on some students (maybe even themselves). This is the "state" interpretation of anxiety, meaning anxiety that is triggered by a situation, rather than the "trait" anxiety, which is called neuroticism and is a general characteristic of a person's functioning. This phenomenon is discussed in the chapter on motivation, so I'll just remind you that this is an area that produces trouble for a lot of students and could be a big source of individual differences in performance.

Chapter 7 on motivation suggested how instructors can use motivational theories to enhance student motivation, so I won't repeat them here. However, in almost all cases of motivational differences, student learning is being affected by the goals they set and how they see themselves in relationship to those goals. You will never overcome this area of individual difference by trying to find the one-size-fits-all solution. The instructor's best shot at motivating students is to help them find the relationship between their own goals and those of the course and to encourage them and support them in pursuit of those goals.

The Model of Domain Learning: A Synthesis

Interestingly enough, these three theoretically important components of individual differences in learning are borne out by research and model building of Patricia Alexander (1997) and her colleagues. She calls her synthesis the Model of Domain Learning (Alexander, 1997) and developed it both theoretically and empirically by looking at the clusters of students that emerged when a set of theoretically significant characteristics were measured and analyzed according to cluster analysis. This procedure results in groups of students who are most similar to one another and most different from students in other groups. The qualities of students in each group can then be characterized along the dimensions included. As a result of several experiments using a wide range of areas of knowledge and groups of students, Alexander has proposed three stages of development that an individual goes through in learning about an area of content: acclimation (where knowledge is accumulated), competence (where knowledge becomes organized around foundational principles), and expertise (where original contributions to the knowledge base become possible). Individuals move through these three stages because of transformation in the three dimensions of subject matter knowledge (prior knowledge), interest (motivation), and strategic processing (learning strategies). Differences in these three areas result in different clusters of students with differential probabilities of success at learning. Alexander refers to these clusters as profiles. For example, in one study, students who entered the class with a moderate level of subject matter knowledge and high interest were described as the learning-oriented group, and they were able to do pretty well on the test tasks. A second group, the strong knowledge group came in with a lot of prior knowledge but not much interest, and their performance was not as good as the learning-oriented group. A third group, the low profile group had the least prior knowledge, only moderate interest, and not much strategic use, and theirs was the lowest performance. Over the course of a semester, the students in this last group split into two subgroups: one that tried hard but were unsuccessful at deeper understanding and had to settle for more surface processing of the material (they could only reach the acclimated level of proficiency) and one that didn't put forth much effort at all and learned very little. Unfortunately, this last group was the largest in the final results. The findings of this research indicate that no one strength is sufficient to result in good performance; students need strengths in more than one area in order to succeed (Alexander, 1997). Alexander's work is supported by other researchers who found similar patterns. She suggests that a better understanding of how these individual differences are distributed in a class might help teachers target their instruction more specifically to help students develop in their weak areas.

OTHER PROPOSED AREAS OF DIFFERENCE

Although I've concentrated on aspects of individual differences that have a good basis in the literature and that instructors can use, many other difference dimensions have been proposed. These include personality, general ability or intelligence, stimulus mode preferences, and epistemological level. The first two of these are conceptualized as trait variables within the learner and not amenable to much intervention on the part of the instructor. Modal preferences have a lot of face validity but may be based on processing differences instead of sensory modality preferences. Nevertheless, those who propose we consider modal preferences offer suggestions to both instructors and students about how to deal with them. Epistemological level appears to be important for learning and instructional design, but is hard to pin down empirically. In general, instructors wouldn't be able to make many changes in these areas in the short time that we interact with the students. Mostly what we have to do with these dimensions is recognize them and design with them in mind. We'll look briefly at each of these areas just to raise awareness of them.

Personality Differences

This is a huge area in psychology, as you might expect, and it bleeds over into instruction because we are after all dealing with human beings and who they are makes a difference in all they do. One perspective on this connection (Schmeck, 1988a) proposes a model of how personality, motivation, and stage of development lead to a prevalent learning style, which in turn causes the learner to adopt a particular learning strategy in a given situation, which then leads to a learning outcome (Figure 8.2). For example, Schmeck connects stable introvert, intrinsic motivation, reflective, field-independent, internal locus of control, high self-confidence, highly individuated as a personality cluster with a deep processing learning style, which is characterized by learning strategies that involve conceptualizing, such as the learning tactics of categorizing, comparing and contrasting categories, hierarchically organizing ideas in networks, abstracting, which result in a learning outcome of synthesis and analysis, evaluation of conclusions, subsumption, schema development, theory development. He draws similar relational links between other personality clusters and the types of learning they support. I'm somewhat skeptical about these links because I believe that good learners select a learning strategy on the basis of the demands of the task rather than their personal tendencies. In fact, that's what we often mean by good learners in the first place. Perhaps this is a case where how good or flexible the learner is determines whether a personality model applies. Less flexible learners may be more influenced by their personality characteristics than other learners.

Figure 8.2
Interconnectedness of Style and Strategy
as Described by R. Schmeck (1988)

Personality → Learning style → Learning strategy → Learning tactics → Learning outcome

Stable introvert → Deep processing → Conceptualizing → Comparing → Synthesis and analysis

Researchers and theorists in cognitive theory rarely consult the personality literature and vice versa. However, extensive work (Ackerman, Kyllonen, & Roberts, 1999; Talbert & Cronbach, 2002) on redefining "aptitude" by several very prominent researchers in the field offers some insight into the possible connections. But as always, further research is needed.

Richard Snow and Talbert and Cronbach (2002) proposed a model laying out the constructs of mood that should influence learning. They related traits of temperament to personality factors and characteristic moods. For example, the five personality factors that find the most support in the literature are: 1) agreeableness, altruism, affection; 2) extroversion, energy, enthusiasm; 3) intellectual openness, originality, flexibility; 4) conscientiousness, control, constraint; and 5) neuroticism, negativism, anxiety. You can feel how these traits might impact learning, but, unfortunately, their impact has not yet been demonstrated satisfactorily (Talbert & Cronbach, 2002) and might be only indirectly related to learning through their influence on behavior.

Perhaps the biggest obstacle to researching this area further is the lack of reliable, valid instruments for measuring personality constructs. Several instruments are used widely for identifying types of learners, most prominently the Myers Briggs Type Indicator. Many studies of this instrument have yielded mixed results. In one particularly thorough analysis of its validity (Pittenger, 1993), it was found wanting. That reviewer states:

> There is insufficient evidence to justify the specific claims made about the MBTI. Although the test does appear to measure several common personality traits, the patterns of data do not suggest that there is reason to believe that there are 16 unique types of personality. Furthermore, there is no convincing evidence to justify that knowledge of type is a reliable or valid predictor of important behavioral conditions. (p. 483)

Perhaps more important for our purposes, however, is that this inventory and many other inventories based on personality theories are often used in inappropriate situations by individuals without the background to interpret them as cautiously as they should be interpreted.

We are wiser to stick with more targeted instruments that refer specifically to learning preferences—the MSLQ, the LASSI, the GAMES survey for better studying. By helping students clarify what they actually do when they're learning, we are better able to help them spot areas where they are not as well-balanced. However, use of a more broadly based instrument that is more reflective of style differences—the Kolb Learning Styles Inventory (Kolb, 1981)—is fairly effective at beginning the conversation about differences. It is also short, easy to score, and most people enjoy the process of describing their "type." This instrument asks individuals to rate how well a dozen statements describe their learning (see Figure 8.3 for a sample of items from the Kolb). The responses are tabulated and grouped along two dimensions: how an individual prefers to take in information (directly through experience or indirectly) and what the individual likes to do with information (apply it directly or reflect on it). The underlying model for the Kolb is the experiential learning cycle, which proposes that in learning we go through four phases: direct experience, reflection on the experience, creation of an abstraction to describe the experience, and testing of the abstraction in a new setting. Individuals are classified into four groups depending on their preferences for different parts of the cycle. These four groups then are described as preferring different instructional strategies. Nancy Dixon and I wrote a brief article about how instructors might use the experiential cycle to design instruction, but we did not emphasize the differences among learners (Svinicki & Dixon, 1987). Rather we suggested that fuller learning would occur if all learners went through the cycle each time they tackled a new area.

Figure 8.3
Sample Items From Kolb's Learning Style Inventory

When I learn:
I like to deal with my feelings.
I like to think about ideas.
I like to be doing things.
I like to watch and listen.
I learn best when:
I listen and watch carefully.
I rely on logical thinking.
I trust my hunches and feelings.
I work hard to get things done.

However, just as I cautioned earlier, instruments like the Kolb need to be accompanied with admonitions not to be too rigid or to expansive in applying the results. The group differences are not as well defined as one would like, and really skillful learners can tailor their learning strategy to the task at hand. There is not much an instructor can do to change personality differences among students, and without appropriate training it is dicey to get too involved with those differences anyway. It's best to simply recognize that there are differences and to vary instruction or offer choices as a way of dealing with them.

General Ability, Aptitude, Intelligence

Here is another huge area of work in psychology that comes to mind when we mention individual differences. Most of us feel that some students are just more intelligent than others. You truly don't want to get too far into this area; it is very complex, and there is little you can do about it anyway. It is best to concentrate on the differences in prior knowledge discussed earlier, because that is something you can work with. I introduce this area, however superficially, only in the interest of being thorough in discussing individual differences.

Returning to the research and theory on intelligence that we are most familiar with, the question is whether there is a set of traits that constitute intelligence or a general overall component representing intelligence across domains. Most recent versions of intelligence theory fall into three camps: a three stratum theory of aptitude, multiple intelligences theory, and the triarchic theory of intelligence. What follows is a general idea of each theory and what they might mean for you as an instructor.

The Three Stratum Theory of Aptitude: A Factor Analysis Approach

This theory is closer in content to the original meanings of intelligence as an individual's aptitude for learning. Proposed by Carroll (1993, 1996) and based on a wide range of studies, this model asserts that there are three levels of abilities:

- Stratum I: Specific skills representing different clusters of abilities, such as general sequential reasoning, induction, verbal language comprehension, memory span, visualization, and so on.
- Stratum II: Clusters of specific skills that have different properties from other clusters, such as fluid intelligence, crystallized intelligence, general memory and learning, and so on.

- Stratum III: General intelligence, which is what we think of as broadly based ability.

While interesting to psychologists, this theory doesn't offer much to classroom instruction except a conceptualization of the types of skills that might be considered part of overall intelligence ability and that might differentially affect the tasks we assign.

Multiple intelligences theory. This theory has had a lot of publicity since it was first proposed by Howard Gardner (1983) and for good reason. Through this particular theory, he asserts that it is wrong to think that there is only one kind of intelligence as usually represented in IQ tests and general intelligence theories. Rather, he proposed multiple ways in which individuals could excel and be intelligent. For example, many of the areas that are normally labeled as gifted, such as musical ability or physical ability he included as intelligences. He also classified areas such as interpersonal awareness and knowledge of self (intrapersonal awareness) as intelligences. He has in essence tried to raise the public's awareness of the complexity of the construct of intelligence. He suggested a set of very carefully thought out criteria by which an ability area could be classified as an intelligence. Those criteria included changes in the behavior associated with an intelligence when there was physical brain damage, the existence of savants and prodigies, a distinctive developmental sequence, and several other measures. Anything claiming to be an intelligence had to present evidence in each of these areas. The seven intelligences that he settled on were linguistic, spatial, logical-mathematical, bodily-kinesthetic, musical, interpersonal, and intrapersonal. Gardner believed that individuals excelled in one or more of these areas, but probably not all. In addition, all of them represented ways in which new knowledge could be represented in education.

More recently, he clarified his intended purpose for the multiple intelligences theory, which was to create deeper understanding from instruction by using multiple entry points into a concept along with multiple representations (Gardner, 1999). Although some might have interpreted this as playing to learners' strengths, I think that Gardner's intention was to help any learner reach a deeper level of processing by seeing a concept introduced and represented in multiple ways—a fairly different interpretation from the more popular ideas about letting an individual learn according to his or her strength. I also think it is a more justified and workable strategy for teaching. I think that's why he refers to this method as "multiple approaches to understanding©" and has copyrighted that phrase. Gardner proposes six ways to approach a topic, each favoring one or more of the intelligences: narrational (tell stories), quantitative/numerical (use statistics or numbers), foundational/existential (couch the topic in terms of large philosophical questions), aesthetic (use artistic materials), hands-on (use activities), and social (use group settings and methods). He suggests first that each instructor select a few highly significant topics on which to concentrate. These topics should be connected to the large themes of the discipline such that they give the learner a deeper structural understanding of the field. Then the instruction can introduce the topic by using one or more of the multiple intelligence modes. For example, you might tell a story or show a film for the narrational approach. Then the instruction segues to analogies and examples to deepen the understanding of the main concepts. The instruction cycles through the concepts using several different representational modes and spends a significant amount of time on each so that the students have a much better and broader understanding of it. Finally, demonstration of proficiency also takes many different modes so that the knowledge gained is flexible in its application. In this representation of Gardner's theory, the focus is not on how students differ, but on the recognition that learning can occur in many ways and that instruction should be varied accordingly. This conclusion is a much better way of thinking about how to acknowledge and use differences in learning.

The triarchic model of intelligence. The triarchic theory of intelligence is mostly concerned with how the components of intelligence work together (Sternberg & Ben-Zeev, 2001). Sternberg has suggested that there are three abilities in intelligence, represented by the way an individual interacts with the world. There is an analytic ability, which is used to understand and judge the outside world; a creative ability, which imagines or invents new ways of understanding or interacting with the outside; and a practical ability, which puts into practice what the other components develop. Sternberg also proposes three types of tasks we have to accomplish to function: we must understand and control our internal world; we must be able to use our past experience in present situations; and we must apply what we know to many different kinds of problems in the external world. You can see how the abilities would be put in play in these situations. There are a few other aspects to this theory, but the analytic/creative/practical aspects have the most to offer in terms of instruction. Sternberg believes we should broaden our educational system to help students achieve real gains in their abilities to cope with the world. He also believes we should change our assessment systems to allow a wider variety of students to succeed.

A more general perspective on intelligence. I'd like to add one more perspective on intelligence, one that I think is very important in the way we think about and use the concepts of intelligence, regardless of the theory. This is the question of whether intelligence is fixed or malleable. Original models of intelligence believed that you were born with a certain level of it and that level could not or did not change. Intelligence was the underlying factor in success and you were forever limited by the amount of intelligence determined by your genetic structure. Pitted against that view is the idea that intelligence is not a fixed quantity, but something that can be altered through experience and effort. These two views of intelligence or ability suggest very different approaches to instruction and learning. If you believe that intelligence is a fixed quantity (the entity theory), then effort on your part can only bring you up to the level determined by that quantity. Under this perspective, an instance of failure could signal that you have reached your maximum potential and can go no further. This is not a very motivating perspective.

Opposed to that perspective is the idea that intelligence is not a fixed, inborn level of potential, but an indication of what you have achieved so far (the incremental theory). Your potential changes as you gain more experience and exert more effort. Under this perspective, an error is a temporary state, that can be changed with more or different efforts. This perspective is motivating because it says you can get better.

Work in this area by Dweck and Leggett (1988) has shown that these two perspectives on ability produce very different behaviors in learners. Recalling the chapter on motivation, there is a big difference between learners who adopt performance versus mastery goals. One of the complicating factors is whether they also have an entity or an incremental view of intelligence or ability. In Dweck's analysis, individuals who have an incremental view of intelligence are also more likely to adopt a mastery orientation and engage in mastery type behavior patterns. For example, they will be willing to try new things (because that's how you increase your abilities) and they will be more likely to persist in the face of failure (because they don't take that as a sign of low ability). On the other hand, individuals who hold an entity view are more likely to have performance goal orientations. If at the same time they believe they have high intelligence, they will be convinced that they will be able to do a task eventually and will not be deterred by occasional setbacks. However, if they believe their ability is low, they are more likely to adopt a learned helplessness behavior pattern, such that they avoid challenge and give up at the first sign of failure. Some theorists expand this model to say that there is probably a continuum of beliefs that are specific to an ability area. For example, you might act like an entity believer about some of your skills ("I'm just not good at sports") and an incrementalist about other skills ("I'm learning to be more creative") (Pintrich & Schunk, 1996).

The same attitudes about ability and intelligence exist in instructors, of course, and can have great impact on how we respond to students. If we believe that our students are either smart or they're not, we're not as inclined to put forth the effort for those in the bottom half of the class. It would be viewed as wasted effort. If we believe that effort makes a difference in achievement, we may be more likely to think that almost all students can learn in our course; we just have to find the right mix of instructional methods. Our beliefs also can easily be communicated to our students, either intentionally or unintentionally, influencing the view of ability they adopt in our classes.

Why is this perspective important in instruction? Obviously, we want our students to believe that hard work and effort will eventually pay off. In order to believe that they must believe either that ability is incremental or that they have high ability. It is far easier for us as instructors to encourage the incremental view of ability than to convince all the students that they have high ability. We can do this through our words as well as our deeds. As noted earlier, if you talk about student work as if you believe they can do it, they are more likely to adopt that same attitude. If you also provide them with multiple ways to demonstrate and expand their understanding, they actually are more likely to succeed, thus reinforcing the belief that intelligence is not a fixed quantity, at least not in your class. If, when a student makes an error, you view it as an opportunity for him or her to learn something new, then you support the view that mistakes don't signal lack of ability, just lack of understanding. Indeed, these and all the other strategies designed to encourage students to adopt mastery goals (see Chapter 7 and the section on goal orientation earlier in this chapter) will help them change their perspective on ability, if only in your subject matter. They are definitely worth considering.

Epistemological Development Level

The last individual difference area that is worth discussing is based on the individual's cognitive development or epistemological development level—or the way an individual thinks about knowledge and how it is acquired or verified. Let me give an example that every instructor in higher education has experienced. We have all been in the position of giving a thorough presentation contrasting two theories, each explaining the same phenomenon, but with very different approaches. We finish and then ask if there are any questions, when a student raises his or her hand and asks the dreaded question, "But which one is the right one, Professor Smith?" Those of us in the social and behavioral sciences always give the same answer to this affront to advanced thinking: "It depends!"

The idea behind epistemological development is that learners have different beliefs about what it means for something to be right. One of the early researchers in this field was William Perry (1970). After studying college students for several years at Harvard University, he developed a four-stage theory of intellectual or epistemological development. He said that freshmen entered the university as dualists, believing that there was a right answer and a wrong answer and the authorities knew which was which. The students' responsibility was to find out what the authority knew and learn that. Unfortunately, in college, students are exposed to many "authorities" who sometimes disagree on what is correct, which confuses the students terribly. They change their beliefs about knowledge and truth to ones in which there are multiple possible truths, each of which is equally valid. Perry called this the multiplistic stage. Of course, we know that this particular stance is incorrect; that some answers are better than others, but it depends on the circumstances. When students learn this, they move up to the relativist stage of epistemology. Perry claimed that most students were at this stage when they graduated from Harvard, but that there was one more stage beyond that. This he called the relativist with commitment, because in this stage the individual is able to select a "truth" that works for him or her based on everything he or she has considered, while still acknowledging that others might differ in opinion.

From an instructional standpoint, where students are in their development will determine how they respond to instruction. Students in the dualist stage are waiting for the instructor to tell them what the correct answer is; multiplists will argue with the instructor and refuse to accept his or her word for it; relativists are capable of structuring an argument to fit any need; and relativists with commitment make wonderful dinner companions! The task of a college education is to help students move along the continuum.

Several other models of epistemological development make for very interesting reading (Baxter-Magolda, 1992; Baxter-Magolda, 2000; Hofer & Pintrich, 1997). Most of the work in this area derives from more qualitative research methods than the positivist methods that underlie the other theories in this book. Nevertheless, a great deal of high quality work being is done, and the results can be very informative with regard to teaching. In general, the individual differences identified in this area deal with beliefs about learning, and these can have a huge impact on students' approaches to learning. For example, Ormrod (1999) describes five beliefs about learning that many students hold, and I've paraphrased them below.)

1) The certainty of knowledge: Is knowledge an absolute, unchanging set of facts or does it change with circumstances?

2) The simplicity and structure of knowledge: Is knowledge composed of discrete facts or is there a cohesive structure to it?

3) The source of knowledge: Do we get what we know from outside experts or is it constructed from our own experiences and thinking?

4) The speed of learning: Does learning occur quickly or not at all? Or does it take a long time?

5) The nature of learning ability: Similar to the entity versus incremental theory of intelligence. Can you improve yourself? (p. 336)

What does this mean for teaching? It means that students are faced with the task of leaving behind their old ideas and trying out new ones, a difficult task even for adults. We must be prepared to recognize when students are operating under a belief that is hampering their growth (like believing that if they can't solve a problem immediately, they never will) and to help them see the alternative, higher level of complexity that makes for an educated adult. Ormrod (1999) reports that students who adopt the higher-level epistemological beliefs also tend to achieve more at the college level. Research shows that these beliefs change over time and with experience. It is important for us to model the higher cognitive levels we hope the students will achieve, to challenge the beliefs they hold now, and to support them as they try to understand a different way of thinking about knowledge. However, it is also important for us to realize that growth in these areas is slow and painful and requires many years and lots of experiences from different directions. Relatively few curricula are so well integrated that they can guide the students throughout their college years. One institution that has accepted that challenge and done an excellent job of it is Alverno College in Milwaukee, Wisconsin, a small liberal arts college for nontraditional female students. The book *Learning that Lasts* (Mentkowski, 2000) describes how the entire college—faculty, staff, and students—works together to foster long-term development in the students. It is a wonderful discussion of what might have to be done to produce the kind of epistemological development that we have always believed was the goal of higher education. Although we might not be able to replicate the results in our own institutions, we might aspire to them in our interactions with our students and thus produce some of the same type of long-term growth.

9

PUTTING IT ALL TOGETHER

Have I convinced you that there is a lot you can learn about learning and motivation? That was my goal when I began this book. Now that we've examined the dominant theories and research on learning and motivation, how does it all fit together in the end when it's time to design or redesign instruction? In this last chapter I'm going to show how the main theories can inform decisions about instruction in a very practical way by applying them to a hypothetical class, a freshman seminar class similar to those at almost all colleges and universities. I hope that this scenario can then serve as a memorable model about the interaction between theory and practice in education.

Let's begin with a brief description of the course. This freshman seminar has the following goals:

1) The students will know how to draw on the university's resources to work through questions of an academic nature.

2) The students will be able to raise a fairly complex question, research it, and write a well-documented and organized answer to it.

3) The students will be able to do the above in the area of introductory psychology—that is, they will be able to use the terminology and principles of basic psychology correctly in most contexts.

4) The students will be able to apply theories of psychology to explain everyday scenarios.

Each section of this course is an independent topic representing the area of expertise of the instructor assigned to teach it. Students are not required to participate in the program, but are allowed to choose a section on a topic of interest to them, if it is available. Individual sections of the course have a maximum of 18 students. They generally meet for two one-hour classes each week.

Given this basic description of the course, how would I use the theory-derived principles we've been talking about to design this course?

PRINCIPLE 1: EMPHASIZE A FEW KEY IDEAS

The first aspect of learning that should be addressed is the key ideas and skills that students will be expected to learn in this course. Cognitive theory says that we must be sure that the key ideas are highlighted and stressed in both the overall course and in each class session. The first and second objectives have a heavy component of skill learning since they are asking students to 1) use university resources to answer questions and 2) ask and research questions. The third objective is primarily a basic content objective—to learn the definitions and principles of psychology at the introductory level. The fourth objective is back to learning a skill because it requires students to apply what they've learned to everyday scenarios.

In order to plan the appropriate sequencing of instruction, these objectives must be broken down into finer components, like the steps in a procedure for using university resources or applying a given theory to a scenario. In the case of the content objective (objective 3), this breakdown would list the main theories, terms, and principles that the student should be able to use. Thinking along the lines of structural knowledge, I would probably want to create my own concept map relating the main theories to the scenarios they best fit. In order to increase the probability of transfer to other situations and within the course itself, I would want to determine whether a particular order of topics or skills needed to be followed. I would certainly be attuned to what future settings were likely to require the use of these principles. For example, if the class is very generic, with students from several disciplines, I would want to teach using a wide range of example situations. If all my students were going to be psychology majors, I would concentrate on more discipline-related examples.

PRINCIPLE 2: BE AWARE OF PRIOR KNOWLEDGE

Once I know where my class is going in terms of content and skills, I would like to learn about their prior knowledge. As you know, what they bring to the class will determine to a great extent what they take from it. I could probably get some idea about their prior knowledge from their incoming transcript. For example, have they had a psychology class before? Was that class here or at another school? (Another school might use different terminology or focus on different aspects of the content, thus influencing preparation and bias.) I should examine the contents of all the prerequisite classes for main ideas they should already know in some detail.

I might also be able to get some demographic information on the learners—such as gender, ethnicity, geographic origin, major, and previous educational institution—and speculate on their prior knowledge. Gender and ethnicity shouldn't matter too much except in the area of interests to pursue or prior knowledge about that area of psychology (e.g., female students may be more interested in pursuing gender-based areas of psychology, or they may have already done some reading in that area). Their geographic origin might provide some ideas about their upbringing and customs. Their major should be a good clue about interests and therefore motivations as well as related courses. For example, students interested in social sciences may have done reading in psychology already. The type of educational institution they previously attended could have significance for ease of learning and transfer from a similar situation. For example, if they already have some experience using university resources or a comparably complex system of information access from a previous institution, we might be able to build on that knowledge as they learn about this institution. On the other hand, there will undoubtedly be differences, and those, too, can be used to our advantage. Their old skill set can be contrasted with what they're being taught about this one in order to emphasize key skills.

Although some of this information would be available in their transcripts, a lot of the potentially more interesting information would need to be gathered directly from the students at the beginning of the semester. Therefore, I might want to prepare a background survey of key prerequisites or influential variables to administer on the first day. This information might help me decide how quickly I can move through the course or in what particular area I might want to focus.

PRINCIPLE 3: TAP INTO MOTIVATIONAL SOURCES

I should pay a little attention to motivation during the planning of the course, as well as early in the sequence. How much motivation will the learners bring to the course, and how much do I have to provide? As noted in the course description, this is not a required course; the students have chosen to enroll. That works in my favor in terms of the value they already place on the course content. Remember that task value is a key arm of the amalgamated theory from Chapter 7. I will want to emphasize connections between what we're learning and their own lives as another source of value for the content.

An advantage of early courses in psychology is that the order in which theories are studied is not that crucial. Thus, some choice might be built into the course sequence, allowing students to determine what we study when. This gives them some value based on self-determination. I could certainly do that with regard to the second objective about being able to research a question. Allowing the students to choose a topic for their question would give them some control, another source of motivation.

A disadvantage in this particular course is that these students, being freshmen, may have low expectations for success when they first enter the class. They will be on unfamiliar ground, which may cause some anxiety. Therefore, I'll want to do something to make them feel more efficacious. For example, starting with some simple assignments similar to what they had done in high school might help. I could then build on the simplicity of that initial assignment by increasing its complexity and pointing out the contrast between high school and college-level expectations. If we do this in a fairly low stakes environment at first, just for practice, and if they receive positive feedback as well as constructive criticism, they should begin to feel both the challenge and the possibility that they can succeed—a combination that should increase their motivation and lower their anxiety.

PRINCIPLE 4: BUILD STRUCTURAL KNOWLEDGE TO ACHIEVE UNDERSTANDING

Now it is time to establish the class content for real. I don't want the students to look on each theory in psychology as an independent entity with no interconnectedness so I want to build some structural understanding into the course. In this case, I have several options that all revolve around the same principle. The idea is to generate a set of questions that highlight the key components of any theory in psychology and that can be used to understand the basics of each theory. For example, every theory in psychology focuses on some aspect of human behavior and offers a mechanism by which that aspect of behavior is changed; thus, we'd want it to have a research base to support it, and we'd want to know its implications for everyday life. This set of questions can be a type of structural knowledge about psychology that would be highlighted in a chart that might look like Figure 9.1.

Figure 9.1
One Form of Structural Knowledge of Theories of Psychology

THE THEORY	What aspect of behavior is the focus of the theory?	How is behavior change explained according to this theory?	What is the research evidence supporting this theory?	How is this theory related to other theories studied?	What is the significance of this theory for explaining everyday life?
Behavior theory					
Cognitive theory					
Psycho-dynamic theory					

The students who can figure out what to put in the cells of this table will be accomplishing the third and fourth objective. The last column on this table could be the focus of the questions referred to in objective two. Students could choose to write their paper on something that fits in the "what is the significance" column. Having an opportunity to hear what other students have written about is a good way to make sure that everyone learns something about the significance of every theory. The fourth column encourages the students to make connections among the theories, which from a cognitive standpoint will make all the theories easier to recall and use in the future.

PRINCIPLE 5: STRUCTURE LEARNING TO SUPPORT ENCODING OF THE CONTENT

I can use this structural table as the format for studying each of the theories of psychology, and it would stay the same for all the theories studied. This regularity of inquiry would hopefully become the routine by which the students attack the study of any theory in psychology in the future. The table would be the encoding strategy, in this case both encoding based on organization and encoding based on elaboration. And to some extent the table supports visual encoding because the structure of the table itself provides retrieval cues for the information (i.e., there are five questions in five columns).

In class I could select for the first theory to be analyzed one that is not too difficult. This is a form of scaffolding in that I am picking a straightforward example to use first, thus holding off on some of the more difficult variables until the students have the table structure down pat. But once we have gone through this first theory as a group, I would want the students to be more actively in charge for the future theory analyses. So after the first theory has been used as a modeling opportunity (cognitive apprenticeship theory), the students choose the next theory and they are responsible for filling in the column cells for that theory by reading the textbook or other sources. This actively involves the learners in processing information at a deeper level because they are making the decisions and getting feedback on the consequences of their decisions. One way to organize this activity would be to have groups of students become the experts on different theories. Each group chooses a theory, explores the details of that theory by answering the questions in the table, and then presents its analysis to the rest of the class.

PRINCIPLE 6: USE MODELING TO TEACH SKILLS

Note that I start teaching the use of the table to analyze theories by having the whole class do the first one together. Presumably, I would lead this analysis and involve the students at appropriate points through questions and invitations to contribute. As I did so, I would be modeling the behavior (and attitudes) I wanted them to learn and talking aloud about the kinds of decisions involved in such an analysis. This is essentially the cognitive apprenticeship approach to teaching a skill.

Having the students work in groups on the other theories is another opportunity for modeling to occur. Making sure there is a range of students in each group increases the probability that some of the students will serve as models for the others on the parts they understood the best or enjoyed the most. The differences among the perspectives the students bring to the group allow them to experience the task through different eyes as they work on it together. This group work is also very fundamental to a constructivist approach to learning, especially a social constructivist approach.

This active involvement of the students in analyzing each theory is rife with possibilities for modeling. We can see examples of different ways to resolve disputes, approach a problem, deal with frustration, find information, work together, and the list goes on and on. Another benefit is that students become less dependent on the instructor as the source of all information, and thus they develop epistemologically.

PRINCIPLE 7: GIVE LOTS OF ACTIVE, COACHED PRACTICE

Now that the students are analyzing the theories, they are actively involved, which, as noted earlier, promotes deep processing. But another benefit of their active involvement is that it gives them opportunities to practice their understanding of our table system for analyzing theories in psychology and to receive feedback on their progress. The students will get feedback as the instructor focuses primarily on the accuracy of their analysis. They will receive feedback from the other students in their group and the other students in the class on the clarity with which they explain themselves. Remember that in the GAMES model of Chapter 6, the practice of explaining your ideas is a strong support for learning.

It would be nice if they could work on more than one theory so they have multiple opportunities to practice the analysis steps. This could be achieved by having each group work on each theory independently and then come together as a whole class and compare their analyses. The class as a whole could then fashion the best explanation of each theory.

This option might not be as strong from a motivational perspective as the original one proposed. When each group is responsible for teaching the whole class about their particular theory, there is a greater incentive to get it right than when everyone is eventually going to compare notes. So in this case I'd forego multiple theory practice for each group and stick to each group becoming the resident experts on a given theory.

PRINCIPLE 8: TEACH IN WAYS THAT PROMOTE TRANSFER

I actually had another reason for sticking to the one group–one theory approach. It sets the class up nicely for a transfer situation. Remember that in transfer we want the learners to be able to use their newly developed knowledge beyond the confines of the situation in which it was learned. In fact, this is the point of the final objective: to apply theories of psychology to explain everyday scenarios. We've now come to that part of the course plan.

To give the students lots of practice using their understanding of theory, I would present a series of case studies to which those theories could be applied. Since each group is now an expert in their particular theory, they would be asked to analyze the case from the perspective of that theory. Then as a whole class we would compare how different theories would approach each case. Because each group is the expert on its particular theory's explanation of the scenario, it should make for an interesting discussion. The best part is that it gives the students practice applying theories to different situations, an important component of transfer.

PRINCIPLE 9: HELP STUDENTS BECOME AWARE OF THEIR OWN LEARNING STRATEGIES

This principle is a more pervasive one that needs to be emphasized throughout the learning. The construction of the table itself is one way to help students become metacognitively aware of their learning. I might also ask them to reflect on what we did after the entire class completed the first example. Having them describe the steps we went through and the decisions we made brings that systematic process to their attention.

Then I could also require as part of anything they wrote about their theory an analysis of how they arrived at their conclusions. Self-reflection through journaling is a good strategy for helping students monitor their learning. Of course, I would have modeled self-reflection while doing the initial analysis in front of the class and hopefully emphasized my thinking and awareness of it.

PRINCIPLE 10: RESPECT INDIVIDUAL DIFFERENCES IN LEARNING

By respect, I don't just mean tolerance of differences. I mean building into the class some flexibility about how each student approached learning. For example, I might create the groups by putting together students who have complementary strengths or interests. A student who is good at writing might not be good at presenting and vice versa. Allowing the groups to present their analysis in different modes (visual, web-based, written, oral), allows preferences to be accommodated. Use of this approach would depend on how important it was that all the students in the class understand every theory.

There will be times when options are not an option. If everyone must learn each theory well, then there can't be too much flexibility in what is presented. Each presentation would have to include certain key components, no matter how the groups felt about it.

AND OVER AND OVER

The above thinking and decision process would occur at least twice more in the design of this freshman course, once for teaching the students how to ask and research a question, and again for teaching them how to use the university's resources. For example, I would have to identify the key skills and knowledge involved in using the university's resources. I would be well-advised to find out what the students already know, but more important what they don't know. As faculty we tend to think that everyone knows how to use the library, but differences in resources at high schools could have created a huge gap in student knowledge about researching. And lest we be too smug, information resources change so quickly these days that we aren't always up to date on all the possibilities. This work should be scheduled so as to maximize motivation. Learning about resources is best done just before they are needed, so instruction in using the library should occur around the time the students are about to work on their question of interest paper. I'd want to model using the resources, give them practice and coaching and feedback and be aware of transfer issues. Just as I'd stepped through all the principles when it came to the third and fourth objectives of the course, I would have to step through them with regard to the first and second objective of the course.

APPLYING THESE IDEAS TO OTHER EXAMPLES

I hope that you can glean the key ideas from this example from my own teaching and apply them to your situation. There will be differences, of course, in the actual implementation, but the principles are universal enough to inform any instructional design or redesign. To facilitate transfer of these ideas, I've created three typical course scenarios and shown how each of the principles would play out in them (Table 9.1). The three courses are an upper division undergraduate skills course such as statistics, a large undergraduate survey course such as government, and a graduate class in current disciplinary topics.

I've only briefly described how I might use the principles to generate ideas in each scenario. As in most complex situations like this, there is no one right answer, nor can all the possible options be fit into one small chart. I hope only to make the application of the principles clearer through a broader range of examples, and to stimulate your own thinking about applying the principles to your situation.

USING THE PRINCIPLES IN PROBLEM SOLVING

The principles of instructional design can also help if you get stuck with an instructional problem. I suggest turning them into a series of questions to ask yourself and then looking to the theories to help you think of ideas to solve your problems. Here are some examples.

1) How am I making clear the key points to learn? Are there too many? Are they inconsistent? Do the students need them in a different format or at a different point in their learning?

2) What have I assumed about student prior knowledge? Is it possible that they don't have some requisite skill or background information? How serious is this lack? How can I remediate it?

Table 9.1

Applying the Principles to Different Scenarios

Principle	Upper division undergraduate skills course, such as statistics	Large lower division undergraduate survey course, such as government	Graduate course in current topics in the discipline
1) Key ideas	Classify analyses by type of situations. Highlight key measures that go across statistical methods.	Keep number of points down in a class period. Highlight visually, verbally. Provide outline notes or study guide.	Emphasis is on process steps for critiquing research. Students generate topics, specifics.
2) Prior knowledge	Point out everyday uses. Assess prior experience with similar math.	Know prerequisite course content. Use broad present examples. Use asides and elaborations to give common background. Give beginning of semester survey.	Respect variety of experience. Respect professional expertise of students. Students may have more self-knowledge.
3) Motivation	Give examples of everyday use. Follow statistics with case example. Move beyond number crunching to the interesting stuff.	Use broad examples. Use current events. Use student opinion surveys to contrast with research data.	Tie into professional experiences. Give more choice and control. Treat as colleagues in training.

continued on page 232

	Use computers to do the above. Low self-efficacy and math anxiety are likely.	Keep up with student interests.	Use of role models, self, and others.
4) Encoding	Keep symbols constant across measures to ease encoding. Help develop mnemonics for things that have to be memorized. Reduce necessity of memorization through "cheat" cards.	Provide mnemonics when memorization is needed. Use visual images to support encoding. Have students provide their own elaboration. Provide outline notes to be filled in.	Relate specifics to the professional needs of students. Have students generate their own applications.
5) Structure	Compare statistics across situations. Create key questions to use in deciding on statistic.	Provide a concept map that overviews the content. Use progressive disclosure when presenting ideas. Include essay questions based on underlying concepts to encourage synthesis.	Have students generate the structural relationships. Have students compare different structures that are used in the discipline.
6) Modeling	Instructor should model while thinking aloud.	Be enthusiastic in class.	Create the process model. Use student groups to discuss the material.

	Use students as models.	Use popular culture figures and events.	Use self-disclosure by the instructor on interest and questions about content.
	Use group work in problem solving.	Provide personal referents for key ideas from your own experiences.	
	Provide lots of practice problems with explanations.		
7) Practice with coaching	Use lots of practice problems with explanations.	Ask questions inclass. Use think-pair-share model.	Think of the class as a learning community.
	Use group problem solving.	Have online practice quizzes.	Learn along with the students.
	Create a list of common errors and their origins and solutions.	Give group instead of individual feed-back.	Use group work.
8) Transfer	Use real data for practice.	Create meaningful transitions between ideas.	Use case studies to apply ideas.
	Teach "when" to use statistics by comparative case studies.	Model transfer by bringing in current events and uses of content.	Use student generated cases based on their own experiences.
9) Self-regulation	Administer survey of learning strategies.	Teach study strategies to use with the text, test, note taking.	Students may already be more self-aware, or their habits may be too ingrained.
	Help students develop emotional control for anxiety.	Have students reflect on test performance for extra credit.	Offer constructive feedback.
			Use peer feed-back.

continued on page 234

10) Individual differences	Provide different ways to learn.	Use variety in the presentation of information.	Recognize and use differences in experience.
	Acknowledge differences in math background.	Allow different ways to demonstrate proficiency.	Allow students to select their own strategies.
	Recognize difference between analytical and holistic learners. Provide overview for the latter.	Provide variety of ways to get help.	Build in self-reflection opportunities to enhance self-awareness.

3) What do the students think about why they're learning this content? Do they see its value? How can I make it more intrinsically valuable? Or do I need to impose extrinsic value on it? Do they have doubts about their ability to learn this material? Have I contributed to those doubts? What can I do to reassure them or help them? Can I give them any more control over their own fates?

4) Are there aspects of this content that have to be memorized? Are there ways to organize this material to make it more memorable? What examples, analogies, or metaphors would help make this content easier to remember? Can I create mnemonics or other tricks to help the students memorize the less meaningful parts? Do I help the students see the difference between memorization and real learning?

5) What is the structure of this material? How do the main points fit together? Is that obvious to the students? Is there a way of representing this structure in more than one format?

6) Am I demonstrating the skills I expect the students to master? Are all the steps clear and visible? Are there too many parts? Does the demonstration need to be done in smaller chunks?

7) Am I giving the students opportunities in class to practice the skills I want them to learn so they can get immediate feedback? Am I giving them enough feedback? Clear feedback? Timely feedback? Can they help one another?

8) Do I present the skills or knowledge in the context in which the students will eventually use it? How can I make the learning situation more realistic? Do the students understand when and where they should use this content?

9) Are there strategies for learning this content that would make students' load easier? What kind of strategies are the students using? Are they good or poor? Can I give them more opportunities to reflect on their learning?

10) What are the individual differences variables that are most likely to impact learning this material? Are some students more at risk than others? Can I help them? How can I vary my instruction to compensate for differences in learner preferences and strengths?

If you find yourself asking these questions, think back to the various models that I've discussed in this book. Within their structure you might find an answer to your dilemma.

To Go Further

Obviously, this book does not cover all there is to know about learning and motivation. I urge you to consider going further and reading in more depth. Any good introductory educational psychology book will provide much detail. The National Research Council's books on learning, (Bransford, Brown, & Cocking, 1999; Druckman & Bjork, 1994), and other general reference books are also quite helpful. Not a lot of journals provide easy access to this kind of analysis, but I'm pleased to say that the series *New Directions for Teaching and Learning* (which I edit) tries very hard to strike a balance between theory and practice similar to that found here. Some newsletters like the *National Teaching/Learning Forum* do a good job of bridging the gap between research/theory and practice. Most faculty development centers around the country have libraries of good books on learning such as those included in the references of this book. The professionals at such centers can help you find additional material on any of the topics contained in this book. If you want to strike out and read the research itself, journals like *Educational Researcher* are accessible to nonspecialists. The many good references throughout the chapters here should also be helpful in your desire to go further.

I only ask that you do try to go further, to educate yourself about learning and motivation. I believe that only through really understanding the principles behind the learning you see in your students will you be able to make them and yourself as efficient as you can be at what is a very complex task. The theorists and researchers in these areas will continue to look for better ways of understanding learning and motivation and translating those into practical strategies to help both you and your students.

APPENDIX

THE THEORIES IN A NUTSHELL

This appendix summarizes the key theories in learning and motivation that are behind the strategies presented in this book. These short descriptions are a good start toward understanding the more detailed theories that shape thought and practice in psychology today. For a more complete explanation of various theories, I recommend the following:

For Learning Theories

Halpern, D. F. (1996). *Thought and knowledge: An introduction to critical thinking* (3rd ed.). Mahwah, NJ: Lawrence Erlbaum.

Langer, E. J. (1997). *The power of mindful learning.* Reading, MA: Addison-Wesley.

Ormrod, J. (2002). *Human learning* (4th ed.). Upper Saddle River, NJ: Prentice-Hall.

Schunk, D. H. (2000). *Learning theories: An educational perspective.* Upper Saddle River, NJ: Prentice-Hall.

For Motivation Theories

Pintrich, P., & Schunk, D. H. (1996). *Motivation in education: Theory, research, and application.* Englewood Cliffs, NJ: Merrill/Prentice-Hall.

And now the theories in a nutshell.

LEARNING THEORIES

Cognitive Theory (or Information Processing Theory)

The primary focus of this theory is how information gets processed, stored, and retrieved from long-term memory. The unit of interest is the change in long-term memory storage rather than external behavior. (For comparison, in behavioral theories of learning, the external behavior is believed to be a manifestation of what is stored in memory as influenced by the current situation.)

In the cognitive model of learning, information comes in from the environment and stimulates the sensory registers (one for each sense), which are temporary holding cells in which the stimulus remains until it is either processed or new information comes into the same sense and pushes the previous stimuli out before they can be processed. If the learner pays attention to the stimulus in a register by focusing on it, that information will move into working memory to be processed for storage. Working memory is similar to what we think of as consciousness. It holds the limited amount of information that we can work with in a given time period. If too much information tries to crowd into working memory, something will be squeezed out. Working memory is also limited in duration, so information won't stay there long unless the learner does something to keep the memory fresh, like repeating it over and over (called rehearsal). While in working memory, incoming information is compared with what already exists in long-term memory. If there is a match, the learner recognizes the new information as similar to the old and attaches it to that old storage link (this is called perception). If the new information doesn't match anything encountered before, the learner has to make a new category to store this new information. Knowledge stored in long-term memory is dispersed and interconnected. What really gets stored is the gist of the incoming information rather than an exact copy. Different aspects of that gist are connected with different previously stored information. To retrieve the information from long-term memory, one needs a retrieval cue that stimulates the new information directly or stimulates something else connected to it. There are many ways we think of memory storage. Memories can be of specific events (called episodic memories) or general knowledge (semantic memories). They can be in verbal form (like a word or description) and/or visual form (like a picture). Knowledge stored in long-term memory can be of facts (called declarative knowledge) or processes (called procedural knowledge) or conditions (conditional knowledge, when something applies).

The most important part of long-term memory is the interconnectedness of what is stored there. The more connections that a learner has for a given bit of information, the more meaningful it is. The more meaningful, the easier to remember (retrieve). Therefore, the goal of learning is to create meaningful connections among information through the process of encoding. This is done by presenting new information in an organized fashion that emphasizes the relationships of ideas to one another (structural knowledge). Presenting more details (elaboration) and vivid images (imagery) are also strategies for better encoding. Once information has been encoded and stored in long-term memory, it should be retrieved frequently so that new associations and more practice with existing associations can strengthen the connections. At another level of learning, learners can become aware of their own thought processes and thereby exercise some control over them. This is the process of metacognition, and it involves the learner in directing how his or her own learning occurs.

The significant points of instructional intervention in this theory.

1) Attention—Instructors can see to it that the learners attend to the important ideas.

2) Working memory—Instructors can arrange for ideas to be present simultaneously in working memory by presenting them in close temporal or physical proximity to make the link. Instructors also need to be careful about the limits in capacity and duration of working memory so it doesn't get overloaded.

3) Encoding—Instructors should present new information in ways that encourage students to see connections between ideas, to provide their own examples and elaborations on those ideas, and to create visual images as well as verbal descriptions of the information. Although instructors can do this for students, learning is better if the learners make their own associations.

4) Long-term memory storage—Instructors should know what prior knowledge the learners already have in long-term memory in order to build on what's there or counter incorrect information that might have been learned before. Helping learners create a structural understanding of content provides the most solid foundation for learning.

5) Retrieval and active processing—Instructors should give the learners multiple, varied opportunities to practice what has been learned so storage connections can be strengthened.

6) Metacognition—Learners can become aware of and control their own learning when they are taught about metacognition strategies, such as self-monitoring, self-correcting, self-evaluation, and other goal-directed thinking. Instructors should make learners aware of these control processes by articulating them and offering practice in them.

Concept Learning Theory (a Subset of Cognitive Theory)

Knowledge is retained in the form of concepts, which are "labeled sets of related characteristics of objects, symbols, or events that share common characteristics" (Schunk, 2000, pg. 184). Concept learning theory is our beliefs about how those concepts are formed. The process is extremely important since all learning revolves around creating concepts. Concept learning involves identifying the key characteristics of the concept so that when future instances are encountered they can be accurately identified. The process involves comparing positive and negative instances of the concept in order to focus in on what the positive instances have in common that the negative instances don't.

Significant points of instructional intervention in this theory.

1) Definition of the concept—The instructor can hasten the process by providing a clear definition of the concept at the beginning of learning. Later, it is useful if the learners can articulate the definition themselves.

2) Key examples—The instructor needs to provide examples that are clearly positive examples of the concept during the

initial learning. These later become the benchmarks against which learners compare future instances.

3) Positive and negative instances—The instructor should contrast examples of the concept with other examples that are not related to the concept. The sequencing of example comparisons can help eliminate dependence on irrelevant features and help the learners focus on the key features that truly define the concept. It helps if these comparisons are done simultaneously rather than successively, probably due to working memory constraints.

Social Cognitive Theory (Formerly Social Learning Theory)

This theory was originally proposed as a contrast to behavior theory, in which all attention is focused on the overt, observable behavior that a learner displays. Behaviorists give little attention to the thinking behind the behavior because they believe that the learning is a consequence of behavior. Social cognitive theory asserts that there are other ways to learn and other forces that influence behavior. Specifically, this theory posits that learners learn a great deal by observing. They observe models engaging in behaviors, which they then duplicate. They observe the consequences that those models experience, which influence their own likelihood of engaging in that behavior. (Seeing someone else get rewarded for a response increases our likelihood of making the same response in anticipation of getting the same reward.) Social cognitive theory is based on the idea that there is mental activity that mediates the interaction between the learner and the environment. When observing a model, the learner creates a mental representation of the behavior seen and then can use that mental model to later reproduce the behavior. The environment then reinforces or punishes that response, which in turn influences future occurrences. This interaction between the learner's mental representations and interpretations, the overt behavior, and the environmental consequences determines future occurrences of that behavior.

Significant points for instruction in this theory.

1) Models are used as ways of showing learners how to engage in the response to be learned. Models can be live, represen-

tations, instructions, or other forms of depiction. The learner's probability of learning from a given model is a function of the characteristics of the model as well as the learner's goals and motivations.

2) The consequences to the model will influence learner behavior. If a model is reinforced for the behavior, the learner is more likely to engage in that behavior. Therefore, instructors should arrange for learners to see the positive consequences of the behaviors they are trying to teach.

3) In order for a behavior to be learned through observation, it must be observable. Therefore, instructors need to be sure that the key steps in any target behavior are made observable to the learners, including the thinking that is going on.

4) The learner characteristics that influence the ability and propensity to learn from a model are the learner's level of development and ability to create mental models, his or her motivations, and his or her belief that the behavior is doable. The latter is called the learner's self-efficacy, and it must be moderately high to ensure that modeling occurs.

Constructivist Theory (Another Refinement of Cognitive Theory)

Constructivist theories (there are several) are all related to cognitive theory in that they focus on the mental representation of information by the learner. They do not focus on the overt behavior that is the manifestation of that representation. They differ from early cognitive theory in the degree to which they assert that the learner is engaging in reconstruction of long-term memory representations of external events and the degree to which those representations are accurate reflections of the environment. The primary controversy around constructivism is the relationship between the learner's construction of reality and the reality itself. Some constructivists hold that all of a learner's constructs of reality are unique because they are a result of that specific learner's experiences and prior knowledge. No two learners can have the exact same constructs, and a teacher cannot impose a construction of reality on a learner, almost by definition. Other theorists believe that there is an external reality and that the learner's representation of that reality can coincide with it and with others' constructions, and, as a result, it is possible for a teacher to mold a learner's construction. For constructivist theorists, instruction needs to be focused on the learner's questions and ideas. In fact, a strict constructivist would say that no matter what the instructor does, the learning will derive from the learner's questions and ideas. If the teacher is lucky, those ideas and questions will be similar to what the teacher intended; if not, there's not much that can be done about it.

The processes involved in learning in the constructivist model are like those in the cognitive model. The difference lies in who is creating the construction: the learner or the environment (teacher, classroom, materials, etc.). Constructivist methods put the learner at the center of the process and in the driver's seat. Learning will follow the path dictated by the learner's activities. The best instructional methods in constructivist classrooms are based on student discovery and active interaction with the environment and among students. It is in the context of those activities that the learner forms his or her construction of reality from the experiences.

A more radical form of constructivism is social constructivism, which places a couple of additional restrictions on instruction and learning. First, social constructivists place a very strong emphasis on the development of understanding through dialogue and interaction with other learners. Learners are said to negotiate meaning or refine their understanding by contrasting their perspectives with those of other learners and the teacher. Learning comes about as the learners change their world views in response to the views of others. The second, and more radical, version says that meaning lies not in the individual learner's interpretation of the situation, but in the collective understanding that we achieve as we experience the world together. Constructivist theory is very similar to social cognitive theory in its assertion that learning is an interaction between the learner, the environment, and the behavior to be learned.

Significant points of instructional intervention in this theory.

1) Active construction of understanding by the students—The instructor needs to step out of the center of the activity around learning and allow the students to experience the environment directly. It is through these experiences that the learner creates a world view.

2) Problem-based learning in authentic environments with authentic questions—The instructor structures the classroom around real problems representing fundamental concepts and skills. Learning in authentic environments is the only way that learners will have the full picture of what they are learning. The classroom is an artificial or at least a different environment.

3) Authentic testing—Because the environment is an integral part of the learner's construction of understanding, any form of assessment must be done in that authentic situation. To give pencil and paper tests of active learning concepts is contrary to the principles of constructivist teaching.

4) Roles of teacher and students change—Instructors in a constructivist class are not authorities and sometimes not even resources. They are more likely to be viewed as fellow learners, but more advanced in their strategies and abilities. Students learn from observing the teacher learning as well.

MOTIVATION THEORIES

Expectancy Value Theory

In this theory, motivation level is a function of the value that the learner places on whatever is being learned and the expectancy for success at that learning. Both value and expectancy must be present in a situation for the learner to have any motivation to continue with the task.

Value is influenced by such things as novelty and variety, challenge (but not too much), complexity, utility, degree of learner control, and a tie-in with the learner's ultimate goals. Value also can be externally influenced—for example, by the promise of rewards or approval if the learning is completed.

Expectancy is influenced by the learner's past experiences in the area (success or failure), by his or her beliefs about the difficulty level of the task, by his or her general self-confidence, by what others say (encouragements or warnings), by beliefs about what causes success or failure, and by other environmental variables present.

Significant points of instructional intervention in this theory.

1) Increase the value of the learning to the learner—Instructors can manipulate the tasks to make them more valuable to the learner as a way of increasing motivation. However, it is important to get the learner to believe that the choices being made are under his or her control, if possible. Otherwise motivation will be damaged.

2) Increase the learner's self-efficacy with regard to this task—Instructors can manipulate the success probabilities by starting with simpler tasks and building to more complex ones, by helping learners remember past successes and related skills, and by encouraging accurate assessments of the learner's capabilities. Focusing on smaller, more immediate goals makes success more likely and can help the learner begin to believe in eventual success at the whole task.

Attribution Theory

In this theory, an individual's level of motivation is tempered by his or her explanations of the causes of behavior outcomes. In general, individuals seek to maintain an image of competence and avoid that which threatens that image. As a result, they want to take credit for good things that happen to them and avoid the blame when things go wrong. They attribute their success or failure to various causes in an attempt to understand and master their world. In the original theory, the causes of outcomes that a learner would perceive at work were ability, effort, luck, task difficulty, outside intervention by others, health, mood, and so on. These causes had certain characteristics revolving around the dimensions of locus of control, stability, and controllability. For example, the cause of an outcome could be something attributable to the learner's actions or qualities (internal locus) or to the actions of others (external locus). If the cause was internal, the learner would possibly be in a position to do something about it and therefore might be motivated to try. If the cause was external, there might be nothing the learner could do to change things, and therefore he or she would not be motivated to try.

The stability dimension referred to whether the conditions were likely to change. For example, physical characteristics such as height are stable once adulthood is reached. They are not likely to change. Therefore, the learner might as well not try to change anything and would not be motivated to try. But if change can happen, is it controllable? For example, luck is unstable (likely to change) but uncontrollable, whereas health is also likely to change but is controllable to some extent. If control is possible, the individual might be motivated to attempt to exercise that control.

The theory also asserts that individuals are often characterized by a particular explanatory style. For example, some students exhibit an external locus of control—they believe their fate is always in the hands of others—while other students feel they are always responsible for what happens to them. Although it might seem that adopting an internal locus of control is desirable, what we really should strive for is appropriate attributions. Accept responsibility when you have control and don't take responsibility for things that are beyond your control.

Significant points of instructional intervention in this theory.

1) Help students make the connection between the choices they make and the outcomes of those choices. A good way to do this is to encourage student reflection on their work.

2) Avoid making attributions as a teacher that do not necessarily have a base in real data. We are all subject to attributional bias at times, but instructors must lead the way in terms of modeling appropriate attributions.

3) Give accurate feedback to students, being neither too kind nor too critical. Help them develop good skills at evaluating their own work by modeling constructive criticism and how to respond to it.

Achievement Goal Orientation Theory

In this theory, individuals approach goals with different outcomes in mind. In general, the theories talk about two different approaches to goals: mastery versus performance goals. Individuals who exhibit a mastery goal orientation have as the ultimate outcome mastery of the skill and a focus on learning. Conversely, the desired outcome of individuals who exhibit performance goal orientation is to demonstrate ability or to do better than others. These two orientations result in very different behaviors and attitudes. When adopting a mastery orientation, individuals are more willing to take a chance at something that is difficult if it will help them learn more quickly or reach a higher level of achievement. Because they are more likely to take chances, they also are more willing to take a chance on making mistakes. For individuals with a mastery orientation, mistakes are seen as opportunities to learn rather than indictments of them as individuals. They don't mind putting forth additional effort because they don't interpret that as evidence of their lack of ability. Rather they take pride in the fact that they are trying to get better. They are also more willing to ask for help because they don't interpret this as a sign of weakness.

Individuals with performance orientations have a very different approach to the situation. Their goal is to demonstrate competence or at least to appear competent. Therefore, they are unlikely to take risks but prefer to stay with tasks they know they can do. For them, mistakes are an indication of lack of ability and are to be avoided or hidden. This keeps them from seeking help if they run into trouble. They tend to use surface learning strategies rather than putting forth the effort needed to process information deeply. In fact, they take having to put forth effort as a sign of lack of ability.

Although the original versions of these theories pitted these two orientations against one another as if an individual had one or the other approach all the time, more recent thinking says that an individual can display both mastery and performance goals even within the same situation. This is a much better reflection of reality.

Significant points of instructional intervention in this theory.

1) Encourage students to adopt a mastery orientation with regard to their studies by emphasizing progress rather than comparison with others.

2) Try to give evaluation that is focused on how they can improve and do it in a private manner if possible.

3) Through your attitude, demonstrate that mistakes are opportunities to learn.

4) Give students some measure of choice and control to allow them to work at their own pace and to feel they are in control of their work.

Self-Determination Theory

In this theory, individuals are seen as being most highly motivated when they perceive themselves to be in control and operating autonomously. Indeed, this desire to be in control is one of many basic human needs, and is one of the bases for intrinsic motivation. Tasks are intrinsically motivating if they help fulfill this need for autonomy and competence. In the expanded version of self-determination theory, motivation occurs at several levels of internalization. Beginning with total extrinsic motivation, the perceived locus of control in some situations is totally in the hands of others. For example, when one is paid for a job, the motivation is extrinsic. However, an individual can begin to focus on doing a good job in order to obtain the approval of others, regardless of pay. At this level, the motivation is called introjected motivation. It is less extrinsic because it is more in the perception of the individual but still based on what others think. At the next level of internality, called identification, an individual begins to adopt the values of the others who used to provide the extrinsic motivation. He or she begins to express the goals as things of value without respect to the opinions of others. Eventually, the individual integrates the values of society into his or her own value system, which is a form of intrinsic motivation. The goal of socialization in a community is to have the individual reach this level of integration with regard to the values of that community.

Significant points of instructional intervention in this theory.

1) Give the learners opportunities to make choices among the alternative ways to learn in the class.

2) Give the learners some control over their work.

3) Model the values that you wish students to adopt and base your policies and feedback to them on those values. Support them when they begin to exhibit behaviors consistent with those values.

As you might expect, there is much more to be learned about each of these theories. These thumbnail sketches may give you enough of a feel for them to be able to use them in making instructional decisions. They also may intrigue you enough to motivate you to look into them more fully.

BIBLIOGRAPHY

Ackerman, P. L. (1999). Traits and knowledge as determinants of learning and individual differences. In P. L. Ackerman, P. Kyllonen, & R. Roberts (Eds.), *Learning and individual differences: Process, trait and content determinants* (pp. 473–460). Washington, DC: American Psychological Association.

Ackerman, P. L., Kyllonen, P., & Roberts, R. (Eds.). (1999). *Learning and individual differences: Process, trait, and content determinants.* Washington, DC: American Psychological Association.

Alexander, P. (1992). Domain knowledge: Evolving themes and emerging concerns. *Educational Psychologist, 27*(1), 33–51.

Alexander, P. (1997). Mapping the multidimensional nature of domain learning: The interplay of cognitive, motivational, and strategic forces. In M. L. Maehr & P. Pintrich (Eds.), *Advances in motivation and achievement* (Vol. 10, pp. 213–250). Greenwich, CT: JAI Press.

Alexander, P., & Murphy, P. K. (1998). Profiling the differences in students' knowledge, interest, and strategic processing. *Journal of Educational Psychology, 90*(3), 435–447.

Ames, C. , & Ames, R. (1991). Motivation and effective teaching. In L. Idol & B. Jones (Eds.), *Educational values and cognitive instruction: Implications for reform* (pp. 247–296). Hillsdale, NJ: Lawrence Erlbaum.

Anderson, C., & Roth, K. (1989). Teaching for meaningful and self-regulated learning of science. In J. Brophy (Ed.), *Advances in research on teaching* (Vol. 1, pp. 265–306). Greenwich, CT: JAI Press.

Angelo, T., & Cross, P. (1993). *Classroom assessment techniques.* San Francisco, CA: Jossey-Bass.

Atkinson, R., & Raynor, J. (1978). *Personality, motivation, and achievement.* Washington, DC: Hemisphere.

Ausubel, D. (1960). The use of advance organizers in the learning and retention of meaningful verbal materials. *Journal of Educational Psychology, 51,*
267–272.

Bandura, A. (1986). *Social foundations of thought and action: A social cognitive
theory.* Englewood Cliffs, NJ: Prentice-Hall.

Bandura, A. (1997). *Self-efficacy: The exercise of control.* New York, NY: W. H.
Freeman.

Baxter-Magolda, M. B. (1992). *Knowing and reasoning in college: Gender related
patterns in students' intellectual development.* San Francisco, CA: Jossey-Bass.

Baxter-Magolda, M. B. (Ed.). (2000). *Teaching to promote intellectual and personal maturity: Incorporating students' worldviews and identities into the learning process.* San Francisco, CA: Jossey-Bass.

Bereiter, C., & Scardamalia, M. (1985). Cognitive coping strategies and the
problem of "inert knowledge." In S. Chipman, J. Segal, & R. Glaser (Eds.),
Thinking and learning skills (Vol. 2, pp. 65–80). Hillsdale, NJ: Lawrence Erlbaum.

Beyer, B. K. (1997). *Improving student thinking: A comprehensive approach.*
Boston, MA: Allyn and Bacon.

Biggs, J. (2001). Enhancing learning: A matter of style or approach? In R. J.
Sternberg & L.-f. Zhang (Eds.), *Perspectives on thinking, learning, and cognitive styles* (pp. 73–102). Mahwah, NJ: Lawrence Erlbaum.

Borkowski, J., Carr, M., Rellinger, E., & Pressley, M. (1990). Self-regulated
cognition: Interdependence of metacognition, attributions, and self-
esteem. In B. Jones & L. Idol (Eds.), *Dimensions of thinking and cognitive
instruction* (pp. 53–92). Hillsdale, NJ: Lawrence Erlbaum.

Bransford, J., Brown, A., & Cocking, R. (Eds.). (1999). *How people learn.*
Washington, DC: National Academy Press.

Bransford, J., & Schwartz, D. (1999). Rethinking transfer: A simple proposal
with multiple implications. In A. Iran-Nejad & P. D. Pearson (Eds.),
Review of Research in Education, 24 (pp. 1–30). Washington, DC: AERA.

Bransford, J., Vye, N., Kinzer, C., & Risko, V. (1990). Teaching thinking and
content knowledge: Toward an integrated approach. In B. Jones & L. Idol
(Eds.), *Dimensions of thinking and cognitive instruction* (pp. 381–414). Hillsdale, NJ: Lawrence Erlbaum.

Brookfield, S. (1995). *Becoming a critically reflective teacher.* San Francisco, CA:
Jossey-Bass.

Brooks, L. W., & Dansereau, D. F. (1983). Effects of structural schema training and text organization on expository prose processing. *Journal of Educational Psychology, 75*(6), 811–820.

Carroll, J. (1993). *Human cognitive abilities: A survey of factor-analytic studies.* New York, NY: Cambridge University Press.

Carroll, J. B. (1996). A three-stratum theory of intelligence: Spearman's contribution. In I. Dennis & P. Tapsfield (Eds.), *Human abilities: Their nature and measurement* (pp. 1–17). Mahwah, NJ: Lawrence Erlbaum.

Chi, M., & Bassok, M. (1989). Learning from examples via self-explanations. In L. Resnick (Ed.), *Knowing, learning, and instruction: Essays in honor of Robert Glaser* (pp. 251–282). Hillsdale, NJ: Lawrence Erlbaum.

Chinn, C. (1998). A critique of social constructivist explanations of knowledge change. In B. Guzzetti & C. Hynd (Eds.), *Perspectives on conceptual change: Multiple ways to understand knowing and learning in a complex world* (pp. 77–115). Mahwah, NJ: Lawrence Erlbaum.

Chinn, C., & Brewer, W. (1993). The role of anomalous data in knowledge acquisition: A theoretical framework and implications for science instruction. *Review of Educational Research, 63*(1), 1–49.

Collins, A., Brown, J., & Newman, S. (1989). Cognitive apprenticeship: Teaching the crafts of reading, writing, and mathematics. In L. Resnick (Ed.), *Knowing, learning, and instruction: Essays in honor of Robert Glaser* (pp. 453–494). Hillsdale, NJ: Lawrence Erlbaum.

Corkill, A. (1992). Advance organizers: Facilitators of recall. *Educational Psychology Review, 4,* 33–67.

Corno, L. (1993). The best-laid plans: Modern conceptions of volition and educational research. *Educational Researcher, 22*(1), 14–22.

Corno, L. (2000). Conceptions of volition: Studies of practice. *International Journal of Educational Research, 33*(7–8), 659–663.

Covington, M. V. (1992). *Making the grade: A self-worth perspective on motivation and school reform.* Cambridge, England: Cambridge University Press.

Csikszentmihalyi, M. (1990). *Flow: The psychology of optimal experience.* New York, NY: Harper & Row.

Damasio, A. (1994). *Descartes' error: Emotion, reason, and the human brain.* New York, NY: Avon Books.

Deci, E., & Ryan, R. (1987). *Intrinsic motivation and self-determination in human behavior.* New York, NY: Plenum.

Decyk, B. (1994). Using examples to teach concepts. In D. F. Halpern (Ed.), *Changing college classrooms: New teaching and learning strategies for an increasingly complex world* (Vol. 89, pp. 39–63). San Francisco, CA: Jossey-Bass.

Derry, S. (1990). Learning strategies for acquiring useful knowledge. In B. Jones & L. Idol (Eds.), *Dimensions of thinking and cognitive instruction* (pp. 347–380). Hillsdale, NJ: Lawrence Erlbaum.

deWinstanley, P., & Bjork, R. (2002). Successful lecturing: Presenting information in ways that engage effective processing. In D. Halpern (Ed.), *Applying current learning theory* (Vol. 89, pp. 19–31). San Francisco, CA: Jossey-Bass.

DeWitte, S., & Lens, W. (2000). Exploring volitional problems in academic procrastinators. *International Journal of Educational Research, 33*(7–8), 733–750.

Dillon, J. (1988). *Questioning and teaching: A manual of practice*. New York, NY: Teachers College Press.

Donald, J. (1995). Disciplinary differences in knowledge validation. In N. Hativa & M. Marincovich (Eds.), *Disciplinary differences in teaching and learning: Implications for practice* (pp. 7–18). San Francisco, CA: Jossey-Bass.

Druckman, D., & Bjork, R. (1991). Enhancing long term retention and transfer. In D. Druckman & R. Bjork (Eds.), *In the mind's eye: Enhancing human performance* (pp. 23–56). Washington, DC: National Academy Press.

Druckman, D., & Bjork, R. (1994). *Learning, remembering, believing: Enhancing human performance*. Washington, DC: National Academy Press.

Duit, R. (1991). Students' conceptual frameworks: Consequences for learning science. In S. Glynn, R. Yeany, & B. Britton (Eds.), *The psychology of learning science* (pp. 65–85). Hillsdale, NJ: Lawrence Erlbaum.

Dweck, C., & Leggett, E. (1988). A social-cognitive approach to motivation and personality. *Psychological Review, 95,* 256–273.

Entwhistle, N., McCune, V., & Walker, P. (2001). Conceptions, styles, and approaches within higher education: Analytical abstractions and everyday experience. In R. J. Sternberg & L.-f. Zhang (Eds.), *Perspectives on thinking, learning, and cognitive styles* (pp. 103–136). Mahwah, NJ: Lawrence Erlbaum.

Entwhistle, N., & Ramsden, P. (1983). *Understanding student learning*. London, England: Croon Helm.

Fleming, N. D. (1995). *I'm different; not dumb. Modes of presentation (VARK) in the tertiary classroom*. Paper presented to Research and Development in Higher Education, Proceedings of the 1995 Annual Conference of the Higher Education and Research Development Society of Australia.

Fromme, D. K., & Daniell, J. (1984). Neurolinguistic programming examined: Imagery, sensory mode, and communication. *Journal of Counseling Psychology, 31*(3), 387–390.

Gardner, H. (1983). *Frames of mind*. New York, NY: Basic Books.

Gardner, H. (1999). Multiple approaches to understanding. In M. Reigeluth (Ed.), *Instructional-design theories and models: A new paradigm of instructional theory*. (Volume II, pp. 69–89). Mahwah, NJ: Lawrence Erlbaum.

Gick, M. L., & Holyoak, K. J. (1987). The cognitive basis of knowledge transfer. In S. M. Cormier & S. D. Hagman (Eds.), *Transfer of learning: Contemporary research and applications* (pp. 9–46). San Diego, CA: Academic Press.

Gilovich, T. (1991). *How we know what isn't so*. New York, NY: Free Press.

Guzzetti, B., & Hynd, C. (1998). *Perspectives on conceptual change: Multiple ways to understand knowing and learning in a complex world*. Mahwah, NJ: Lawrence Erlbaum.

Halpern, D. F. (1996). *Thought and knowledge: An introduction to critical thinking* (3rd ed.). Mahwah, NJ: Lawrence Erlbaum.

Haskell, R. E. (2001). *Transfer of learning: Cognition, instruction, and reasoning*. San Diego, CA: Academic Press.

Hayes, J. (1985). Three problems in teaching general skills. In S. Chipman, J. Segal, & R. Glaser (Eds.), *Thinking and learning skills* (Vol. 2, pp. 391–405). Hillsdale, NJ: Lawrence Erlbaum.

Heckhausen, H., & Kuhl, J. (1985). From wishes to action: The dead ends and short cuts on the long way to action. In M. Frese & J. Sabini (Eds.), *Goal directed behavior: The concept of action in psychology* (pp. 134–160). Hillsdale, NJ: Lawrence Erlbaum.

Hillocks, G., & Shulman, L. (1999). *Ways of thinking, ways of teaching*. New York, NY: Teachers College Press.

Hofer, B. K., & Pintrich, P. R. (1997). The development of epistemological theories: Beliefs about knowledge and knowing and their relation to learning. *Review of Educational Research, 67*(1), 88–140.

Isen, A., & Daubman, K. (1984). The influence of affect on categorization. *Journal of Personality and Social Psychology, 47*, 1206–1217.

Jaspers, F. (1994). Target group characteristics—Are perceptual modality preferences relevant for instructional materials design? *Educational & Training Technology International, 31*(1), 11–18.

Jonassen, D., & Grabowski, B. (1993). *Handbook of individual differences, learning and instruction.* Hillsdale, NJ: Lawrence Erlbaum.

Keller, J. M. (1999). Using the ARCS motivational process in computer-based instruction and distance education. In M. Theall (Ed.), *New directions for teaching and learning: No. 78. Motivation from within: Approaches for encouraging faculty and students to excel* (pp. 39–47). San Francisco, CA: Jossey-Bass.

King, A. (1992). Facilitating elaborative learning through guided student-generated questioning. *Educational Psychologist, 27*(1), 111–126.

King, A. (1994). Inquiry as a tool in critical thinking. In D. F. Halpern (Ed.), *Changing college classrooms: New teaching and learning strategies for an increasingly complex world* (Vol. 89, pp. 13–38). San Francisco, CA: Jossey-Bass.

Klein, G., & Hoffman, R. (1993). Seeing the invisible: Perceptual-cognitive aspects of expertise. In M. Rabinowitz (Ed.), *Cognitive science foundations of instruction* (pp. 203–226). Hillsdale, NJ: Lawrence Erlbaum.

Kolb, D. (1981). Learning styles and disciplinary differences. In A. W. Chickering (Ed.), *The modern American college: Responding to the new realities of diverse students and a changing society.* San Francisco, CA: Jossey-Bass.

Kolodner, J., & Guzdial, M. (2000). Theory and practice of case-based learning aids. In D. Jonassen & S. Land (Eds.), *Theoretical foundations of learning environments* (pp. 215–242). Mahwah, NJ: Lawrence Erlbaum.

Kuhl, J. (1985). Volitional mediators of cognition-behavior consistency: Self-regulatory processes and action versus state orientation. In J. Kuhl & J. Beckman (Eds.), *Action control: From cognition to behavior* (pp. 101–128). New York, NY: Springer-Verlag.

Langer, E. J. (1997). *The power of mindful learning.* Reading, MA: Addison-Wesley.

LeDoux, J. (2002). Emotion, memory and the brain. *Scientific American, 12*(1), 62–71.

Martin, D., & Arendale, D. (Eds.). (1994). *New directions for teaching and learning: No. 60. Supplemental instruction: Increasing achievement and retention.* San Francisco, CA: Jossey-Bass.

Marton, F. (1988). Describing and improving learning. In R. Schmeck (Ed.), *Learning strategies and learning styles* (pp. 53–82). New York, NY: Plenum.

Mathews, S., Yussen, S., & Evans, R. (1982). *Remember that story? An investigation of the robustness and temporal course of the story schema's influence.* Unpublished manuscript, University of Wisconsin–Madison.

Mayer, R. (1995). Student learning outcomes differ because student learning traits differ: The return of trait theories of individual differences. *American Journal of Psychology, 108*(1), 144–148.

Mayer, R., & Wittrock, M. (1996). Problem-solving transfer. In D. Berliner & R. Calfee (Eds.), *Handbook of educational psychology* (pp. 47–62). New York, NY: Simon & Schuster.

Mentkowski, M. (2000). *Learning that lasts: Integrating learning, development, and performance in college and beyond.* San Francisco, CA: Jossey-Bass.

Naveh-Benjamin, M., & Lin, Y. (1994). Measuring and improving students' disciplinary knowledge structures. In P. Pintrich, D. Brown, & C. Weinstein (Eds.), *Student motivation, cognition and learning* (pp. 51–78). Hillsdale, NJ: Lawrence Erlbaum.

Oettingen, G., Honig, G., & Gollwitzer, P. (2000). Effective self-regulation of goal attainment. *International Journal of Educational Research, 33*(7–8), 705–732.

Ormrod, J. (1999). *Human learning* (3rd ed.). Upper Saddle River, NJ: Prentice-Hall.

Paris, S., & Winograd, P. (1990). How metacognition can promote academic learning and instruction. In B. Jones & L. Idol (Eds.), *Dimensions of thinking and cognitive instruction* (pp. 15–52). Hillsdale, NJ: Lawrence Erlbaum.

Pask, G. (1976). Styles and strategies of learning. *British Journal of Educational Psychology, 46*, 128–148.

Perkins, D., & Salomon, G. (1987). Transfer and teaching thinking. In D. Perkins, J. Lochhead, & J. Bishop (Eds.), *Thinking: The second international conference* (pp. 285–303). Hillsdale, NJ: Lawrence Erlbaum.

Perry, W. (1970). *Forms of intellectual and ethical development in the college years: A scheme.* Troy, MI: Holt, Rinehart, and Winston.

Peterson, C., Maier, S., & Seligman, M. (1993). *Learned helplessness: A theory for the age of personal control.* New York, NY: Oxford University Press.

Pintrich, P. (2000). An achievement goal theory perspective on issues in motivation terminology, theory and research. *Contemporary Educational Psychology, 25*, 92–104.

Pintrich, P., & Schunk, D. H. (1996). *Motivation in education: Theory, research, and application.* Englewood Cliffs, NJ: Merrill/Prentice-Hall.

Pintrich, P., Smith, D., Garcia, T., & McKeachie, W. (1993). Reliability and predictive validity of the Motivated Strategies for Learning Questionnaire (MSLQ). *Educational and Psychological Measurement, 53,* 801–813.

Pintrich, P. R., Marx, R. W., & Boyle, R. A. (1993). Beyond cold conceptual change: The role of motivational beliefs and classroom contextual factors in the process of conceptual change. *Review of Educational Research, 63*(2), 167–199.

Pittenger, D. (1993). The utility of the Myers Briggs Type Indicator. *Review of Educational Research, 63*(4), 467–488.

Posner, J. G., Strike, K., Hewson, P., & Gertzog, W. (1982). Accommodation of a scientific conception: Toward a theory of conceptual change. *Science Education, 66,* 211–227.

Pressley, M. (1983). Making meaningful materials easier to learn: Lessons from cognitive strategy research. In M. Pressley & J. Levin (Eds.), *Cognitive strategy research: Educational implications* (pp. 239–266). New York, NY: Springer-Verlag.

Pressley, M., & McCormick, C. (1995). *Advanced educational psychology for educators, researchers, and policymakers.* New York, NY: HarperCollins.

Pressley, M., Wood, E., Woloshyn, V., Martin, V., King, A., & Menke, D. (1992). Encouraging mindful use of prior knowledge: Attempting to construct explanatory answers facilitates learning. *Educational Psychologist, 27*(1), 91–109.

Renzulli, J., & Dai, D. Y. (2001). Abilities, interests, and styles as aptitudes for learning: A person-situation interaction perspective. In R. J. Sternberg & L.-f. Zhang (Eds.), *Perspectives on thinking, learning, and cognitive styles* (pp. 23–46). Mahwah, NJ: Lawrence Erlbaum.

Resnick, L. (1989). Introduction. In L. Resnick (Ed.), *Knowing, learning, and instruction: Essays in honor of Robert Glaser* (pp. 1–24). Hillsdale, NJ: Lawrence Erlbaum.

Riding, R. (1997). On the nature of cognitive style. *Educational Psychology, 17*(1–2), 29–50.

Riding, R. (2001). The nature and effects of cognitive style. In R. J. Sternberg & L.-f. Zhang (Eds.), *Perspectives on thinking, learning, and cognitive styles* (pp. 47–72). Mahwah, NJ: Lawrence Erlbaum.

Riding, R., & Cheema, I. (1991). Cognitive styles—An overview and integration. *Educational Psychology, 11*, 193–215.

Riding, R., & Rayner, S. (1998). *Cognitive styles and learning strategies: Understanding style differences in learning and behaviour.* London, England: David Fulton Publishers.

Rissland, E. (1985). The structure of knowledge in complex domains. In S. Chipman, J. Segal, & R. Glaser (Eds.), *Thinking and learning skills* (Vol. 2, pp. 107–126). Hillsdale, NJ: Lawrence Erlbaum.

Rohwer, W. D., & Thomas, J. W. (1989). Domain-specific knowledge, metacognition, and the promise of instructional reform. In C. McCormick , G. Miller, & M. Pressley (Eds.), *Cognitive strategy research: From basic research to educational applications* (pp. 104–132). New York, NY: Springer-Verlag.

Romainville, M. (1994). Awareness of cognitive strategies: The relationship between university students, metacognition and their performance. *Studies in Higher Education, 19*(3), 359–366.

Rosenthal, H., & Jacobson, L. (1968). *Pygmalion in the classroom.* New York, NY: Holt, Rinehart, and Winston.

Ryan, R., & Deci, E. (2000). Intrinsic and extrinsic motivations: Classic definitions and new directions. *Contemporary Educational Psychology, 25*, 54–67.

Sagan, C. (1995). *The demon-haunted world: Science as a candle in the dark.* New York, NY: Random House.

Schmeck, R. (1988a). Individual differences and learning strategies. In C. Weinstein, E. Goetz, & P. Alexander (Eds.), *Learning and study strategies: Issues in assessment, instruction, and evaluation* (pp. 171–191). San Diego, CA: Academic Press.

Schmeck, R. (1988b). Strategies and styles of learning: An integration of varied perspectives. In R. Schmeck (Ed.), *Learning strategies and learning styles* (pp. 317–347). New York, NY: Plenum.

Schmeck, R., Ribich, F., & Ramanaiah, N. (1977). Development of a self-report inventory for assessing individual differences in learning processes. *Applied Psychological Measurement, 1*, 413–431.

Schon, D. A. (1983). *The reflective practitioner: How professionals think in action.* New York, NY: Basic Books.

Schraw, G. (1994). The effect of metacognitive knowledge on local and global monitoring. *Contemporary Educational Psychology, 19*, 143–154.

Schraw, G., Dunkle, M. E., Bendixen, L. D., & Roedel, T. D. (1995). Does a general monitoring skill exist? *Journal of Educational Psychology, 87*(3), 433–444.

Schunk, D. H. (2000). *Learning theories: An educational perspective.* Upper Saddle River, NJ: Prentice-Hall.

Sherwood, R. as part of The Cognition and Technology Group at Vanderbilt. (1993). Toward integrated curricula: Possibilities from anchored instruction. In M. Rabinowitz (Ed.), *Cognitive science foundations of instruction* (pp. 33–55). Hillsdale, NJ: Lawrence Erlbaum.

Snow, R. (1998). Abilities as aptitudes and achievements in learning situations. In J. J. McArdle & R. W. Woodcock (Eds.), *Human cognitive abilities in theory and practice* (pp. 93–112). Mahwah, NJ: Lawrence Erlbaum.

Snow, R., Corno, L., & Jackson, D. (1996). Individual differences in affective and conative functions. In D. Berliner & R. Calfee (Eds.), *Handbook of educational psychology* (pp. 243–310). New York, NY: Macmillan.

Snowman, J. (1986). Learning tactics and strategies. In G. Phye & T. Andre (Eds.), *Cognitive classroom learning: Understanding, thinking, and problem solving* (pp. 243–275). London, England: Academic Press.

Sorcinelli, M., & Elbow, P. (Eds.). (1997). *New directions for teaching and learning: No. 69. Writing to learn: Strategies for assigning and responding to writing across the discipline.* San Francisco, CA: Jossey-Bass.

Speck, B. (1998). Unveiling some of the mystery of professional judgment in classroom assessment. In R. Anderson & B. Speck (Eds.), *New directions for teaching and learning: No. 74. Changing the way we grade student performance: Classroom assessment and the new learning paradigm* (pp. 17–31). San Francisco, CA: Jossey-Bass.

Spiro, R., Feltovich, P., Coulson, R., & Anderson, D. (1989). Multiple analogies for complex concepts: Antidotes for analogy-induced misconception in advanced knowledge acquisition. In S. Vosniadou & A. Ortony (Eds.), *Similarity and analogical reasoning* (pp. 498–531). New York, NY: Cambridge University Press.

Steadman, M., & Svinicki, M. (1998). CATs: A student's gateway to better learning. In T. Angelo (Ed.), *New directions for teaching and learning: No. 75. Classroom assessment and research: An update on uses, approaches, and research findings* (pp. 13–20). San Francisco, CA: Jossey-Bass.

Stellwagen, J. B. (2001). A challenge to the learning style advocates. *The Clearing House, 74*(5), 265.

Sternberg, R. J., & Ben-Zeev, T. (2001). *Complex cognition: The psychology of human thought*. New York, NY: Oxford University Press.

Svinicki, M., & Dixon, N. (1987). The Kolb model modified for classroom activities. *College Teaching, 35*(4), 141–146.

Symons, S., Snyder, B., Cariglia-Bull, T., & Pressley, M. (1989). Why be optimistic about cognitive strategy instruction? In C. McCormick, G. Miller, & M. Pressley (Eds.), *Cognitive strategy research: From basic research to educational applications* (pp. 1–32). New York, NY: Springer-Verlag.

Talbert, J., & Cronbach, L. (Eds.). (2002). *Remaking the concept of aptitude: Extending the legacy of Richard E. Snow*. Mahwah, NJ: Lawrence Erlbaum.

Theall, M., & Franklin, J. (1999). What have we learned? A synthesis and some guidelines for effective motivation in higher education. In M. Theall (Ed.), *New directions for teaching and learning: No 78. Motivation from within: Approaches for encouraging faculty and students to excel* (pp. 99–109). San Francisco, CA: Jossey-Bass.

Vosniadou, S., & Ortony, A. (Eds.). (1989). *Similarity and analogical reasoning*. New York, NY: Cambridge University Press.

Vygotsky, L. S. (1978). *Mind in society: The development of higher psychological processes*. Cambridge, MA: Harvard University Press.

Walvoord, B., & Anderson, V. J. (1998). *Effective grading: A tool for learning and assessment*. San Francisco, CA: Jossey-Bass.

Weinstein, C. (1996). Learning how to learn: An essential skill for the 21st century. *Educational Record, 4*, 49–52.

Weinstein, C., Palmer, D., & Schulte, A. (1987). *LASSI: Learning and study strategies inventory*. Clearwater, FL: H&H Publishing.

Wentzel, K. (2000). What is it that I'm trying to achieve? Classroom goals from a content perspective. *Contemporary Educational Psychology, 25*, 105–115.

Whimbey, A., & Lochhead, J. (1999). *Problem solving and comprehension*. Mahwah, NJ: Lawrence Erlbaum.

Whitehead, A. N. (1929). *The aims of education*. New York, NY: Macmillan.

Wigfield, A., & Eccles, J. (2000). Expectancy-value theory of achievement motivation. *Contemporary Educational Psychology, 25*, 68–81.

Wlodkowski, R., & Ginsberg, M. (1995). *Diversity and motivation: Culturally responsive teaching*. San Francisco, CA: Jossey-Bass.

Zimmerman, B. J. (2000). Self-efficacy: An essential motive to learn. *Contemporary Educational Psychology, 25*, 82–91.

INDEX